Using Gramsci

Reading Gramsci

General Editors:
Peter Ives, Professor of Politics, University of Winnipeg
and
Adam Morton, Professor of Political Economy, University of Sydney

Also available:

Solidarity without Borders
Gramscian Perspectives on Migration and Civil Society Alliances
Edited by Óscar García Agustín and Martin Bak Jørgensen

Gramsci, Culture and Anthropology
An Introductory Text
Kate Crehan

Gramsci on Tahrir
Revolution and Counter-Revolution in Egypt
Brecht De Smet

Language and Hegemony in Gramsci
Peter Ives

Subalternity, Antagonism, Autonomy:
Constructing the Political Subject
Massimo Modonesi
Translated by Adriana V. Rendón Garrido
and Philip Roberts

Unravelling Gramsci:
Hegemony and Passive Revolution in
the Global Political Economy
Adam David Morton

Using Gramsci

A New Approach

Michele Filippini

Translated by Patrick J. Barr

First published 2017 by Pluto Press
345 Archway Road, London N6 5AA

www.plutobooks.com

British Library Cataloguing in Publication Data
A catalogue record for this book is available from the British Library

ISBN 978 0 7453 3569 8 Hardback
ISBN 978 0 7453 3568 1 Paperback
ISBN 978 1 7868 0007 7 PDF eBook
ISBN 978 1 7868 0009 1 Kindle eBook
ISBN 978 1 7868 0008 4 EPUB eBook

Typeset by Stanford DTP Services, Northampton, England
Printed and bound by CPI Group (UK) Ltd, Croydon, CR0 4YY

To Daniela

Contents

Series Preface

Antonio Gramsci (1891–1937) is one of the most frequently referenced political theorists and cultural critics of the twentieth century. His pre-disciplinary ideas and especially his articulation of hegemony are commonly referred to in international relations, social and political theory, political economy, historical sociology, critical geography, postcolonial studies, cultural studies, literary criticism, feminism, new social movements, critical anthropology, education studies, media studies and a host of other fields. And yet, his actual writings are steeped in the complex details of history, politics, philosophy and culture that shaped Italy's formation as a nation-state as well as in the wider turmoil of twentieth-century world history.

Gramsci began his practical and intellectual odyssey when he moved to Turin University (1911). This move to mainland industrial Italy raised cultural and political contradictions for the young Sardinian, whose identity had been deeply formed by the conditions of uneven development in the 'South'. These issues were pursued by Gramsci whilst he devoted his energy to journalism (between 1914 and 1918) in the newspapers *Il Grido del Popolo*, *Avanti!* and *La Città Futura*. His activity centred on the Factory Council movement in Turin – a radical labour mobilization – and editorship of the journal *L'Ordine Nuovo* (1919–20). Exasperated by the Italian Socialist Party's lack of leadership and effective action during the *Biennio Rosso*, Gramsci turned his attention to the founding and eventual leadership of the Italian Communist Party (PCd'I) as well as the organization of the workers' newspaper *L'Unità* until 1926. Gramsci spent from May 1922 to December 1923 in the Soviet Union actively involved in organizational issues within the Communist International (Comintern). This included functioning on the Executive Committee of the Comintern in Moscow as the representative of the PCd'I and as a member of various commissions examining organizational, political and procedural problems that linked the various national communist parties. During this period, Gramsci had direct contact with Leon Trotsky and led discussions on the 'Italian Question', including the united front tactics to tackle Fascism, the trade union relationship, and the limits of party centralism. These issues were developed by Gramsci through the work of ideological hegemony carried out by the PCd'I and, following his Moscow period, as a central author and architect of 'The Lyon Theses' – a collection of positional statements on the tactics and strategies needed in response to Fascism. The theses are regarded as a major survey of the conditions of uneven development confronting social forces within Italy and the European states-system at the time.

By 1926, after drafting his famous essay 'Some Aspects of the Southern Question', Gramsci was arrested as a Communist Party deputy by the Fascist authorities and was incarcerated until a few days before his death in 1937. Gramsci wrote almost 500 letters in prison; over half were to his sister-in-law, Tatiana Schucht, who was living in Rome and became his key supporter and his most frequent visitor. She also conveyed Gramsci's ideas to another significant patron, Piero Sraffa, the Italian economist then at Cambridge. These letters constitute a rich mixture of intellectual, cultural and political analysis as well as representing the daily struggle of prison life including Gramsci's increasingly severe health problems. But the most enduring and influential component of his legacy is the 33 notebooks penned between 1929 and 1936 that together constitute the *Quaderni del carcere* (*Prison Notebooks*). Tatiana Schucht hid these notebooks in a vault at the Banca Commerciale Italiana while she arranged for their transportation to Moscow. Publication of the *Prison Notebooks* in Italian ensued from the late 1940s onwards and has continued in various languages ever since.

The breadth of the above political and intellectual journey is perhaps matched by the depth of detail and coverage contained within Gramsci's pre-prison and prison writings. The study of intellectuals in Italy, their origins and grouping according to cultural currents; his engagement with, and critique of, Italy's most important intellectual of the time, Benedetto Croce; the study of comparative linguistics and the Italian language question; analysis of the Sicilian writer Luigi Pirandello and the potential his plays offered for transforming Italian culture and society; and discussion of the role of the serialized novel and popular taste in literature would be later expanded into a wider plan. This chiefly focused on Italian history in the nineteenth century, with special attention being directed to Italy's faltering entrance into capitalist modernity under conditions of 'passive revolution', including the imposition of a 'standard' Italian language; the theory of history and historiography; and the expansion of the capitalist labour process through assembly plant production techniques beyond the United States under the rubric of 'Americanism and Fordism'. In summary, issues of hegemony, consciousness and the revolutionary process are at the centre of Gramsci's attention. It is for such reasons that Antonio Gramsci can be regarded as one of the most significant Marxists of the twentieth century, who merits inclusion in any register of classical social theorists.

Reading Gramsci, however, is no easy task. He plunges into the complexities of debates of his time that are now obscure to many readers and engages in an enormous range of topics that at first seem unrelated. Moreover, the prison conditions and his own method yield a set of open-ended, fragmented and intricately layered *Prison Notebooks* whose connections and argumentation do not lead linearly from one note to the next, but seem to ripple and weave in many directions. This has sometimes led to aggravation on the part of Gramsci scholars when they see how often his name is invoked by those with quite partial or superficial understanding of these complexities. It has also generated frustration on the part of those who want to use Gramsci's ideas to illuminate their own studies, analyses and political acumen. After all, while Gramsci himself was a meticulous researcher with a rigorous philological method, he was deeply committed to people understanding their own political and cultural contexts in order to engage and change them. These points, about the necessity of deploying an openness of reading Gramsci to capture the branching out of his thought *and* the necessity of deploying a practical interest in understanding the here and now of contemporary events, were central to Joseph Buttigieg's original idea for initiating this 'Reading Gramsci' series. Buttigieg's contributions to Gramscian scholarship extend also to his monumental and superbly edited and translated English critical edition of the *Prison Notebooks* (Columbia University Press), the final volumes of which are still in process. In keeping with Buttigieg's initial goals, this series aims to provide expert guides to key features and themes in Gramsci's writings in combination with the pressing political, social and cultural struggles of our time. Rather than 'applying' Gramsci, the point of the series is to provide monographs that think through and internalize Gramsci's method of thinking about alternative historical and contemporary social conditions. Given that no single study can encapsulate the above political and intellectual depth and breadth, each volume in the 'Reading Gramsci' series is focused in such a way as to open readers to specific aspects of his work as well as raise new questions about our contemporary history.

Peter Ives
Adam David Morton

Acknowledgements

This book owes a great deal to a large number of people, including a number of colleagues with whom I have shared research work in fields other than that of Gramscian studies, but who have provided me with constant stimuli, and this has indirectly contributed to my reading of Gramsci and my 'use' of his writings. Thus, I would like to thank the following: Giuseppe Allegri, Livio Boni, Fortunato Maria Cacciatore, Matteo Cavalleri, Roberto Ciccarelli, Luisa Lorenza Corna, Dario Gentili, Peter Ives, Dhruv Jain, Pietro Maltese, Jamila Mascat, Samuele Mazzolini, Sandro Mezzadra, Massimiliano Mita, Adam David Morton, Mauro Pala, Damiano Palano, Maurizio Ricciardi, Federico Tomasello, Bernardo Venturi. I would also like to thank the translator of this book, Patrick John Barr, with whom I have had a highly productive exchange of ideas regarding the choice of terminology, which has helped me clarify certain theoretical passages of this work. The responsibility for the contents of this volume remains that of the author, of course.

The history of the English translations of Gramsci's writings has been a long and difficult one. The sources of quotations chosen for this book, offered in the attempt to constantly provide the most recent, correct translation, is clear evidence of this.

All quotations from the *Prison Notebooks* contained herein are shown in the form Qx§y (where x indicates the number of the Notebook, and y indicates the number of the note). This specification (which applies to all editions) is then followed by the edition from which the translation was taken. At present there are only three volumes of the English translation (*Prison Notebooks*, translated and edited by J. Buttigieg) of the critical edition of the *Quaderni del carcere* published in Italian in 1975 and edited by Valentino Gerratana, which continues to be the most complete and accurate edition, pending publication of the National edition of Gramsci's writings. These three volumes comprise the first eight of the twenty-nine notebooks that Gramsci wrote in prison (except those of translations). Consequently, when a quotation is taken from one of the first eight notebooks, it is taken from the Buttigieg edition and abbreviated using the acronym PN followed by the number of the volume (PN1, PN2,

PN3) and by the corresponding page number. For the notes contained in the subsequent notebooks (9–29), quotations are taken from various anthologies of Gramsci's writings published in English: in the main they are taken from *Selections from the Prison Notebooks* (SPN), from *Further Selections from the Prison Notebooks* (FSPN) and from *Selections from Cultural Writings* (SCW). In those rare cases where a quotation is not to be found in any of the aforementioned editions, we have translated it into English ourselves: in such cases, the reference given is to the Italian critical edition of the *Quaderni del carcere* (QC) followed by the wording 'author's translation'.

Existing translations have been amended on occasion, either when clearly wrong or when the choice of terms is deemed to impair the richness of Gramsci's language: in such cases a note has been included indicating the amendment made.

Inside Gramsci's quotations, square brackets are used to contain amendments designed to facilitate the reading of the text (e.g. [that]) or omitted words (e.g. […]), whereas angle brackets <…> are used to contain phrases present between the lines in Gramsci's manuscripts, that is, phrases added by Gramsci after the initial drafting of the work in question.

Between 1931 and 1935, after having commenced drafting his notes in 1929, Gramsci began reorganizing those writings he had already written, classifying them within 'special notebooks'. Thus, the writings are subdivided by convention, according to a classification introduced by Valentino Gerratana (QC: XXXVI–XXXVII) in the critical edition of the *Prison Notebooks*, between: rough writings (a), writings drafted just once (b), redrafted writings (c). In the latter case, Gramsci takes the previously drafted writings and re-writes them, often unifying them and sometimes changing the contexts to a significant degree.

Quotations from, and reference to, any secondary literature that has not been translated into English have been kept to a minimum where possible. Those who wish to further pursue the topics in question may avail themselves of a number of powerful digital tools, such as the Gramsci Foundation's *Bibliografia Gramsciana* [Gramscian Bibliography] (bg. fondazionegramsci.org) or the digital library www.gramsciproject.org (which in addition to Gramsci's writings, also contains the *Dizionario gramsciano* [Gramscian Dictionary] and offers readers the opportunity to carry out a series of cross searches).

The bibliography at the end of the volume makes no claims to be complete, but is designed to be of help in regard to the 'uses of Gramsci'.

Readers interested in discovering whether there is an English translation of a given Gramscian writing may consult the extremely useful concordance tables to be found on the International Gramsci Society's website: www.internationalgramscisociety.org/resources/concordance_table and www.internationalgramscisociety.org/resources/pre-prison-index.

Abbreviations

ON   *L'Ordine Nuovo 1919–20* [The New Order 1919–1920], edited by V. Gerratana and A.A. Santucci, Turin: Einaudi, 1987.

QC   *Quaderni del carcere* [Prison Notebooks], 4 vols, Istituto Gramsci's critical edition, edited by V. Gerratana, Turin: Einaudi, 1975.

QT   *Quaderni di traduzioni (1929–1932)* [Translation Notebooks (1929–1932)], 2 vols, edited by G. Cospito and G. Francioni, part of *Quaderni del carcere* [Prison Notebooks], National edition of the works, Rome: Istituto della Enciclopedia Italiana, 2007.

SF   *Socialismo e fascismo. L'Ordine Nuovo 1921–1922* [Socialism and Fascism: The New Order 1921–1922], edited by E. Fubini, Turin: Einaudi, 1974.

Introduction

> Those who do not produce things (in the wide sense) cannot produce words.
>
> Antonio Gramsci
>
> 1912

In 1987, Eric J. Hobsbawm wrote an article for the Italian journal *Rinascita*, informing readers that Antonio Gramsci was among 'The 250 most cited authors in the Arts and Humanities Citations Index 1976–1983'.[1] Together with Gramsci, this ranking, which included famous names from the sixteenth century onwards, only included another four Italians: Giorgio Vasari, Giuseppe Verdi, Benedetto Croce and Umberto Eco. Gramsci died on 27 April 1937, and his fame was very much of a posthumous nature, starting at the end of the Second World War with the publication of the thematic volumes of his prison writings.[2] So, what exactly happened during the thirty-year period from the late 1940s to the end of the 1970s? Well, during that period a leading political figure, the Secretary of the Italian Communist Party, who had been imprisoned by the Fascist regime and had subsequently died just a few days after his release, became not only a leading intellectual figure for the international left and for critical thought in general, but also a classic in political theory.[3] This success was influenced in particular by the political-cultural atmosphere in Europe and the USA during the 1960s and 1970s, as well as by an intense period of anti-colonial and emancipation movements in the rest of the world. During this period, Gramsci's writings were divulged to the four corners of the world, in the wake of the publication of a famous anthology of the *Prison Notebooks* in English (SPN). This initial phase of the internationalization of Gramsci's thought was characterized by the explicit political use of his writings within the context of emancipatory struggles that were quite different from the struggles Gramsci himself had been involved in: struggles against Latin American dictatorships, against colonial regimes in Asia and Africa, for civil rights in Europe and the USA and also in favour of Eurocommunism.

This initial phase has since been accompanied by a second phase coinciding with the start of the new millennium.[4] In the last fifteen years, in fact, there has been a strong revival of interest in Gramsci's work, thus marking a strong reversal in the trend that had characterized the final twenty years of the previous millennium. This second wave of interest appears not only more substantial, but also of a more far-reaching nature than the previous one. It has proven capable of reaching the most varied of cultural contexts and disciplines. While the first phase was characterized by its evocation of the historical experience of international communism, aided by the hagiography of the martyr of the Fascist regime, and based on the attempt to identify a version of socialism different from that of the USSR, the second phase has been distinguished by a less constrained approach to Gramsci's historical experience. The focus this time around has been on the use of Gramscian concepts within various disciplines, in particular in the social sciences. Although this has at times led to interpretations and 'uses' of Gramsci's writings of a somewhat misleading or little documented nature, and the arbitrary disengagement of his concepts from the Marxist and materialist sphere in which they were forged, nevertheless in the majority of cases the 'political character' of Gramsci's writings, together with their emancipatory and critical spirit, have been largely preserved.

The new approach to Gramsci's work adopted in the present volume is set within the context of this 'shifted' use of Gramsci's theoretical instruments in a broad range of disciplines (political science, education and pedagogy, language, cultural studies, international relations, subaltern and postcolonial studies, anthropology, geography). The present is an attempt to provide scholars of these disciplines with an interpretation of Gramsci's writings offering a precise historical/theoretical reconstruction that is, however, devoid of all the esoteric features that normally characterize a restricted and specific community of scholars. Hence, the decision to organize the book into a number of chapters, each of which is dedicated to a specific key theme, which at first sight may not appear to reflect the traditional instruments of Gramscian analysis, but which on the contrary refer to the central questions of political and social thought: ideology, the individual, collective organisms, society, crisis and temporality. Gramsci's conceptuality, consisting of a series of well-known formulas – passive revolution, historical bloc, hegemony etc. –, is in the end based around these key themes, and will be analysed within this context. In contemporary debate, Gramsci's concepts are in danger of being diluted to such an extent that they are no longer useful, on the one hand, and of remaining hostage to the historical circumstances that produced them, on the other hand. To get around the first of these two problems, Gramscian discourse needs to be reconnected to the large-scale changes taking place at the time he wrote; however, in order to resolve the second problem, said discourse needs to be rendered available, as all classics, to contemporary analysis, which sees the present characterized by different, but nonetheless epoch-making, changes.

An indication of this kind was offered by Gramsci himself when he wrote that the 'Search for the *Leitmotiv*, for the rhythm of the thought as it develops, should be more important than that for single casual affirmations and isolated aphorisms'.[5] As rightly claimed by Alberto Burgio – a meticulous scholar who can afford to adopt this approach to Gramsci's writings without risking the philologists' ire – what is felt here is 'the genuine concern that an overly respectful reader may prove the least well equipped to understand. Gramsci is aware of the paradox whereby the actual fetishism of writings may, in the case of the *Prison Notebooks*, produce perverse effects, causing the author to be attributed with positions and thoughts that in reality may be the exact opposite of those actually held'.[6] One of the aims of this new approach is thus to follow the rhythm of Gramscian thought, and to provide a solid basis for those wishing to utilize his categories in the fields of sociology, political science and the social sciences in general. The path followed is somehow in an upward direction, from the individual to society, although the central theoretical problems remain the same, all of which are linked to the changes brought by the advent of mass politics, which had generated 'social governance' needs previously unheard of. Looked at from this point of view – that of a mass, politicized society – Gramsci reformulated the Marxist vocabulary of his time, and one century later has provided us with a conceptual toolkit that can be used to understand the contemporary crisis of a world that Gramsci himself had witnessed emerging.

1

Ideology

Ideologies must become dramas if they are not to remain mere ink
printed on paper.

Antonio Gramsci

13 October 1917

THE PROBLEM OF IDEOLOGY

In his study of ideology, Michael Freeden cites Karl Mannheim, Louis
Althusser and Antonio Gramsci as the three twentieth-century figures
who made the greatest contribution to the broadening of our understanding of ideology. According to Freeden, their merit 'was that they
transformed our conception of ideology from the transient epiphenom-
enon Marx and Engels had made it out to be into a permanent feature
of the political'.[1] This view, whilst perhaps somewhat reductive in regard
to Marxian writings, nevertheless grasps a fundamental advancement
witnessed in the social sciences during the first half of the twentieth
century. It is not surprising that the disciplines that suffered this
'ideological tribulation' were in fact those ascribable to the aforementioned three figures: that is, sociology, philosophy and political theory.

In the case of sociology, the transition from a purely instrumental
conception of ideology to the establishment of a specific field of study
regarding the formation of ideas – the sociology of knowledge – was
completed without too much difficulty.[2] In the case of philosophy, the
process proved more uneven, and ended up grinding to a standstill when
the attempt was made to interpret the effects and structure of ideology in
a 'constructive manner', by considering ideology as a constantly coherent
expression of social totality. In this case, the gap between ideological
forms and economic structure was bridged, and ideology was reduced to
the status of an objective function of the system.[3] Finally, in the case of
political theory, the transition to a more complex conception of ideology
was attempted only occasionally, and in fact Gramsci remains, almost a

century later, the main source of ideas for those wishing to deal with the question from a non-reductionist Marxist point of view.[4]

Gramsci agrees with, or rather pre-empts, the Althusserian view of ideology as an organic part of a social totality (Gramsci's 'historical bloc'), whilst at the same time maintaining the flexibility of the concept, so that he can consider ideological, on the one hand, the disjointed *senso comune*[5] that is not aimed at, or functional to, any specific historical bloc a priori; and, on the other hand, philosophy, which is, in fact, in keeping with, and functional to, political domination. The various levels of ideology that Gramsci analyses – common sense, folklore, religion, philosophy (and science in part) – can thus be arranged according to a scale of internal consistency, where common sense and philosophy represent the extremes of such a scale. This scale, as we shall see, coincides with the level of consciousness of the bearer of this ideological thought system. In Gramsci's view, the knowledge, understanding and development of these ideological elements represent the core of revolutionary political theory.

This approach to the formation of historical subjects – and thus to the various ideological forms that distinguish such – reveals Gramsci's conviction that the historical bloc underlying each type of domination never derives mechanically from the morphological structure of society, but is, on the contrary, the result of the composition of elements that may be arranged in various different ways.

In order to deal with this tangle of problems, however, we need to first examine the context within which Gramsci wrote, and the level of debate on ideology at that time. His *Prison Notebooks* were written in the early 1930s, in a period in history that had only recently witnessed the introduction of the concept of ideology into the political vocabulary.

THE HISTORICITY OF THE CONCEPT OF IDEOLOGY

The first evidence of Gramsci's interest in defining ideology can be found in a note from Notebook 4, in which he muses on the origin of the concept:

'Ideology' is an aspect of 'sensationalism', that is, of the eighteenth-century French materialism. It used to mean 'science of ideas', and since analysis was the only method recognized and applied by science, it meant 'analysis of ideas', that is, also, 'search for the origin of ideas'.

Ideas had to be broken down into their <original> 'elements', which could be nothing other than 'sensations'.[6]

From here, Gramsci goes back to the definition of ideology formulated by Destutt de Tracy, whom he considered to be the 'literary propagator of ideology [...], among the most renowned and popular, because of the ease of his exposition'.[7] In Tracy's original design, ideology is a genuine 'political science of the social',[8] the aim of which is to deal scientifically with the new field of study that actually has emerged with the advent of the French Revolution. The science that is to operate in this new field of study must provide answers to the questions: how are the ideas formed of those free, equal, fraternal individuals who, no longer being subjected to traditional or personal powers, produce ideas that are no longer foreseeable? What impact do such ideas have on the political order, and how can their effects be foreseen? In this case, the basis for the scientific study of ideas and their formation was laid by the historical circumstance that permitted such ideas to be 'freed' from their original, constant subjugation to traditional powers. That which, after 1789, became unforeseeable for such traditional powers, which up until then had regulated the formation of ideas, could become predictable for a science.

Thus, Gramsci was aware of the transformation that the concept had undergone, and he immediately displayed a strong awareness of its historicity. In truth, it was the very semantic and political evolution of the term following the post-revolutionary watershed that Gramsci was interested in, that is, 'How did the meaning of "ideology" change from "science of ideas" and the search for the origins of ideas, to "a system of ideas?"'.[9] We know that this transition took place very early in the history of the concept, in a period somewhere between Napoleon's famous attack on the *Idéologues* and the emergence of Marxist criticism,[10] which Gramsci saw as a 'distinct advance [*superamento*]'[11] on sensationalism. But if 'In logical terms, the process is easy to understand – Gramsci continued –, how did it come about historically?'[12] Gramsci's interest in this transition already marks an important point: ideology had followed a rapid process of formation, politicization and, finally, criticism, as a result of the historical process triggered by the French Revolution. Therefore, it did not possess any independent character, since it was modelled on its own connections with historical-political events. Thanks to historical materialism, ideology thus took the form of the political element of the superstructure, to be analysed from a historical perspective.

The distinction between the two meanings of the term is indicated in the *Prison Notebooks* by the use, or otherwise, of the capital 'I'. The science of ideas, the capitalized 'Ideology' of the *Idéologues* and of Tracy, is the science of a physiological nature that studies the formation of ideas on the basis of their derivation from sensations;[13] 'ideology' with a small 'i', on the other hand, refers to the system of ideas that each person possesses, which does not depend on physiological causes but on historical-political ones.

In this latter meaning of ideology, the concept becomes a vast analytical terrain that in the *Prison Notebooks* is broadened and specified to constitute a multitude of further concepts, whilst at the same time revealing an area of theoretical engagement in which debate rages over ideology's independence or dependence, its cognitive richness or its mystifying aspects, the rigidity it entails or the movement it stimulates. In fact, while the *Prison Notebooks* also features a non-specific use of the *term* – often with 'ideological' employed as a negative adjective – there are also signs of a knowing, albeit incomplete, construction of an independent *concept* of ideology on Gramsci's part.[14] This process of construction begins with Gramsci distancing his analysis from two other attempts made to do likewise within the Marxist field: Bukharin's venture to provide Marxism with a sociology, and a theory of ideology based on this sociology; and that of the so-called 'reflection theories' that perceive ideology as a variable that is closely dependent on the economic structure, thus nullifying its importance from the knowledge point of view.

As far as regards the first of these two attempts, Gramsci's criticism of Bukharin's *Historical Materialism: A System of Sociology* submitted in Notebook 11,[15] is that this work had remained tied to a concept of ideology similar to the one shared by the *Idéologues*, namely, a science that reconstructs the components of human thought, such components being taken as stable and uniform insofar as they are rooted in people's consciousness and expressed by their common sense. Thus, Gramsci believed that Bukharin 'really capitulated before common sense and vulgar thought, for he did not pose the issue in correct theoretical terms and was therefore practically disarmed and impotent'.[16] The correct theoretical terms, on the other hand, are those of historical materialism, which compared to this meaning of ideology 'represents a distinct advance [*superamento*] and historically is precisely in opposition to Ideology [capital letter]'.[17] Marx himself, Gramsci continues, in connoting the concept of ideology negatively, thus attributing a value judgement to it, had pointed out the historical – and thus criticizable – origin of ideas rather than their physiological origin. By linking ideology to historical elements and to social relations, Marx marked a transition, a historical achievement for historical materialism (the philosophy of praxis in Gramsci's vocabulary).

The second Marxist attempt to define ideology that Gramsci criticized was that of the so-called 'reflection theories'. In fact, in the 1920s Gramsci found himself faced with a use of the concept, particularly by Marxists, which, on the one hand, had adopted the originality of the historicity of the 'system of ideas', but which, on the other hand, tended to interpret ideology as mere appearance, that is, as a simple reflection of the economic structure, within a rigid framework that once again renders useless the development of a proper concept, at the very time when the notion of ideology had been freed from its naturalistic origins.[18] Gramsci reacted against this simplification:

> For Marx, 'ideologies' are anything but appearances and illusions: they are an objective and operative reality; they just are not the mainspring of history, that's all [...]. Marx explicitly states that humans become conscious of their tasks on the ideological terrain of the superstructures, which is hardly a minor affirmation of 'reality' [...]. This topic of the concrete value of superstructures in Marx should be studied thoroughly. Recall Sorel's concept of the 'historical bloc'. If humans become conscious of their task on the terrain of superstructures, it means that there is a necessary and vital connection between structure and superstructures, just as there is between the skin and the skeleton in the human body. It would be silly to say that a person stands erect on his skin rather than his skeleton, and yet this does not mean that the skin is merely an appearance and an illusion – so much so that the condition of a flayed person is not very pleasant.[19]

Reference is being made here to the human organism, something that we shall often encounter in the *Prison Notebooks*, to describe the workings of modern society. For now we are simply going to point out that Gramsci's analogy between the relationship of skeleton to skin, and that of structure to ideology, serves not only to express the mutual interdependence of the pairs of terms, but also alludes to a general systemic function that ideology (like skin) performs within the overall mechanism. There can be no (living) skeleton without skin, and likewise there can be no skin (performing its function) without a skeleton. The two things only operate together, without, however, any necessary hierarchical relationship between them given that both, albeit in different ways, are determined by the presence of the other. This approach thus negates the simplistic vision of ideology as a mere instrument.

THE COMPLEXITY OF IDEOLOGY

A second characteristic of Gramsci's conception of ideology is its complexity. In fact, for Gramsci ideology represents a 'complex form of the social world',[20] not only in the sense of 'complicated', but more precisely – and etymologically speaking – in the sense of a non-linear object, composed of different parts and several elements, that depends on various determinations. Thus, ideology in the *Prison Notebooks* cannot be conceived as a unitary moloch, a pre-established, coherent block of ideas and positions, constructed in order to be instilled in the minds of subalterns by intellectuals, ideologists or party officers. On the contrary, in Gramsci's view there are those who are privy to an ideology due to their standing in the world of production, or because of their position in the disjointed world of common sense; there are those who produce ideology from their position as major intellectuals, and those who do so as the 'dominant group's "underlings"'.[21] There are also those who operate in a manner inconsistent with their own ideology, and thus who express an 'ideology in practice' that is different from that of their words:

> The average worker has a practical activity but has no clear theoretical consciousness of his activity in and understanding of the world; indeed, his theoretical consciousness can be 'historically' in conflict with his activity. In other words, he will have two theoretical con-sciousnesses: one that is implicit in his activity and that really unites him with all his fellow workers in the practical transformation of the world and a superficial, 'explicit' one that he has inherited from the past. The practical-theoretical position, in this case, cannot help becoming 'political' – that is, a question of 'hegemony'. Consciousness of being part of a hegemonic force (that is, political consciousness) is

the first stage on the way to greater self-awareness, namely, on the way to unifying practice and theory.[22]

This citation from Gramsci clearly alludes to the problem of class consciousness and its development. However, one thing that seems to be of a certain importance in this context is the refusal to consider that theoretical consciousness that is inconsistent with its own practice as mere mystification. The elements of this (allegedly false) consciousness, in fact, appear disjointed in common sense; they are the result of the stratification of hegemonic intellectual traditions that have been transcended, producing what Gramsci calls the 'folklore of "philosophy"'.[23] At certain times these fragments condense and are rearticulated[24] to form an integral part of a new historical bloc. A 'hegemonic force'[25] is such when it comprises, and manages to develop for its own purposes, this entire series of ideological 'remains'.

The true/false model that economic reductionism applies to the ideological sphere is thus replaced by an approach based on the possibility/impossibility of an ideological element being included within a given historical bloc. This possibility/impossibility thus depends on the relationship that is established between two, mobile elements, rather than on the level of consistency of the 'derived' term with the 'immobile' term. The historical bloc, or rather its specific forms, are thus not determined a priori but depend on how the ideological elements present in society are politically designed (or able) to be combined (and developed).

The political openness of this approach is clear: ideology becomes the battlefield for the conquest of hegemony, whilst Gramsci's image of the historical bloc replaces the Marxian base/superstructure metaphor. The study, modification and articulation of this stratification of still active ideological remains is the task that the philosophy of praxis must engage in, and also lies at the heart of the concept of ideology that Gramsci attempts to develop in the *Prison Notebooks*:

Obviously, it is impossible to have 'statistics' on ways of thinking and on single individual opinions that would give an organic and systematic picture: the only thing possible is the review of the most widely circulated and most popular literature combined with the study and criticism of previous ideological currents, each of which 'may' have left a deposit in various combinations with preceding or subsequent deposits. A more general criterion becomes part of this same sequence of observations: changes in ways of thinking, in beliefs, in opinions do not come about through rapid and generalized 'explosions', they come about, for the most part, through 'successive combinations' in accordance with the most disparate 'formulas'. [...] in the cultural sphere diverse ideological strata are variously combined, and what has become 'scrap iron' in the city is still an 'implement' in the provinces.[26]

The composition of this historical bloc depends first and foremost on the 'relations of force', upon which Gramsci formulates a genuine draft copy of revolutionary political theory in the lengthy note 17 to Notebook 13.[27] In this note, which gathers together and transcribes other notes previously drafted under the heading title *Machiavelli. Relations of force* (sometimes *forces*), Gramsci tries to 'accurately pose [...] the problem of the relations between structure and superstructure',[28] offering a dynamic interpretation of such in the light of a series of elements that are to remain key to the *Prison Notebooks*. They are all cited here together, within the space of a few pages.

The difference between organic and conjunctural (or occasional, cf. Chapter 5, section 'The political science of crisis') movements: the former are permanent and of historical significance, and are independent of individuals; the latter are occasional, cyclical and affect the small ruling groups;

- The two principles set out in Marx's 'Preface' to *A Contribution to the Critique of Political Economy* (1859), according to which 'no society sets itself tasks for whose accomplishment the necessary and sufficient conditions do not already exist' and 'no society breaks down and can be replaced until it has first developed all the forms of life which are implicit in its internal relations' (cf. Chapter 5, section 'A new understanding of the crisis').[29]
- The political realism of Machiavelli that demands for the 'history maker' 'an objective and impartial analysis' against 'One's own baser and more immediate desires and passions'.[30]
- The different levels of the relations of force, with the second level – the political one – presenting much wider space for manoeuvre: not conditioned by structure as the first level (tied to the base and independent of people's will), nor conditioned by the contingency

of the battle as the third level (military relations of force, cf. Chapter 5, section 'Crisis and organization').

- The relativization of the concept of crisis, freed from 'collapse theory' and reconsidered as the terrain of political struggle (cf. Chapter 5).

Thus it can be argued, going back to these questions, that in Gramsci's view the historical bloc is formed through an organic movement, within the context of the decline of a social form, by means of political action based on realism that can be deployed in political relations of force in particular, taking advantage of the crisis as a terrain of political struggle.

It is clear that the above is a constructive, almost geometric, model forcing the analysis in the direction of the production of a historical subjectivity capable, at the end of the process, of transforming the ideological elements found to be disjointed within society. In fact, the note ends with the following words:

> The decisive element in every situation is the permanently organised and long-prepared force which can be put into the field when it is judged that a situation is favourable (and it can be favourable only in so far as such a force exists, and is full of fighting spirit). Therefore the essential task is that of systematically and patiently ensuring that this force is formed, developed, and rendered ever more homogeneous, compact, and self-aware.[31]

However, the 'ideological path' of this force cannot be propelled forward by an image of ossified consistency between class position and class consciousness, a view that basically aims to bridge a presumed original gap and to achieve a 'no-longer ideological' condition. On the contrary, this force, if it wishes to be increasingly homogeneous, strong and conscious, must study and understand its existing forms, all of which are constantly undergoing transformation. The world of the ruled, in fact, is always impregnated with various different ideologies.

It is here that Gramsci's realism moves a step forward from the other conceptions of ideology in existence at that time. In fact, he interweaves the study of the ideological reality curbing revolutionary action with a constant reflection on how the conditions of validity of this stable config-uration can be surmounted. The analysis of society's ideological network serves to realistically frame the analysis of the modern, complex forms of consensus organization and of political mediation, in order to be able to pose the question: what are the practical and theoretical preconditions for a possible revolution in the West? At the same time, this analysis does not exhaust the Gramscian 'question of ideology' that works towards a change in premises designed to radically modify the meaning and practical consequences of ideological 'conditioning'. Thus, far from being utopian, Gramsci's thinking, within this interwoven process, is revealed to be a dynamic form of political realism that is careful to emphasize the contingency of ideological phenomena associated with specific power relations, and to negate the objectivity of such phenomena deriving from any indeterminate 'human nature'.

The development of ideologies in Gramsci thus takes the form of a circular movement that at certain moments is characterized by intensification and organization, and at others by crisis and decay. The scale ranging from incoherence/disintegration at one end, to unity/ organicity at the other, sees ideology deriving from the latter of these two poles, in strict relationship with a given social group, before taking an independent, unforeseen direction, disintegrating and coming together again in another form when said social group declines. There are then many different types of ideological articulation within capitalism itself, and they operate as factors legitimizing the capitalist order, even in opposing ways. For example, in 1917, in an article entitled 'Tre principii, tre ordini [Three Principles, Three Orders]',[32] Gramsci notes that each historically established liberal order is based upon one specific principle, as follows: the principle of freedom underlying the English order (economic liberalism and free competition); the principle of rationality underlying the German order (protectionism and organization). In liberal Italy, on the other hand, it has no guiding principle, because 'Italy has missed out completely on that period of gradual development which made possible the England and the Germany of today'.[33] Thus, in Italy there is no order in the rationalizing form to be found in the other two countries, because the ideological development of the bourgeois forces never happened, leaving Italian society's ideological forms in a disjointed state. The 'third order' of Gramsci's article is thus the one that the working class is to establish on the basis of the principle 'that all citizens should be able to develop their own, human personality to the full'.[34] In Gramsci's view, there is thus no specific ideology of the capitalist class,[35] but simply a disjointed series of ideological remains held together by a hegemonic force, which differs from one country to another, and which may only be overcome through a struggle for the coherence and unity of an opposing ideology.

Finally, it is interesting to note that the formation and development of that specific form of ideology represented by common sense, which Gramsci identifies in the subsequent sedimentation of the philosophies of intellectual groups representing social classes in decline, at least partly conflicts with the Marxian argument contained in *The German Ideology*, according to which 'Morality, religion, metaphysics, all the rest of ideology and their corresponding forms of consciousness, […] have no history, no development; but men, developing their material production and their material intercourse, alter, along with this their real existence, their thinking and the products of their thinking'.[36] While it is undoubtedly true that for Gramsci as well, men's actions are what alter their consciousness, it is also true that common sense is characterized by some sort of development, albeit unguided, and a history, albeit disjointed, and that this is one of the primary reasons for its persistence, for its constituting an inexorable restraint on any higher, critical self-consciousness organic to any political project. Investigating both the history of ideological forms and their complex contemporary stratification was one of Gramsci's primary objectives when writing the *Prison Notebooks*.

THE TRUTH/FALSITY OF IDEOLOGY

Ferruccio Rossi-Landi, in what may be considered to be one of the most systematic discussions ever of the concept of ideology, identifies eleven meanings of the term that are then grouped into two categories: on the one hand, ideology as false consciousness (critical-negative meaning) and, on the other, ideology as a vision of the world (positive-descriptive meaning).[37] In the theoretical tradition of Marxism, which has probably offered the greatest number of definitions of ideology, such a distinction may be boiled down (of course, by trivializing it just like the majority of twentieth-century Marxism has done, in fact) to the difference between the Marx of *The German Ideology* – in which ideology inverts real relations – and the Lenin of *What is to be Done?* – which on the contrary refers to the opposition of socialist and bourgeois ideologies.[38]

If we had to place Gramsci in relation to these two positions, we would put him somewhere between the two: close to Marx's position when he, Gramsci, acknowledges, in any case, the mystifying character of bourgeois ideologies, insofar as they are 'instrument of government of the dominant groups'.[39] In this case, ideologies have a 'rapid transience in that they tend to hide reality – namely struggle and contradiction';[40] they do not mystify reality as such, but rather its intrinsic contradictive nature, that is, the class struggle. Gramsci finds himself tending towards the latter position (that of Lenin), however, when, situating the concept within the framework of the class struggle – insofar as ideologies mainly '"organize" the human masses'[41] –, he identifies a concept of truth that is not absolute, but is the result of political struggle. In fact, if the superstructures represent the level at which a 'struggle of political "hegemonies"'[42] is fought, which determines people's consciousness, and if the connection between theory and practice is constitutive of social activity, rather than having to be artificially created, then the result of the ideological struggle itself establishes the reality of people's lives.

At this point we encounter the Gramscian argument criticizing the concept of the 'objective reality of the external world' as exemplified by Bukharin's book – but originating from Lenin's *Materialism and Empirio-criticism* (1908) – which presupposes the existence of an 'objective' external world that is independent of the subjects that inhabit it. In this conception, Gramsci finds traces both of the religious idea of God the Creator, who establishes the world before, and regardless of, Man, and of the naive metaphysics of philosophical materialism, which idealizes nature as an objective external entity.[43] Here, reality is perceived as already formed, independent of and external to the subject, who can only try to perfect the cognitive means with which to master that reality. Gramsci's opposition to this theory does not consist of any idealistic subjectivism – despite not being a reductionist, he nevertheless remains within the materialist ranks – but of an objectivity of the real that can only exist in relation to the practice of ideological struggle:

Objective always means 'humanly objective' which can be held to correspond exactly to 'historically subjective': in other words, objective would mean 'universal subjective'. Man knows objectively in so far as knowledge is real for the whole human race historically unified in a single unitary cultural system. But this process of historical unification takes place through the disappearance of the internal contradictions which tear apart human society, while these contradictions themselves are the condition for the formation of groups and for the birth of ideologies which are not concretely universal but are immediately rendered transient by the practical origin of their substance. There exists therefore a struggle for objectivity (to free oneself from partial and fallacious ideologies) and this struggle is the same as the struggle for the cultural unification of the human race.[44]

With the 'ideological problem' defined in these terms, the debate over the intrinsic truth or falsehood of ideologies loses not only its interest, but also its meaning. In fact, the element that establishes the objectivity-truth of ideology becomes historically determined, ultimately corresponding to that of historical efficacy. An efficacy that is to be evaluated on the basis of the distinction between 'historically organic ideologies' and 'arbitrary, rationalistic, "willed" ideologies',[45] as a counterpoint to the previously mentioned distinction between organic movements and conjunctural movements in relations of force: the former are necessary for a given structure – they constitute, as we have seen, its 'skin'; the latter, on the other hand, are the result of 'individual "movements"'[46] that do not organize or mobilize people, but merely serve the interests of individuals or small groups.

At this point however, the concept of ideology reaches its point of maximum tension, as it finds itself describing a series of phenomena that share apparently contradictory features. In fact, on the one hand, Gramsci sees common sense, folklore and religion as powerful forms of a mystifying ideology; on the other hand, shunning reductionism and economism, he argues that such forms of consciousness possess their own historical 'truth', insofar as they are effectual.[47] Likewise, he perceives the dangers of conceiving socialist ideology as being true, scientific and immutable, without any direct interaction with the historical struggle that 'renders it valid'.[48]

Gramsci's conception of ideology is debated within this very space characterized by the confrontation of the effectuality of those ideologies present with the struggle of future ideology to 'prove its truthiness'. It is a productive concept for the very reason that it is forced to contend with the duplicity of its content that is determined, in each case, by the political struggle. This characteristic also distinguishes the concept of hegemony, which in fact is applied both in the analysis of the West's 'fortresses and emplacements'[49] that prevent an East-style revolution and in relation to the transition to the hegemonic phase in the USSR with the New Economic Policy.[50] It comes as no surprise to discover that there is only one definition of ideology in the *Prison Notebooks*, where it is described as a 'scientific, energetic, educational hypothesis that is verified <and criticized> by the real development of history, that is, it is *turned into science*'.[51] This concise definition establishes certain fundamental principles, nonetheless:

- Firstly, it is a 'hypothesis', and thus it does not contain any principle of truth deriving from the position in the economic structure of the bearer of such ideology, but is open to a 'truth procedure'.[52]
- It is of an 'educational' character, that is, it is strictly linked to the transformation of those subjects it affects, and is 'energetic' in that it acts as a stimulus to the transformational action.
- Thirdly, it is connected to the 'real development of history', and is thus susceptible to gradual adjustments and never formalized in any doctrine.
- Finally, ideology, during the practical 'truth procedure', must be 'turned into science', that is, it must contain all the elements required for scientific prevision, where the adjective 'scientific' means, as we shall see in the next section, a certain degree of objectivity (always understood as historically subjective).

At this point it should be noted that Gramsci's pursuit of a suitable definition of ideology came at a time in history prior to the semantically heavy duty understanding of the concept that was to persist throughout the entire twentieth century – mediated by the famous Marxian metaphor – whereby ideology was seen as the inversion of reality.[53] Ideology had not yet been conceived in such terms by Marxists writing during the period in which Gramsci drafted his notes. The concept in question was still undergoing formulation, its suggestive character still limited at that time, and as such it was open to other contiguous terms and concepts that placed the emphasis on other aspects of social reality, and that were utilized in the fields of philosophy, sociology or psychology. Thus, the *Prison Notebooks* offer a 'conceptual constellation' centring around the question of ideology. This constellation includes some of the concepts that have characterized Gramscian analysis, such as 'hegemony', 'historical bloc', 'folklore', 'religion', 'philosophy' and 'science', which we shall now examine at the points where they intersect.

THE CONCEPTUAL CONSTELLATION
OF IDEOLOGY INCLUDING HEGEMONY

Of the family of terms that gravitate around the concept of ideology, one stands out in particular, that is, hegemony: 'the moment of hegemony and consent [must be understood] as a necessary form of the concrete historical bloc'.[54] It is to be found, in fact, 'in the organic life of civil society and the State',[55] and it expresses the socio-political capacity of a ruling class to construct a system of legitimization in which individuals' actions are framed within those preordained forms of conduct permitted by the political powers that be. While hegemony is sometimes considered or used with a great emphasis on the organization of consent, Gramsci also consistently sees it as involving degrees of coercion. Hegemony, together with its coercive side that Gramsci, in reference to Machiavelli, calls dictatorship, in fact regards the 'preservation and defence of organic structures',[56] and specifically includes 'the State [...] as an organism',[57] that has to create 'an equilibrium of parties within an organic whole in which the strongest party would be hegemonic'.[58] Within this context, ideology with its political mobilizing power and its need to 'be turned into science' in practice becomes the terrain for the hegemonic struggle ('ideological terrain', not surprisingly, is one of the most common expressions to be found in the *Prison Notebooks*). Hegemony, in turn, becomes the political process that aspires to conquer the ideological terrain. 'Ideological terrain', which should not be confused with 'opinion', is strictly connected (the skin and bones metaphor applies once again) to a practical movement for the creation or reproduction of an order. Once such terrain has been seized, and ideology has been 'verified <and criticized> by the real development of history',[59] as happened, for example, with the October Revolution, then according to Gramsci, another level is reached that is not only practical but also theoretical: 'The realisation of a hegemonic apparatus, in so far as it creates a new ideological terrain, determines a reform of consciousness and of methods of knowledge: it is a fact of knowledge, a philosophical fact.'[60] The theoretical-practical notion of ideology to be found in the *Prison Notebooks* is thus a precondition for the development of the theory of hegemony. Both concepts developed in an ambivalent, albeit productive manner, as the result of an analysis that not only predicted the forms of the new order, but also tried to investigate the resistance offered by the existing order.

The concept of 'historical bloc', seen from the point of view of its connection to the concepts of ideology and hegemony, on the other hand, describes the capacity of a 'social system'[61] to conform and organically develop, accounting both for its complex structure – which in Gramsci's view is embedded with 'a succession of sturdy fortresses and emplacements'[62] – and its duration. Gramsci borrows the concept from Georges Sorel – probably thinking of a summary of a passage from *Reflections on Violence* contained in a book by Giovanni Malagodi, given that it is absent in Sorel's own works[63] – and uses it to describe the successful result of the hegemonic attempt to conquer the ideological terrain. This action established (and continues to establish) a new ideological terrain on which a specific articulation of forces inscribes society's movements.

The historical bloc is never definitively established, and it does not always manage to include – either through coercion or consent – all of the social forces expressed by society. This dynamic is also the concept's strong point, and it derives from one specific feature of the historical bloc, namely, the organic character of the relations within that bloc. We have already come across the organic systematic 'adjectivation' of ideology, and we shall encounter it again when discussing the notions of party and intellectuals. We therefore need to specify straightaway the Gramscian use of the unique sociological opposition of organic and disorganic. In fact, in the *Prison Notebooks* the latter term does not seem to express the 'inorganic' nature of a relationship, its inherent 'not-organic being' (Gramsci rarely uses such expressions[64] preferring the notion of the crisis of a given organicity, or of the allusion of a possible, but yet to be created, alternative organicity). Thus, in Gramsci's view, social relations are always organic, and their disorganic character is only the result of the crisis of an organic unity, or from the impossibility to create another organic unity.

Gramsci thus appears to support a model of historical development based on the co-existence of moments of disintegration and organic recomposition, during which the two phases – the revolutionary phase (during an 'organic crisis'[65]) and the ethico-political phase ('the moment of hegemony'[66]) – must arise at the same time if a system of power is to be threatened. The new order may only derive from the sum of the objective disintegration of the society in crisis such as at times of war, and the subjective condition of the systematic organization of a new social structure and order supported by a new historical bloc capable of organically reassembling the parts.

At this point, key to our discussion of ideology are the notions of 'common sense' and 'folklore', which Gramsci defines in opposition to the notion of 'philosophy'. However, this opposition differs in the two cases. While there is a fundamental difference between folklore and philosophy regarding the rigidity of the former compared to the latter, the difference between common sense and philosophy does not concern their theoretical constitution, but their respective coherence and systematic character:

> Every social stratum has its own 'common sense' which is ultimately the most widespread conception of life and morals. Every philosophical current leaves a sedimentation of 'common sense': this is the document of its historical reality. Common sense is not something rigid and static; rather, it changes continuously, enriched by scientific notions and philosophical opinions which have entered into common usage. 'Common sense' is the folklore of 'philosophy' and stands midway between real 'folklore' (that is, as it is understood) and the philosophy, the science, the economics of the scholars. 'Common sense' creates the folklore of the future, that is a more or less rigidified phase of a certain time and place.[67]

Common sense is thus an intermediate entity lying between folklore and philosophy. It is changeable, and when it 'sets' it creates folklore in the true sense of the word, which is stronger and preserves a certain consistency as the remaining part of a certain way of thinking that has crystallized over time. Therefore, folklore inevitably has a negative, almost invariably reactionary value, which should be historically analysed as a sign of a previous dominance in the realm of thought.[68] Common sense, on the other hand, may contain progressive elements insofar as it is still a flexible expression of actual contradictions, an expression of emergent classes. Therefore, while folklore must be rejected and criticized as ideological terrain, common sense has to be considered the 'raw material' of a new conception of the world, since it also contains the seeds of the new 'systems of ideas' connected to the emerging classes.

However, common sense also contains elements of past conceptions, mainly derived from 'religion', another element that Gramsci identifies as characteristic of the ideology of the popular strata: 'not only by the religion that happens to be dominant at a given time but also by previous religions, popular heretical movements, scientific concepts from the past'.[69] 'Science' is an antidote to these religious elements representing 'the most widespread and deeply rooted ideology':[70] science is the last element that Gramsci introduces in this semantic opening of the concept of ideology. A science that is not to be understood as 'objective knowledge', as the philosophical foundation of the philosophy of praxis, as Bukharin seems to understand it. Considering science as 'the conception of the world *par excellence*, which lifts the veil formed by ideological illusion',[71] reveals a double misunderstanding. On the one hand, with regard to the presumption of mechanically transposing natural scientific methods to the field of social phenomena:

> Since it 'appears', by a strange inversion of the perspectives, that the natural sciences provide us with the ability to foresee the evolution of natural processes, historical methodology is 'scientifically' conceived only if, and in so far as, it permits one 'abstractly' to foresee the future of society. Hence the search for essential causes, indeed for the 'first cause', for the 'cause of causes'. But the *Theses on Feuerbach* had already criticized in advance this simplistic conception. In reality one can 'scientifically' foresee only the struggle, but not the concrete moments of the struggle, which cannot but be the results of opposing forces in continuous movement.[72]

On the other hand, the misunderstanding concerns the theoretical constitution of science, which must be duly interpreted in order to relativize the 'pure' notion of objectivity that positivism has helped establish as the theoretical 'armour' protecting science.[73] In describing the merits of science in disproving the most archaic, superstitious positions adopted by common sense and folklore, Gramsci describes, as we have seen, a 'spurious' notion of objectivity, which must be a characteristic of science as well, or rather, a relative notion of objectivity in which 'relative' is meant to refer to those very people who create, use and falsify science itself:

> One thus establishes what is common to everyone, what everyone can control in the same way, one independently from another, as long as each has observed to an equal degree the technical conditions of ascertainment. 'Objective' means this and only this: that one asserts

to be objective, to be objective reality, that reality which is ascertained by all, which is independent of any merely particular or group standpoint. But, basically, this too is a particular conception of the world, an ideology.[74]

Gramsci grasps, in a surprising manner, the philosophical meaning of the revolution in physics during the twentieth century, which radically altered the status of the hard sciences during the very years of Gramsci's imprisonment. This revolution, which Gramsci followed from the outset from within his prison cell, was to increasingly question the clear distinction that classical physics had made between subject and object, and to move towards a probabilistic view of reality influenced by observation.[75] The reflections on science contained in the *Prison Notebooks* may thus be considered part of a dual critique: that of Bukharin's essay and of the naive positivism that transforms science into an objective totem; and that of the simplistic idealistic transpositions of scientific theories that trivialize the new knowledge by translating it into an extreme form of subjectivism.[76]

Science, given its 'objective – corresponding to historically subjective' character, is thus part of ideology, being, as it is, 'the union of the objective fact with a hypothesis or system of hypotheses which go beyond the mere objective fact'.[77] However, it is as a result of its very character as 'a historical category' rather than the philosophical basis of historical materialism that 'can be accepted by the philosophy of praxis'.[78] It contributes towards challenging common sense and religion through principles that are falsifiable – one could say 'contractual' at this point – thus sharing what Gramsci perceived as one of the underlying principles of the philosophy of praxis, that is, the 'absolute [...] earthliness of thought'[79] that defines the type of objectivity of which both science and philosophy of praxis are bearers: 'The whole of science is bound to needs, to life, to the activity of humanity. Without humanity's activity, which creates all, even scientific, values, what would "objectivity" be?'[80]

As well as science as such, the philosophy of praxis must adopt a form of politics that conveys conduct that is in keeping with such philosophy. On this level, on the other hand, religion – Protestantism in particular – represents a model that has to be encapsulated by a new conception of the world that wishes to impose itself in practice. According to Gramsci, the thing that religion emphasizes is that 'of a unity of faith between a conception of the world and a corresponding norm of conduct',[81] a topic that in lay terms remains key to any philosophy that wishes to produce a historical transformation. In this regard, Gramsci asks himself: 'why call this unity of faith "religion" and not "ideology", or even frankly "politics"?'.[82] We know for sure that Gramsci had read the very first translation into Italian of Max Weber's *The Protestant Ethic and the Spirit of Capitalism*.[83] It is clear that Gramsci's observation regarding the relationship between ideology, religion and politics is a reference to the German sociologist's studies, and it contributes towards a non-reductive analysis of religion, as shown by the assessment Gramsci offers of the Protestant Reformation, which gave rise to the philosophy of praxis' need to encourage an intellectual and moral reform: 'Historical materialism, in its dialectic of popular culture-high culture, is the crowning point of this entire movement of intellectual and moral reform. It corresponds to Reformation + French Revolution, universality + politics'.[84]

Even from this perspective, ideology plays a fundamental role with regard to the central issue analysed by Gramsci in his *Prison Notebooks*, namely, that of the conditions and possibility of the revolution in the West. The consistency between theory and practice, between ethics and everyday conduct, and ultimately between the formation of a historical bloc and the break-up of a rival bloc, can only be obtained through this new theory of ideology.

2
The individual

Philosophy teaches that to be human one must be part of some social aggregate.

Antonio Gramsci
30 September 1916

THE STRUCTURE OF THE INDIVIDUAL

In the first chapter, we saw how the ideological forms identified and analysed by Gramsci, rather than being dependent on the strict economic determination, are the result of the relations among individuals within society. However, this social formation of ideologies is based on an implicit premise, namely, a specific conception of Man whereby the relationship between the individual and society is perceived as a constituent element of the individual himself. In fact, Gramsci presupposes (and indeed states, as we shall see) a rather unusual conception of individuality that distinguishes him from the Marxists of his generation, and that reveals a sensitivity akin to that of the nineteenth-/twentieth-century social sciences.

However, no attempt shall be made here to identify a Gramscian 'political anthropology' based on the liberal model,[1] designed to generalize certain characteristics in order to render them universal. On the contrary, the focus shall be on identifying Gramsci's approach to individuality as something concerning the structure of the individual, that is, the individual's composition from a series of organic, but also conflicting, interconnected parts. In Gramsci's mind, this structure depends on the individual's social relationships, and is necessarily linked to the individual's mass experience. Thus, this structure may generalize and universalize different contents, depending on relations among individuals and between themselves and society as a whole.

Gramsci's investigation of this type of Man, where every individual is seen as a 'mass-man' or 'collective man',[2] is based on the experience of the early 1920s, where, on the one hand, Soviet Russia attempted to construct a 'New Man', while, on the other hand, Italy witnessed the emergence of Fascism, which produced and reproduced 'social individuality' on the basis of a mechanism of mass inclusion that was original and unknown to the liberal order. Gramsci used this basis to outline the characteristics of a 'new type of Man',[3] which may be reconstructed using the same approach adopted with regard to ideology, by means of certain concepts contained within Gramsci's discourse, namely: Man, human nature, individuality and personality.[4] We come across an initial definition in Notebook 10:

> Man is to be conceived as an historical bloc of purely individual and subjective elements and of mass and objective or material elements with which the individual is in an active relationship. To transform the external world, the general system of relations, is to potentiate oneself and to develop oneself.[5]

The image is clear here: each individual is an aggregation of individual elements and mass elements, both subjective and objective, of personal characteristics and relational characteristics. Thus, each individual is not defined solely on the basis of his own specific characteristics, but owes his genesis to the complex interrelationship between specific subjective factors, on the one hand, and the general social relations in which he is immersed, on the other. The individual is a 'centre of interaction'[6] between individuality, that is, the specific characteristics of each human being, and the outside world, that is, the individual's relations with his peers and with society as a whole. This interweaving, given its dependence on general social relations, is of a dynamic character, and as such is not determined a priori by any 'natural' features, but on the contrary depends on the evolution of relations within society: 'one must conceive of man as a series of active relationships (a process) in which individuality, though perhaps the most important, is not, however, the only element to be taken into account'.[7]

Thus, the reciprocal relationships among individuals are continuously redefined, and their only 'nature' identifiable a priori is that of their dynamic structure, that is, their potentiality understood as a space where forces and relations intersect. Gramsci developed these reflections on the basis of his criticism of both liberal anthropology and Catholicism:

From the 'philosophical' point of view, what is unsatisfactory in Catholicism is the fact that, in spite of everything, it insists on putting the cause of evil in the individual man himself, or in other words that it conceives of man as a defined and limited individual.[8]

The image of the 'individual in himself' – defined by nothing else, and solely responsible for the world's ills – constitutes the basis of Catholic doctrine, and is systematically reflected also in secular philosophies: 'It could be said of all hitherto existing philosophies that they reproduce this position of Catholicism, that they conceive of man as an individual limited to his own individuality and of the spirit as being this individuality.'[9] Here Gramsci clearly makes reference to the speculative philosophy of Benedetto Croce rather than to German idealism in general, given that Hegel remains one of the favoured sources of a relational definition of the individual for Gramsci.[10]

The perception of Man as a monad, on the other hand, which is so dear to both Christianity and to Croce's philosophy, in Gramsci's mind represents an attempt to formulate a general philosophy based on a unitary conception of the individual: a definitive, stable, reactionary theoretical project that is indifferent to social relations and their conflictual dynamics; one capable of advocating a return to the presumed unity of the human species that necessarily acts in a coercive manner in order to direct the sporadically subversive masses towards an abstract unity defended by professional philosophers – Gramsci maintains – who are totally disconnected from the people. On the contrary, 'Man in general' does not exist, and any proposal to suggest that he does represents the premise for a political programme designed to bend individuals' multiplicity and contradictory character to its own purposes. Human nature, on the contrary, may only be identified with 'the ensemble of social relations';[11] it is not a fixed concept but a developing one, not of unity but of inherent contradictions.

The image of Man portrayed by Gramsci is thus unrelated to either his physical or mental constitution, or to his singularity – his self-referential being. This dual negation, however, reveals two positive characteristics of human beings: the *historicity* (or political quality) defining the contingency of each and every individual formation, and that presupposes the transformation of the world in order for people to fully express their individuality; and the *sociality* that sees social relations as a constituent element of an individual's being. The openness of each individual to others that this approach guarantees means that each individual is potentially capable of identifying with the entire human species and its contradictions, through 'The humanity which is reflected in each individuality'.[12] By thus maintaining that the link between individuals and the human species can be found within each individual, Gramsci confirms the Marxian idea, present in *The German Ideology* – a work that Gramsci did not know but which renders the comparison even more interesting – of the creation, through the development of capitalism, of empirically universal individuals:

> only with this universal development of productive forces is a universal intercourse between men established [...], and finally [this development] has put world-historical, empirically universal individuals in place of local ones.[13]

Man, historically determined and defined by his relationship with other men, thus finds himself potentially, and with the emergence of capitalism, effectively, related to humanity as a whole. Consequently, the individual's constitution is established by the relationships that he/she establishes with other people and with the surrounding natural environment. Such relationships are not mechanical, but 'active and conscious',[14] mediated through collective organisms (in the case of relations with other people) or by work and techniques (in the case of the natural world). Awareness of these relations, the relationship that the individual establishes with the world through such, comes about 'organically' rather than 'by juxtaposition', and corresponds to 'the greater or lesser degree of understanding that each man has of them'.[15] Thus, Man is involved in his own formation and in that of his fellow men, and he does so in a more or less conscious, intentional manner.

When individuality, that is, the specific element of each individual, is combined with 'sociality', that is, the relation that determine said individual, and their union is recognized as the battleground on which an individual is effectively constituted, then in Gramsci's mind that individual acquires his own personality: 'to create one's personality means to acquire consciousness of them [the relations], and to modify one's own personality means to modify the ensemble of these relations'.[16] The fact that the acquisition of personality, and thus the critical understanding of one's own constitution, is a necessary precondition for influencing the historical process, is shown by the way in which Gramsci uses this reference not only in relation to individuals, but also with regard to collectivities such as the Nation – 'The national personality (as the individual personality) is a mere abstraction if considered outside the international (or social) nexus'[17] – or the State – 'seeking and finding within itself, within its complex life, all the elements of its historical personality'.[18] The key characteristic of this type of Man tied to the relationship between individuality and sociality is thus ultimately that of being transformable.

This formulation is clearly indebted to the works of Marx and Engels. In fact, the sixth of the *Theses on Feuerbach* establishes that 'the essence of man is no abstraction inherent in each single individual. In reality, it is the ensemble of the social relations',[19] *The German Ideology* also reiterates these social origins of individuality.[20] In the *Prison Notebooks*, however, we find a specific focus on the description of the individual as a stratified, contradictory being, in which the individual elements act upon the social elements, and vice versa. This focus on the social characteristics of individuality, on the one hand, and on its social determinants, on the other, is a sign that reveals a further influence on Gramsci's perception of the individual, namely, the discursive field of French sociology led by its most influential theoretician, Émile Durkheim.

THE SOCIAL PRODUCTION OF THE INDIVIDUAL: GRAMSCI AND DURKHEIM

Gramsci was a careful scholar of French history, and the presence of French culture is clear in the *Prison Notebooks*.[21] They contain numerous references to the positivism of Comte and to his '"organic" concepts',[22] and pay considerable attention to Charles Maurras and *Action Française*.[23] Gramsci also displayed an interest in the work of Henri-Louis Bergson,[24] who found himself at the centre of the reaction to positivism that was to lend an irrational tone to the majority of intellectual works produced during the late nineteenth and early twentieth centuries. By 1921, in fact, in a polemical atmosphere produced by the imminent splitting of the Italian Communist Party from the Italian Socialist Party, faced with the positivist heritage of the Italian workers' movement and comparing this with its French counterpart closely tied to Bergson's ideas, Gramsci had no hesitation in admitting that 'Bergson is a mountain while our positivists were nothing more than frogs in a swamp'.[25] Finally, he was well acquainted with the work of Georges Sorel, who had used the journals *L'Ère Nouvelle* [The New Era] and *Le Devenir social* [The Social Becoming] during the 1890s to divulge the themes of the emerging sociology within the context of Marxist debate.

Thus, from his earliest years in Turin, Gramsci had displayed an interest in the French experience during the Third Republic, in that cultural milieu that searched for answers to the organic crisis of the order in the analysis of society, dealing with the decline in solidarity within an increasingly dynamic society that was losing the binding power of its traditional values as a result, among other things, of France's defeat in the war against Prussia. Gramsci's analysis of how the different French schools of thought tried to understand the limitations, novelties, dynamics of, and divisions within, this new society, meant that the Third Republic became a favoured field of study and comparison, where the hegemonic methods employed by the ruling classes to govern society could be analysed together with the emergence of the social sciences as useful tools with which to deal with demands for order, social organicity and political direction.[26]

In Gramsci's view, fifty years prior to the political turmoil witnessed in Italy, France had seemed one large 'bourgeois laboratory'[27] where solutions to the crisis of the liberal order were tested out. An attempt to govern society that took account of the new 'collective men'[28] produced by industrial development and mobilized by mass politics. Notwithstanding their profound differences, the French republican-democratic system of the turn of the century, and the authoritarian Italian regime of the 1920s and 1930s, thus seemed to express the same need to respond to the changed relationship between individuals and society resulting from the crisis of the liberal order.

The one work that best represents France's pursuit of social cohesion is without doubt Émile Durkheim's *The Division of Labour in Society*, published in 1893.[29] The thing that really stands out here is the way in which some of Durkheim's theoretical perceptions are also to be found in Gramsci's work, in particular the conception of Man deriving from the interweaving of organic and mechanical solidarity within the context of a complex society that perceives such as the two poles around which empirical reality is to be arranged.[30] In fact, Durkheim submits that

> there is in the consciousness of each one of us two consciousnesses: one that we share in common with our group in its entirety, which is consequently not ourselves, but society living and acting within us;

the other that, on the contrary, represents us alone in what is personal and distinctive about us, what makes us an individual.[31]

On this basis, Durkheim distinguishes between two types of solidarity: mechanical solidarity, such that 'to the extent that the ideas and tendencies common to all members of the society exceed in number and intensity those that appertain personally to each one of those members',[32] and organic solidarity, which 'assumes that they [the individuals] are different from one another' and 'is only possible if each one of us has a sphere of action that is peculiarly our own, and consequently a personality'.[33] The prevailing type of solidarity, and the type of relationship between the individual and society, depend on the proportion between these two consciousness.

The proximity of Durkheim's analysis to Gramsci's thoughts in the *Prison Notebooks* derives from the focus on a shared problem, namely, that of the formulation of an image of the individual that is suited to modern industrial society, where the dynamic relationship between the individual and social elements of individuality conditions the stability and reproduction of the system, and where this 'social production of individuals', who are differentiated from one another but rendered uniform in the masses, becomes a key element both for the preservation of the system and for the possibility of its eventual overturning.

In Durkheim's conception of modern industrial society, the differentiation of individuals is generated by the division of labour, which in turns depends on the morphology of societies.[34] Such individuals, however, are 'restrained' by a principle of social cohesion that is inherent to society, that does not derive from the projection of the State over society and that is not available to single individuals or groups thereof. In this regard Durkheim, whilst placing the emphasis on the plurality of, and the at times conflicting dynamics between different parts of society – just like that between the corresponding parts of the individual – does not conceive of the possible existence of a power that is that of just one part of society, or rather, that is not the power of society as a whole. Gramsci, on the other hand, distances himself from Durkheim by acknowledging the political potential of the socially determined elements of the individuality of a specific part of society, that is, of that part connected to the new forms of industrial labour. In this way he galvanizes that side of the individual/society relationship that remains immobile in Durkheim, focusing on the relationship between the social part of individuality and society itself, as the struggle to change the relations within society and, together with this, that very part of individuality that represents the individuation[35] thereof: 'So one could say that each one of us changes himself, modifies himself to the extent that he changes and modifies the complex relations of which he is the centre of interaction.'[36]

The propulsive force behind this change is seen as the conflicting relationship between personality (individuality + sociality) and general social relations. In an industrial society that develops a specific division of labour, this translates into class struggle. The working class's acquisition of personality means acknowledging, whilst modifying, this division; it means overturning the aforesaid social relations. Class struggle is thus the characteristic of the acquisition of personality:

> To transform the external world, the general system of relations, is to potentiate oneself and to develop oneself. That ethical 'improvement' is purely individual is an illusion and an error: the synthesis of the elements constituting individuality is 'individual', but it cannot be realised and developed without an activity directed outward, modifying external relations both with nature and, in varying degrees, with other men, in the various social circles in which one lives, up to the greatest relationship of all, which embraces the whole human species. For this reason one can say that man is essentially 'political' since it is through the activity of transforming and consciously directing other men that man realises his 'humanity', his 'human nature'.[37]

What Gramsci includes in the aforementioned passage – the political actions of part of society on society itself – is a process that can no longer be formulated using the categories of Durkheim's sociology, which deliberately maintains society as a unified whole, as its chosen focus. However, the analysis of the new type of Man, based on the interrelationship between his individual and social elements, appears to be based on an idea shared by both writers. And while, on the one hand, this means that Gramsci's discourse displaces the political within the sphere of partiality rather than that of universality, on the other hand, Gramsci remains aware of the difficulties involved in such a dislocation. In accepting the theoretical moves and the concepts of the social sciences, Gramsci in fact also necessarily develops those political problems and questions to which such concepts refer.

'MAN IS A SOCIAL WORKER': GRAMSCI AND SOREL

Georges Sorel, as we have already mentioned, represents an important juncture in the relationship between French sociology and Marxism. In fact, he can be considered to be one of the principal drivers of the influence that French sociology's field of discourse had on the image of the individual and society outlined by Gramsci in his *Prison Notebooks*. Sorel is actually known above all as the theoretician of revolutionary syndicalism and in particular of the general strike: not as a utopian ideal – a purely intellectual product – but as a myth, that is, a pure expression of will: 'Whilst contemporary myths lead men to prepare themselves for a combat which will destroy the existing state of things' – Sorel wrote in a letter to Daniel Halévy in 1907 – 'the effect of utopias has always been to direct men's minds towards reforms which can be brought about by patching up the system'.[38]

As we know, Sorel's myth of the general strike assigns a key role to class violence. It is perceived by Sorel as being the only way out of the bourgeois system, that is, a necessary step towards the creation of a new order: 'Proletarian violence entirely changes the appearance of all the conflicts in which it plays a part, since it disowns the force organized by the bourgeoisie and wants to suppress the State which serves as its central nucleus'.[39] Certain elements of Sorel's well-known reflections play an important part in the drafting of the *Prison Notebooks*, as the literature concerning the two writers has often shown.[40] A certain similarity may also be seen between Gramsci's experience in the factory councils during the red years (1919–20) and Sorel's writings on the autonomy of the producers. However, hardly anyone has bothered to reconstruct the possible influence on Gramsci of Sorel's theoretical reflections prior to the highly influential *Reflections on Violence*.[41]

In the 1890s, in fact, Sorel had yet to develop his reflections on violence and the general strike. He had had a long career as a civil engineer in the Third Republic, and was influenced by the positivism that pervaded France at that time. He studied and published essays on psychology and criminology, but he also had a sound humanistic background influenced by major liberal-conservative thinkers such as Taine and Renan (as well as Tocqueville).[42] His formation as a socialist thinker was thus still a fairly recent development at that time. In 1894 he published a number of reviews in the French journal Ère nouvelle [The New Era], the first French theoretical Marxist journal, together with an essay entitled 'The

Old and the New Metaphysics'[43] in which Durkheim's recommenda-
tions from *The Division of Labour in Society* were combined with Marx's
class analysis. In the journal *Le Devenir social* [The Social Becoming]
– a publication that Sorel promoted, and which was characterized by
the attempted renewal of French Marxism through the introduction of
elements taken, in fact, from the social sciences – he published other
articles dealing with the same topic. The journal's opening article,
entitled 'Mr. Durkheim's Theories', was a long essay on Durkheim's *The
Rules of Sociological Method*.[44] During this period, Sorel was trying to
establish a non-deterministic science of social facts that took on board
the innovations of historical materialism, in the face of positivism's
structural decline. A 'materialistic theory of sociology'[45] embracing 1)
the more advanced elements of French sociology (Durkheim), 2) the
essential centrality of the class struggle (Marx), and 3) the experimental
methods of the natural sciences.

The themes focused on by Sorel's particular form of revisionism were,
not surprisingly, also dear to Gramsci who took the critique of economic
dogmatism as his basis for the construction of a revolutionary political
theory centred around the interaction between the social and the
political. Gramsci discovered the echoes of the battle of ideas fought by
Sorel during this period not only in his pre-prison readings, but also in
the fundamentally important correspondence between Sorel and Croce
published by *La Critica* [The Critique], which he read carefully and
commented on at numerous points in the *Prison Notebooks*.[46]

In the lengthy essay entitled 'The Old and the New Metaphysics', Sorel
examined the problem of determinism and individual freedom, and tried
to establish a 'real metaphysics' connected to industrial development.
This was at the time of Sorel's initial relationship with Marxism, when
the question of Marxism was still dealt with in a very orthodox manner;
however, we can already perceive the key issues that, received from
Durkheim and screened by Marx, reached Gramsci in the form of
suggestions. Sorel criticized that 'formal system' that 'appeared under
the name of social economy',[47] and countered it with a real metaphysics
that enabled people to know 'the laws pertaining to economic concepts'.[48]
This was the scientific socialism of Karl Marx, which combined social
enquiry with a scientific theory capable of establishing class struggle as
an intrinsic feature of bourgeois society.[49] According to Sorel, Marx was
among the few to understand the decisive influence of the environment
on individuals' actions; however, Marx – and this is his true strength –

did not reduce the environment to an external thing determined by the fatalism of natural and biological laws, as Durkheim seemed to do, but he always related it to Man and his actions:

> It is virtually unnecessary to recall the importance of the man-made environment to Karl Marx's doctrine. Just as a cell does not live in any immediate relationship with the cosmic elements, so Man does not develop in isolation. The environment is fabricated, constructed, constantly transformed by his activities, and any science that neglects this environment is a groundless anthropology.[50]

Sorel was thus searching for a new image of Man on which to base his analysis of social facts, of a new relationship between the individual and the environment. He found that image in the writings of Marx, and agreed with the definition of all milieus as artificial, and with the claim that such milieu could be transformed. The opportunity to create a science of social actions thus came about in Sorel's case through his examination of labour: 'Aristotle [...] defined Man as a rational and social animal. Today [...] the term *worker* comprises, for modern-day people, an expression of being alive and being rational, and thus we say that Man is a *social worker.*'[51] Man's working activity underlies both his individuality and his sociality: he is conceived as *homo faber* in the broad sense of creator and transformer of both his milieu and of himself.

The words of Gramsci regarding Man as an 'essentially "political"' being,[52] insofar as he is both transformer and director, re-echo here. However, the influence of Sorel on Gramsci, just like that of sociology on Gramsci's Marxism, is not so much literal as mediated. These are topics, terms and concepts that in moving from one field to another, fortify the analysis to be found in the *Prison Notebooks*, rendering it capable of unexpected departures by means of which Gramsci succeeds in articulating (but not always resolving) those thorny political questions that the social sciences raise vis-à-vis political theory. Questions such as: what are the preconditions for socio-political order in mass societies?; what is the relationship between the individual and society in the age of the intensification of social relations?; what emplacements need to be conquered in order to break up this social formation of individuality and rebuild it on new foundations?

In this setting, for example, it is both surprising and yet in keeping with this reconstruction, to see Gramsci's broad use of the term 'environment'.

The 'determined market' – a concept that Gramsci uses to account for social regularities – is in fact defined as 'an *environment* which is organically alive and interconnected in its movements of development'.[53] The 'real philosopher' who 'cannot be other than the politician', is, instead, 'the active man who modifies the *environment*';[54] likewise 'Every man, in as much as he is active, i.e. living, contributes to modifying the social *environment* in which he develops'.[55] However, this equation also holds in the opposite sense, given that the environment is considered to be the specific agent of social coercion in forming individuality: 'As if there has not always been some form of coercion! Just because it is exerted unconsciously by the *environment* and by single individuals, and not by a central power or a centralized force, does it cease to be coercion?'[56]

It is clear that such a repeated use of a characteristically sociological term by a Marxist thinker is somewhat unusual. In fact, Marxist doctrine has always preferred concepts such as 'material conditions', 'relations of production' or 'ideological relations', depending on requirements. Gramsci, on the other hand, makes ample use of the term 'environment', and further proof of this is given by the translation of the *Theses on Feuerbach* that Gramsci worked on whilst in prison, prior to the writing of his *Prison Notebooks*,[57] where his translation of the third thesis into Italian from the original German reads as follows:

La dottrina materialistica che gli uomini sono il prodotto dell'ambiente e dell'educazione e che pertanto i cambiamenti degli uomini sono il prodotto di altro ambiente e di una mutata educazione, dimentica che appunto l'ambiente è modificato dagli uomini e che l'educatore stesso deve essere educato.[58]

[The materialist doctrine that men are products of their environment and education, and that, therefore, changed men are products of a changed environment and education, forgets that it is men who change the environment and that the educator must himself be educated.]

Gramsci's translation is certainly not the best possible one, as in fact the editors of the Translation Notebooks themselves admit,[59] but it is of particular interest owing to the use of the Italian term *ambiente* [environment] as the translation of the German term *Umstände*. Marx, in fact, uses this term in the German original,[60] which literally speaking should be translated using the Italian word *circostanze* [circumstances, the term that the Italian and English translations of the time in fact use], rather than *Umwelt*, a term introduced by the social sciences at the turn of the century, which corresponds to the Italian *ambiente* [environment]. This would seem to point to the influence of the French term *milieu*, which was to become extremely popular in French social sciences between the nineteenth and twentieth centuries.

Let us conclude our consideration of Sorel by emphasizing how the process whereby people are created, both inside and against one's own *milieu*, is grafted onto Durkheim's model that distinguishes between the individual and the social parts of Man:

> Language reveals to us, very clearly, that all of our actions are of a two-fold character; they are both individual and social: everywhere one finds a pair of expressions, one of which refers to a private force, the other to a public force: sin and crime, repentance and retribution, penitence and punishment, love and marriage, generation and family, agreement and contract, etc.[61]

It is here that the fundamental theoretical divergence from Durkheim's work lies: the social aspect of individuality becomes society's dynamic lever through his class analysis. Thus, 'Producer-Man' is a new type of Man: industrial labour creates a class of producers with political potential deriving from that part of individuality that is socially determined. Here Gramsci follows the same line when he affirms that 'Today [...] collective man is formed essentially from the bottom up, on the basis of the position that the collectivity occupies in the world of production', reiterating that the focus of analysis of this emerging new world must be 'the economic base of collective man: big factories, Taylorization, rationalization'.[62] Consequently, Gramsci's answer to the question 'What is the reference point of the new world in gestation?' is 'the world of production, labour'.[63]

Thus we can summarize Sorel's anthropology as follows: 1) Man is both an individual being and a social being (social worker); 2) the former cannot be scientifically analysed, whereas the latter can be ('personal processes have no common measure and may only be considered in the individual; the objective effects of material transformations constitute phenomena of a similar nature, and may be compared'),[64] 3) the study and understanding of these social phenomena must result from the study of industrial development.[65]

Sorel thus grafted onto Durkheim's model a conception of society and of the individual that was centred around labour and was accompanied by the idea of class struggle. This no longer comprised the 'de-subjectivized' division of labour that Durkheim identified in modern societies as the result of morphological changes, but a definition of the individual founded on his labour, as in the case of the factory worker, and which thanks to this offers at one and the same time a world view, an ethics and a new society opposed to the existing one. In Gramsci's view, this assumption finally clears the way for the political use of the terms and concepts adopted in the social sciences, thus showing that the 'toolbox' utilized by French sociology can be used to formulate a revolutionary theory articulated by a partisan subject capable of organizing itself organically to become the State.

THE THEORY OF PERSONALITY AND
MOLECULAR TRANSFORMATIONS

Finally, let us go back once again to Chapter 1's reconstruction of the broadened concept of ideology to be found in the *Prison Notebooks*. In Gramsci's view, ideology is the environment, internally diversified into different levels of coherence and truth, in which individuals' lives are structured together with their positions vis-à-vis other individuals. However, ideology is also the domain within which both the personality and the individuality of individuals is formed, either casually or in a structured political manner. Thus, we can use this basis to build a genuine Gramscian theory of personality formation,[66] whereby the ideological field represents the space within which individuals are created.

As we have seen, Gramsci believed that each individual comprised a series of internal elements constituting his individuality – such elements often being of a contradictory nature – which in turn reflected the heterogeneity of society and said person's relations with others. Thus, the individual and society reveal an isomorphism: each displays both unitary characteristics and internal conflicts, and neither can be interpreted on the basis of any one principle of coherency that determines them in a linear fashion. Therefore, the theory of personality and the theory of society are, in the *Prison Notebooks*, two expressions of the same problem. This finding means that the ideological struggle within society must also be fought at the level of the formation of individuals.

As with society, in the case of individuals the shifting elements constituting each individual may find their coherent equilibrium if one of them prevails thanks to its hegemonic capacity. It cannot be taken for granted, however, that this equilibrium is attained in this manner, on the basis of a coherent plan and through a coercive/consensual force applied in order to implement that plan. In fact, it may arise in an 'incoherent' form, as a hotchpotch of different, contradictory conceptions that co-exist:

> When one's conception of the world is not critical and coherent but disjointed and episodic, one belongs simultaneously to a multiplicity of mass human groups. The personality is strangely composite: it contains Stone Age elements and principles of a more advanced science, prejudices from all past phases of history at the local level and intuitions of a future philosophy which will be that of a human race united the world over. To criticize one's own conception of the world means therefore to make it a coherent unity and to raise it to the level reached by the most advanced thought in the world.[67]

As further confirmation of the isomorphism between the individual and society, this description of the possible individual contradictoriness is reflected in the social contradictoriness of common sense, which 'is not a single unique conception, identical in time and space. [...] it is a conception which, even in the brain of one individual, is fragmentary, incoherent and inconsequential, in conformity with the social and cultural position of those masses whose philosophy it is'.[68]

Thus, not everyone possesses a coherent individuality; indeed, it is much more likely that a person's individuality is of a transient, fragmentary character, which however – and this is the key point – does not prevent individuals from 'functioning' as such, of being 'mass active individual[s] operating in a practical manner' even in the presence, as we have seen, of a 'theoretical consciousness [...] historically in opposition to [their] activity'.[69] In this case, it should be emphasized, Gramsci is not describing a situation of disorder in which individuals are instable because of their contradictory natures – in view of their fragmentary, transient consciousness – but, on the contrary, a particular form of order. The individual – once again as with society, where no one organizational principle exists – rather than becoming anomic, in fact participates in a societal order that may be formed from a number of contradictory individual orders.[70] Thus, Gramsci's analysis leads to an awareness of the fact that in addition to the sovereign order based on the principle of command and obedience, there is also another, truly social order that is apparently disorderly, but where conflicting individuals fit in perfectly.

The individual's internal contradictoriness is thus reflected in the contradictory nature of society, in the form of conflict among different groups of people. However, this in turn affects individual personalities, which experience a form of internal conflict as a result. In a letter to his sister-in-law Tatiana, Gramsci wrote: 'How many societies does each individual belong to? And doesn't each one of us make continuous efforts to unify his conception of the world in which there continues to subsist heterogeneous fragments of fossilized cultural worlds?'[71] The class struggle, in fact, is also a struggle that goes on within each individual, in the constant effort to render one's own individuality coherent:

> Having ascertained that, given the contradictory nature of social relations, the consciousness of men must also be contradictory, the problem arises as to how this contradiction manifests itself, and how unification can be gradually attained: it manifests itself in the entire social body, with the existence of group historical consciousness (with stratifications corresponding to diverse stages of civilization's historical development and with antitheses in those groups that correspond to the same historical level) and it manifests itself in single individuals as a consequence of such a 'horizontal and vertical' disintegration.[72]

In this regard, it should be said that Gramsci understood the importance of the then emergent Freudian psychoanalysis, by including it in the process of construction of this 'new Man': 'The most salutary and immediately acceptable nucleus of Freudianism is the need to study the unwholesome repercussions entailed in the construction of any "collective man", of any "social conformism".'[73]

The formation of this new man lies at the centre of Gramsci's entire theory of personality, which thus applies to the three momentous phenomena that during his time best expressed this constructive endeavour: the creation of socialism in the USSR; the emergence of Fascist regimes in Europe; and the birth of Fordism-Taylorism in the USA. The connection with the 'sociality' of this new Man constitutes the crux of the emergence of these three different 'mutations'. However, all three cases represent long-lasting processes that not only operate coercively in contingent circumstances, but also produce effects that are felt over a lengthy period of time.

In this regard, Gramsci uses a specific concept to describe the manner in which a new personality emerges, and is subsequently consolidated, within the same individual. This concept is that of 'molecular transformations', which is to be found not only in Gramsci's political reflections in the *Prison Notebooks*, but also in his private reflections contained in the *Letters from Prison*. The meaning of the term refers, in both cases, to the slow, yet inexorable mutation of single elements within an organism (be it individual or collective) that at a certain point metamorphose from quantitative to qualitative, and which redefine the nature and structure of the object in question:

> As I have begun to judge with greater indulgence the catastrophes of character [...]. I say that who is changed 'molecularly' (where this is understood to be by force majeure) is 'morally' more justifiable than who changes suddenly [...]. A typical example is that of cannibalism. One may say that, at the current level attained by civilization, cannibalism is so repugnant that a normal person is to be believed when they say that faced with the choice, they would kill themselves. In reality, the same person, if faced with exactly the same choice – 'be a cannibal or kill yourself' – would no longer reason like this, because there would have come about such changes in the self that 'killing oneself' would no longer present itself as a necessary alternative; those people would become cannibals without giving suicide the slightest thought.[74]

Acting in a molecular, almost imperceptible manner, at least until the transformation has largely come about, the force driving the mutation avoids any direct confrontation, fragmenting and deploying its action on various different fronts, and thus engaging in a genuine war of position in order to conquer the organism, whether a person or a social aggregate.

Gramsci experiments with such dynamics personally, during the more difficult moments of his detention. The hardships of prison life, his precarious state of health, the isolation in which he lives from one day to the next; all of this acts molecularly to cause that catastrophe of the character described when he uses the example of cannibalism. In a letter to Tatiana, Gramsci writes:

the most serious thing is that in these cases there is a split in the personality: one part if it observes the process, the other suffers it, but the observing part (as long as this part exists there is self-control and the possibility of recovery) senses the precariousness of its position, that is, it foresees that it will reach a point at which its function will disappear, that is, there will no longer be any self-control and the entire personality will be swallowed by a new 'individual' who has impulses, initiatives, ways of thinking different from the previous ones. Well, I am in this situation. I don't know what of me may remain after the end of this process of change that I sense is in the course of development.[75]

The splitting of the personality in this case indicates an awareness of the transition from one individual to another, from one personality (individuality + sociality) to another: but 'This fact – Gramsci continues – from being individual may be considered collective.'[76] The *trasformismo* [transformism] witnessed 'from 1860 to 1900' is therefore defined as 'molecular' due to the fact that 'individual political figures moulded by the democratic opposition parties were incorporated one by one into the conservative-moderate "political class".'[77] Likewise, also the Fordist mechanization and rationalization of production that 'has determined the need to elaborate a new type of Man'[78] was studied in terms of its molecular moulding of the workforce through high wages and the strict control over the private lives of workers. Hence, also all those processes that may be included within the category of passive revolution:

> One may apply to the concept of passive revolution (documenting it from the Italian Risorgimento) the interpretative criterion of molecular changes which in fact progressively modify the pre-existing composition of forces, and hence become the matrix of new changes.[79]

From the recognition that all major political and productive changes are the result of gradual, constant molecular changes, one cannot deduce that their development, just like their origin, cannot be influenced by the will of men, according to a form of fatalism that certainly does not pertain to Gramsci. On the contrary, he denies all forms of automatism or mechanicism when he reiterates, time and again, that there has always been a degree of will and hegemonic planning that drives and imposes such changes, and with the advent of mass politics this is now clearer than ever:

this fact [the molecular transformations] ought to be studied as it presently manifests itself. It is not that this circumstance has not arisen in the past, but it is clear that it has taken on a special and [...] calculated form at present. That is, now it is considered that this happens and the event is prepared systematically, which did not happen in the past (systematically, however, means 'en masse' without excluding, of course, special 'attention' to individuals).[80]

This molecular nature of historical change is not restricted to passive, that is, conservative transformations of society, but is of a general character, and also characterizes the war of position that one part of society engages in as it attempts to overthrow that society. Each 'formation of a collective historical movement' in fact proceeds in 'molecular phases',[81] and this process is in no way mechanical or automatic, but depends directly on the political will of a hegemonic force.

The interweaving of individual transformation and social transformation that we have analysed here is, ultimately, the precondition for the question that we shall be looking at in the next chapter, that is, the question of collective organisms:

It will be said that what each individual can change is very little, considering his strength. This is true up to a point. But when the individual can associate himself with all the other individuals who want the same changes, and if the changes wanted are rational, the individual can be multiplied an impressive number of times and can obtain a change which is far more radical than at first sight ever seemed possible.[82]

Social cooperation, which in production creates a value that is greater than the sum of individuals' labours, also creates a surplus in the social sphere that exceeds the mere sum of the individualities that come together. Collective organisms, their internal lives, their relations with individuals, are all Gramscian questions that go well beyond any theory of the political party.

3

Collective organisms

All Italians are capable of the occasional, theatrical heroic act, which may be productive, but which may also appear a fruitless waste of energy. The proletariat has shown itself to be better than this. It is capable of both things. It is a social organism, a living complexity.

Antonio Gramsci
8 September 1917

COLLECTIVE ORGANISMS BETWEEN
CIVIL SOCIETY AND THE STATE

The nature and workings of collective organisms – not only parties, but also trade unions, associations and intermediate bodies in general – represent a specific sphere of reflection in the *Prison Notebooks*, particularly in regard to the new relationship between State and society that in Gramsci's view emerged during the age of mass politics. During the early years of the twentieth century, in fact, there was a growing gap between the exercise of power by the dominant elites, on the one hand, and the new requirements of 'social government' resulting from the political emergence of the masses, on the other. As a result of the First World War, not only had this crisis of the liberal order become increasingly evident, but it had reached a point of no return, in fact. Italy's ruling classes had been legitimized by the national character of the political order established in 1861, which combined modern contractual legitimacy – whereby the command/obedience relationship was guaranteed by its originally contractual roots and was thereafter no longer challengeable[1] – with a reference to the 'community of destiny'[2] of a people, which in its various forms constituted further legitimization and created a link between governed individuals and the governing elites.

This model of national order, despite its fragile nature in a nation that had only recently been unified,[3] had lent support to the creation of a unified administrative machine, of a shared feeling of belonging, and of a bond between individuals and the national State, which was substantially effective from the point of view of the government of a nation. However, from the late nineteenth century onwards this model entered a period of crisis, with an aspect of non-governability resulting from the emergence of new players into the political space. In fact, these new players no longer related to the liberal order in their capacity as neutral individuals, but in a collective mode, that is, in the form of the masses or as emerging intermediate entities. The period bridging the nineteenth and twentieth centuries was thus characterized by the realization of this disunity resulting from, among other things, the emergence of new institutions, hubs of interests and power, which removed certain spheres of mediation and representation from the State that up until then had been considered the only institution qualified to interact with the demands of those individuals under its power.

This problem of legitimacy was also tackled within the formal sphere of law that, during this process of relaxation of the principal channel of command, reformulated its own unitary system of construction. This period witnessed the emergence of the institutional theory of law, whereby law derives from society – in a bottom-up process – and not, on the contrary, from political power, in a top-down process designed to guarantee the conformity of society to a 'legal design'. This approach, which acknowledges the phenomenon of the multitude of associative forms, also acknowledges, as a consequence, a plurality of existing and competing legal systems. Santi Romano, the Italian jurist who commenced this tradition, based his approach on the very consideration that the flourishing of organizations mediating between the State and individuals constitutes the key element of the 'modern State [...], [that] soon manifested itself to be inadequate in regulating, indeed often in failing to acknowledge, groupings of individuals'.[4]

Gramsci tried to reconstruct the origins of this change by going back to the foundation of intermediate organisms as the result of the consolidation of the modern State, which needed to abolish 'many autonomies of the subaltern classes'[5] in order to create room for the new political-State entity. Modern politics thus 'abolishes the state as a federation of classes – but certain forms of the internal life of the subaltern classes are reborn as parties, trade unions, cultural associations'.[6] In re-writing these words four years later, Gramsci was even more explicit when he stated that 'The modern State replaces the mechanical bloc of social groups by subordinating them to the active hegemony of the ruling and dominant group, thus abolishing some autonomies that however re-emerge in another form, as parties, trade unions, cultural associations.'[7]

The autonomy of social groups in the pre-modern age, in fact, permitted a certain freedom of movement and organization, the counterpart to which was the use of force by external powers as the only way of obtaining the obedience of such otherwise autonomous groups. This freedom of movement – which was real despite being constantly threatened by the use of violence – was first eliminated by the central-ization of the power and the bureaucratic-administrative functions of the modern State, only to re-emerge in new forms within the State. The State thus became the mediator of specific, yet organized requests, by introducing consensus-based dynamics into its relations with society.

Within the context of this transformation, the new autonomies were (re-)established with the 'State hallmark': their organization, their action, their very existence was connected to the State, which enabled them to re-emerge within that State's 'own' society. Hence, this autonomy existed, but its roots still lay in the political domination of State power. According to Gramsci, the essence of this problem was already present in the work of Hegel, with the transition from a '"patrimonial" conception of the State'[8] to an 'expansion of the State'[9] that was to include, in fact, the private system of consensus:

Hegel's doctrine of parties and associations as the 'private' fabric of the State [...]. Government by consent of the governed, but an organized consent, not the vague and generic kind which is declared at the time of elections: the state has and demands consent, but it also 'educates' this consent through political and trade-union associations which, however, are private organisms, left to the private initiative of the ruling class. Thus, in a certain sense, Hegel already goes beyond pure constitutionalism and theorizes the parliamentary state with its regimes of parties.[10]

Expanding the concept of the State in view of its relationship with organized consensus – not only that of the dominant, ruling classes, but also that of the subaltern classes – in Gramsci's mind meant rethinking the separation of civil society, meaning the private, economic sphere, from the State, meaning the public, political sphere. In fact, Gramsci broke this dichotomy down further by introducing a third concept, that of 'political society', meaning the repressive, organizational and bureaucratic functions of dominion ('official government'[11]), by using the term State – 'in the integral sense: dictatorship + hegemony'[12] – to describe the combination of political society and civil society. This arrangement also entails the necessary transformation of the concept of civil society: from being the sphere of private economic interests described by classical economists, it becomes the field of forces between individuals and collective organisms in their relations with the State, within which power is not only exercised, but also generated.[13]

This is a conceptual reconfiguration that cannot be considered final, as it is characterized by further oscillations generated by the inherent nature of the *Prison Notebooks*, that is, as a work in progress rather than the finished item. In fact, the same notion of the State is sometimes used by Gramsci to indicate the sum of civil society and political society (consensus + coercion), and at other times as a synonym of political society only (coercion).[14] However, once the non-final nature of Gramsci's writings is recognized, several observations may be made regarding this conceptual reconfiguration. On the one hand, in fact, calling the organizational features of the State itself 'political *society*' has a specific meaning that marks the 'incursion' of society into the coercive mechanisms governing the political order. Gramsci, in fact, appears more interested in the degree to which the 'order of society' figures in State mechanisms than in the State's coercive involvement in society. The latter measure is considered inversely proportional to the ruling classes' ability to 'regulate' society.[15] On the other hand, calling the 'State' the sum of the coercive element (political society) and the consensual element (civil society) makes it possible to broaden the range of figures entrusted with keeping order, through a conception of 'officials' that include those individuals who '"acting spontaneously", [their] action is identified with the aims of the state'.[16] Finally, by also referring to civil society as the 'State', Gramsci aims to relativize and historicize the unity of social life, thus opening the way to the challenging of an order that is only such if perceived from the viewpoint of a 'particular social group'.[17] Society, as we have seen with human nature, does not contain any inherent eternal, transcendent principle; its unfolding depends on the constant recomposition of its unity by the dominant, ruling classes.

The collective organisms that are formed within this State in the integral sense are thus of a dual nature: on the one hand, they remain the principle vehicle for the actions of the subaltern classes, while, on the other hand, they constitute the means by which the dominant, ruling classes exercise their hegemony. It should be pointed out here that this is a case of dual nature, and not of alternate operation. In fact, these collective organisms are never the exclusive product of the autonomy of one social group, and similarly they are never only the instruments by means of which the dominant, ruling classes exercise their hegemony. On the contrary, they perform both functions concurrently within the framework of the interweaving of civil society and State. What does change is the prevalence of the one over the other in their everyday course of action, or rather, the political capacity to subordinate one interest to another through hegemonic action.

What emerges here once again is the discrepancy between the sociological discourse, which postulates the unity of the social sphere through its reification, and the Gramscian argument, which, whilst adopting various insights into the nature of social phenomena taken from sociology itself, nevertheless considers the division of labour to be a source of conflict as well as an organizational principle. Taking up a position outside the conservative organicism of the majority of French sociology, Durkheim himself had acknowledged, in regard to the 'class war', that 'No similar phenomenon is to be observed within the organism'.[18] However, the fact that social reality expresses and contains something more than the organic projection of the dominant, ruling elite, and that this discrepancy may conceal the seeds of a new social order, represents the challenge posited by Gramsci. The dual nature of collective organisms, in fact, enables them to be 'made to operate' both as organic mechanisms rebalancing the power system and as an independent expression of subaltern, potentially revolutionary demands.

The aforementioned terminological oscillation at this point may allude to something more than just non-completion of the argument. In fact, it would appear to refer to an inherent ambivalence in the concept of State (and consequently in that of civil society), which reveals its 'educational' face when the civil society within moves in harmony with the State's plans, but reveals its coercive nature when civil society moves independently in challenging the State. It is no surprise to find that Gramsci writes of an 'identity-distinction between civil society and political society'.[19]

This categorical reformulation is of prime importance not only in terms of the present discourse, but also because Gramsci's very theory of revolution manifests itself within said reformulation, by indicating a series of theoretical steps that evoke this transition: the pre-eminence of the war of position over the war of manoeuvre; the distinction between organic and traditional intellectuals; hegemony as a strategy of class struggle in the age of mass politics.[20] All of these formulations acknowledge the presence of an epochal event consisting in the transformation of the organization of power, of the mechanisms legitimizing that power, and of its relationship with society: a society that no longer consists of an external terrain of conquest and disciplining,[21] but also an internal terrain that determines (and in turn produces) power. A space where, going beyond the perception of the State as a machine, on the one hand, and the individual as a monad, on the other, the collective organisms perform the fundamental function of maintaining (or overthrowing) the social and political order.

BUREAUCRACY AND OFFICIALS: GRAMSCI AND WEBER

Taking Gramsci's approach to collective organisms seriously entails first of all distancing oneself from the idea that they are simply 'parts of society' as opposed, on the one hand, to single individuals, and, on the other, to the State as '*monopoly* of the *legitimate* use of physical force'.[22] On the contrary, collective organisms are both a projection of the 'social' characteristics of individuality and a projection of the very organization of the State. This dual nature gives rise to a fundamental question, namely, that of the connections, the procedures and the relationships that emerge between individuals and the collective organisms, and also within the same organisms. Gramsci deals with this question through his analysis of 'organic centralism' and 'living philology', which shall be examined in Chapter 3, section 'Organic centralism and living philology'. However, a preliminary observation should be made with regard to the question of bureaucratization as a defining feature of the process of formation of increasingly large and complex apparatuses.

With the advent of mass politics, in fact, bureaucratic organization became a characteristic of all collective organisms, raising a series of problems not only in technical-administrative terms, but also from the strictly political point of view when it overlaps with questions of representation, decision making and freedom. As was seen with the formation of collective organisms, reconstructed from the advent of the modern State, once again Gramsci deals with the problem by tracing its origins:

As political and economic forms develop historically, a new type of official is increasingly being produced – what could be described as 'career' officials, technically trained for bureaucratic work (civil and military). This is a fact of prime significance for political science, and for any history of the forms taken by the State. Has this process been a necessary one, or, as the 'pure' liberals claim, a degeneration in respect of the ideal of *self-government*? Certainly every type of society and State has had its own problem of officials, which it has formulated and resolved in its own way; every society has had its own system of selection, and its own type of official to be trained. The reconstruction of how all these elements have evolved is of capital importance.[23]

The argument regarding the new type of Man is taken further here as far as regards the relationship with collective organisms, to become a discourse on the 'new type of official' who imposes himself socially, and who must guarantee, within bureaucratic organizations, the reproduction of relations among individuals.

It was Max Weber, some of whose writings Gramsci knew of,[24] who pointed out that the unique characteristic of the modern State was the emergence of the professional official as the result of the quantitative and qualitative evolution of bureaucracy. This type of official represented a new form of domination (authority),[25] or rather, a specific form of the legitimization of such. This was no longer of the traditional variety, that is, guaranteed by the historical continuity of royal lineage, but of the rational-legal variety, that is, based on the formal legality of procedures (Weber's third type of legitimate domination, the charismatic variety, lacked in continuity, which is indispensable if the State's organization is to be preserved). The legal-rational form of legitimacy consequently results in certain persons being vested with powers of command on the basis of the provisions of law, thus creating a specific type of official. Organized as such, bureaucratic domination 'inevitably accompanies modern *mass democracy*', insofar as it 'usually come[s] into power on the basis of a levelling of economic and social differences'.[26]

The interest in the concept of 'official' – a concept insofar as for Gramsci it 'is a fact of prime significance for political science'[27] – emerges from the question as to whether the formation of said officials is a necessity or simply a perversion of historical development. In this case, it may be asserted that the creation of a group of officials whose task it is to administer organized living is a necessity in Gramsci's view, as shown by his assertion that 'every type of society and State has had its own problem of officials'.[28] Gramsci reiterates this stance in another note when, no longer dealing with the question of the necessity of the bureaucracy – having already stated that 'Bureaucracy [...] has become a necessity' – he examined the question of the relationship between bureaucracy and politics: 'the issue that needs to be raised concerns the formation of an honest and impartial bureaucracy that does not abuse its role in order to make itself independent from the control of the representative system'.[29] This problem arises further in a note in Notebook 14, in regard to the criticism of parliamentarianism:

> That the representative system may politically 'be a nuisance' for the career bureaucracy is understandable; but this is not the point. The point is to establish whether the representative and party system, instead of being a suitable mechanism for choosing elected officials to integrate and balance the appointed civil servants and prevent them from becoming ossified, has become a hindrance and a mechanism which operates in the reverse direction – and, if so, for what reasons. Moreover, even an affirmative reply to these questions does not exhaust the problem. For even allowing (as it must be allowed) that parliamentarianism has become inefficient and even harmful, it is not necessary to conclude that the bureaucratic system must be rehabilitated and praised.[30]

The question of the relationship between the representative form of politics and the bureaucracy thus transcends that of the crisis of the liberal system and of parliamentarianism, and as such is something that those wishing to construct a new order also have to deal with.

In this sense, Weber's analyses are further, and rather unexpectedly, in keeping with those of Gramsci. Weber believed that the process of democratization that levels out differences is both upstream and downstream from bureaucratic development, and constitutes both a precondition for, and a consequence of, such development, even if the two phenomena may find themselves opposed to one another once they become rooted in specific apparatuses of power:

> the democratization of society [...] is an especially favourable basis of bureaucratization [...] [but] 'democracy' as such is opposed to the

'rule' of bureaucracy, in spite and perhaps because of its unavoidable yet unintended promotion of bureaucratization.[31]

Thus, the two powers may find themselves in a struggle against each other, while there is a substantial affinity between the two processes, consisting in the levelling effect of the shared submission to an authority. For Weber, this *levelling of the governed* in face of the governing and bureaucratically articulated group' is the key feature of democratization, which 'does not necessarily mean an increasingly active share of the subjects in government'.[32] His analysis focuses on what he calls the 'process of "passive" democratization'.[33]

Gramsci's use of the term 'passive revolution' – originally coined by Vincenzo Cuoco[34] – is widely known. He employed this expression throughout the *Prison Notebooks* to describe those historical changes that had occurred in the absence of any strong popular action, as a form of transition managed and guaranteed by those classes already holding power.[35] The phenomenon that most interests both Gramsci and Weber would thus appear to be the passivity of the masses that makes history, as the result of that powerful process of 'social disciplining' involving all aspects of human existence; and perhaps it is a coincidence, albeit a revealing one, that both writers use the term 'passivity' to describe this process.

However, the difference between Weber's passive democratization and Gramsci's passive revolution is a reminder of the difference in the two writers' field of discourse. In Weber's case, the problem remains, in fact, that of democracy, a problem that unfolds within the context of an 'unstoppable [...] advance of bureaucratization', in the attempt 'to salvage any remnants of "individual" freedom of movement *in any sense*'.[36] In Gramsci's case, on the other hand, the question is one of revolution: that is, it is the problem of how to break with the association of bureaucracy with passivity, starting from an awareness of the processes leading to the development of the bureaucracy, but offering to a collective organism, rather than to individuals, the opportunity to be agents, and not just passive subjects, of the historical process.[37]

In Weber's work, the impossibility of escaping from the confines of the bourgeois order in the attempt to conciliate liberalism with increasing bureaucratization – thus resolving this contradiction by remaining within the liberal tradition – becomes clear when the extreme edge of such tradition is recouped with the reactivation of charisma, as shown by the proposal in favour of a presidential, plebiscitary republic for post-war Germany.[38] In this regard, Gramsci, on the other hand, shows that he has fully embraced the shift in focus concerning the subject of political action, which can no longer take the form of individuality – each single individual, vis-à-vis society, in fact can only suffer the coercive pressure of that society, as witnessed in Durkheim's analysis – but only that of a collective organism. The revolutionary problem thus manifests itself as the type of relationship to be established between the leading element within this organism and the masses composing such, in the context of the gradual decline of this distinction during the course of the revolutionary process, 'until the demise of political society and the advent of regulated society'.[39]

Despite focusing on the same transformations, Gramsci's and Weber's respective analyses produce different outcomes. In Weber, the political man capable of dealing with the transformations of the existing is described in tragic terms, and is basically the heroic man capable of conciliating the apparently incompatible charisma and bureaucracy. In Gramsci, the party, as the only possible political actor, is willing to promote the construction of a non-fetishistic relationship between the individual and the collective organism, thus creating a new 'mass intellectual' capable of combining technical qualities and strictly political ones.

THE POLITICAL PARTY AND THE POLITICAL CLASS

The analysis of collective organisms conducted so far brings us to the role of the party in modern mass politics. In fact, Gramsci saw the political party as the only body that could enable the subaltern classes to get organized and to fight against, and overturn, the capitalist system so as to subsequently establish a new order. His insistence on the classical question of organization should not be allowed to overshadow the specific perspective from which Gramsci viewed the phenomenon of organization, covering a much broader series of features than just the traditional requirements of decision making and coordination that characterized the communist parties of his time. Gramsci's discourse on the political party, in fact, fits into the framework of the analysis of collective organisms conducted so far: in other words, it is in keeping with those epoch-making processes regarding the form of mass politics, the structure of the State and of society, the process of bureaucratization, and consequently the type of relationship among individuals in a post-liberal age.

In Gramsci's view there are two new vitally important aspects that need to be understood in order to deal with the question at hand. These are: 1) the shifting of the directive function from individuals to collective organisms; 2) the transition from a random standardization to an organized one – whereby, thanks to 'communications, newspapers, big cities [...] the pace of the molecular processes is faster than in the past'.[40] This is something that evaded both Sorel and his conception of myth – 'a "passive activity"' as opposed to the '"active or constructive" phase'[41] of the political party –, and Benedetto Croce with his vision of politics as a 'passion' that reduces 'parties to "individual" party leaders whose "passion" motivates them to construct the instrument that would carry them to victory'.[42] By distancing himself from these two writers, following among other influences the early sociological studies of the matter (especially those of Michels, who was influenced by Weber), Gramsci began to describe certain characteristic traits of modern politics that affect the way the political party is perceived.

First of all, there is the 'Growing complexity of political work, as a result of which party leaders increasingly become professionals'.[43] This quotation is, in truth, part of Gramsci's summary of an article written by Robert Michels,[44] which, however, stands testimony to the attention paid to a phenomenon that was also perceived as a problem for communist parties. The danger of bureaucratization, in fact, is 'the most dangerous in terms of habitude: if it organizes itself as a separate body, compact and independent, the party will end up being anachronistic'.[45] This was a problem that had emerged in those parties analysed by Michels due to the creation, in Gramsci's opinion, of a 'class division within the organization',[46] whereby the leaders not only did not enjoy the trust of the led, but had ended up by representing diverse interests dictated in the main by their own privileged position. In the political party foreseen by Gramsci, given the absence of any such internal division, the organizational and centralization requirements permitted, on the contrary, the creation of a close link 'between great mass, party and leading group; and the whole complex, thus articulated, can move together as "collective-man"'.[47]

However, it is clear (also to Gramsci) that the question cannot be circumvented so easily. Indeed, the strength of Michels' analysis lay precisely in his demonstrating that bureaucratic perversities also occur within the parties of the working class, when such parties' fundamental characteristics should be political involvement and democratic control. The very size of note Q2§75 regarding Michels and the aforesaid problem, despite the caustic criticism contained therein, indicates an unresolved problem that Gramsci continued to reflect upon at length throughout the *Prison Notebooks*. This is a problem that, as Gramsci clearly understood, has no intrinsic or formal solution resulting from any sociological analysis designed merely to overturn Michels' analysis. On the contrary, it needs to be dealt with through that revolutionary praxis that modifies the very premises of Michels' discourse, such as that of the insurmountable division between the rulers and the ruled.[48] The description of social reality offered by political science in fact captures an element of truth in the realistic representation of the persistence of the division between the rulers and the ruled[49] also in 'voluntary' (non-government) organizations such as political parties; but by ignoring the fact that this division refers to a historically determined relationship between individuals and collective organisms, which may take other forms, the opportunity is lost to grasp developments other than those of a fetishistic nature.[50]

In this regard, the party of the working classes is not only asked to create its own leadership, but also to 'educate' one such group that, given the existing conditions, does not reproduce the divisions between intellectual and manual labour, between those representing and those represented, between command and obedience, which characterize those societies divided by class:

> In the Modern Prince [the political party], the question of the collective man; in other words, the question of 'social conformism' or of the goal of creating a new level of civilization by educating a 'political class', the ideation of which already embodies this level. Hence the question of the role and attitude of every physical individual in the collective man.[51]

It is clear that this quote points to the need to foresee in present society those features that are to characterize future society, starting with a realistic analysis of the mechanisms governing that society.[52] In fact, what the working class needs is a 'political class', 'the ideation of which already embodies this [new] level'[53]: a level characteristic of the new order that must create a different relationship between 'the single individual' and 'the collective organism',[54] along the lines of the 'living philology', as we shall see.

For Michels the needs of the organ (the leading entity) compared with those of the organism (the party in the broadest sense of the term) represented a hindrance to the masses' participation in the latter's decisions. In Gramsci's view the needs of the former – the existence and operation of which are established, and which provide the undeniable scientific achievement of political science – may result in a non-oligarchic outcome on the basis of a dynamic, fluid, hegemonic relationship between the masses and the elite. Managing to keep both democracy and technical-administrative processes together is a central problem of political action Gramsci intends to reconsider 'after the expansion of parliamentarism and of the associative systems of union and party, and the growth in the formation of vast State and "private" bureaucracies'.[55]

So, if the level of civilization of the new order has to be foreseen, in some way, in the party, the question becomes: 'which party for which new order?' Once again, Gramsci's writings attempt to provide a series of reflections and warnings regarding a process that can only find any 'truth' through its actual unfolding. One such reflection concerns the fact that the continuity of these voluntary organisms needs to be guaranteed, without losing that dynamism deriving from the close relationship with the group the party represents, which is constantly transformed during the course of its development:

> there is an aspect of the issue that pertains to the organizing centre of a grouping, namely, the question of 'continuity' that tends to create a 'tradition' – not in the passive sense of the term, obviously, but in an active sense, as continuity in constant development, but 'organic development'. This problem contains in a nutshell the entire 'juridical problem', that is to say, the problem of assimilating the whole grouping to its most advanced fraction; it is a problem of education of the masses, of their 'adaptation' according to the exigencies of the end pursued.[56]

Hence, the need to guarantee the continuity of the political organization, but without interrupting the organic development of the grouping, which by its very nature is dynamic: 'There exists, to be sure, the danger of becoming "bureaucratized", but every organic continuity presents this danger, which must be watched. The danger of discontinuity, of improvisation is much greater.'[57] Gramsci terms this principle of continuity an essential ingredient in both 'public' structures and 'private' organizations such as political parties, 'State spirit':

> does there exist something similar to what is called 'State spirit' in every serious movement, that is to say in every movement which is not the arbitrary expression of more or less justified individual-isms? Meanwhile 'State spirit' presupposes 'continuity', either with the past, or with tradition, or with the future; that is, it presupposes that every act is a moment in a complex process, which has already begun and which will continue. The responsibility for this process, of being actors in this process, of being in solidarity with forces which are materially 'unknown' but which nevertheless feel themselves to be active and operational – and of which account is taken, as if they were physically 'material' and present – is precisely in certain cases called 'State spirit'.[58]

The elitist critique of democracy formulated in that period by Michels, Mosca and Pareto from an a-democratic viewpoint,[59] in Gramsci gets transformed into a theory of the 'rationality, historicity or concrete func-tionality'[60] of elites, that is, of their capacity to effectively respond to the needs expressed by social groups who already inherently possess, in their economic activity, a political programme that may only be implemented 'through the mediation of an *élite* for whom the conception implicit in human activity has already become to a certain degree a coherent and systematic ever-present awareness and a precise and decisive will':[61]

> Among the many meanings of democracy, the most realistic and concrete one, in my view, is that which can brought into relief through the connection between democracy and the concept of hegemony. In the hegemonic systems, there is democracy between the leading group and the groups that are led to the extent that <the development of the economy and thus> the legislation <which is an expression of that development> favours the <molecular> transition from the groups that are led to the leading group.[62]

The key feature of democracy, that is, the masses' participation in the political decision-making process, which in Michels' view has been lost forever, which according to Mosca would be a catastrophe if achieved, and which Pareto believed to be pure theoretical abstraction, is on the contrary reformulated by Gramsci, within the framework of a revolutionary theory characterized by these new hegemonic-democratic coordinates.

ORGANIC CENTRALISM AND LIVING PHILOLOGY

Further evidence of Gramsci's specific problematization of the political party as a collective organism can be found in the classification of the party's internal components, based on what Gramsci calls the 'theorem of fixed proportions':[63]

> for a party to exist, three fundamental elements (three groups of elements) have to converge: 1) A mass element, composed of ordinary, average men, whose participation takes the form of discipline and loyalty, rather than any creative spirit or organizational ability. [...] 2) The principal cohesive element, which centralizes nationally and renders effective and powerful a complex of forces which left to themselves would count for little or nothing. [...] 3) An intermediate element, which articulates the first element with the second and maintains contact between them, not only physically but also morally and intellectually.[64]

The proportions in which such elements are to be found is given by historical conditions and the political contingency. However, the second element, which identifies the leaders capable of coordinating and centralizing the 'collective wills'[65] that would otherwise be dissipated, is the one that always plays the key role in the modern political party. If, given favourable 'objective material conditions', such an element exists, then in Gramsci's view 'the other two are bound to exist'.[66]

However, this 'key' element is also the main barrier to the bureaucratization of the party. In fact, how can the political line be maintained if the technical position is imposed for organizational reasons? In this regard, Gramsci makes the distinction, with regard to the organization of a political party, between organic centralism and democratic centralism. The contraposition of these two approaches was originally formulated in the course of the long-standing debate with Amadeo Bordiga – the first ever secretary of the Italian Communist Party and a leading figure among the party's left-wing faction – who in the 1920s argued the need for an 'organic relationship' between the masses and the party, and for an 'organic centralism' in the governance of the party. Bordiga employed these expressions to basically regiment the party and to indicate an immediate (and presumed) correspondence between leadership and class, and thus the significant autonomy of the former. Gramsci began to write the initial notes of his *Prison Notebooks* by countering this organic centralism with democratic centralism, criticizing organic centralism with its underlying principle of '"co-optation" around a "possessor of the truth"',[67] implying 'a caste and priestly type of leadership'[68]. However, in a note in Notebook 9 his view changes:

> The most accurate name [for organic centralism] would be bureaucratic centralism. 'Organicity' can only be found in democratic centralism, which is so to speak a 'centralism' in movement – i.e. a continual adaptation of the organisation to the real movement, a matching of thrusts from below with orders from above, a continuous insertion of elements thrown up from the depths of the rank and file into the solid framework of the leadership apparatus which ensures continuity and the regular accumulation of experience. Democratic centralism is 'organic' because on the one hand it takes account of movement, which is the organic mode in which historical reality reveals itself, and does not solidify mechanically into bureaucracy; and because at the same time it takes account of that which is relatively stable and permanent, or which at least moves in an easily predictable direction.[69]

Thus, organicity cannot be a characteristic of a static, authoritarian vision of political organization, but of political organization operating in a dynamic, democratic manner. From here on, Gramsci always uses the term 'organic centralism' as a synonym of 'democratic centralism', whereas he replaces the preceding (negative) notion of organic centralism with that of 'bureaucratic centralism'.[70]

Thus, organic centralism refers to a form of unitary, yet plural and conflicting, organization, requiring the constant adjustment of organization and class, through the enhancement of the multiplicity of individuals' claims:

> A collective consciousness, which is to say a living organism, is formed only after the unification of the multiplicity through friction on the part of the individuals; nor can one say that 'silence' is not a

multiplicity. An orchestra tuning-up, every instrument playing by itself, sounds a most hideous cacophony, yet these warm-ups are the necessary condition for the orchestra to come to life as a single 'instrument'.[71]

The possibility of influencing the establishment of the collective organism, in a conflicting, organized manner through those forms of mediation present in every organization, becomes a prerequisite of the collective will: 'the vital question is not one of passive and indirect but active and direct consent, and hence that of the participation of single individuals, even though this gives an impression of disintegration and tumult'.[72] Gramsci's words re-echo those of Machiavelli in his *Discourses on Livy*, namely, that 'where the matter is not corrupt, tumults and other scandals do not hurt'.[73] In fact movement, conflict and disagreement are not necessarily perceived as signs of decadence, but as potential factors of strength and liberty, if the organism within which they operate is 'healthy'; that is, going back to Gramsci, if there is the right relationship between individuals and the collective organism. In this regard, Gramsci coined an expression that characterizes that healthy relationship in which the individual is not nullified by the collective organism, but where the two interact without being opposed to one another, thus ensuring that they are both reciprocally enhanced through their interaction:

With the extension of mass parties and their organic coalescence with the intimate (economic-productive) life of the masses themselves, the process whereby popular feeling is standardized ceases to be mechanical and casual [...] and becomes conscious and critical. Knowledge and a judgment of the importance of this feeling on the part of the leaders is no longer the product of hunches [...]. Rather it is acquired by the collective organism through 'active and conscious co-participation', through 'compassionality', through experience of immediate particulars, through a system which one could call 'living philology'.[74]

It is this system of living philology that needs to underlie the formation of a collective organism capable of meeting the need to organize the potentially no longer passive 'great masses of the population'.[75] The tumultuous process by which this organism is created and enhanced is thus the element that characterizes the method of living philology, within the Gramscian assumption of organicity as a metaphor to be used to redefine the semantic field of the revolution. Organicity as a symbol of the centralism of a party, on the one hand, and living philology as an approach to the internal relations of that party, on the other hand, thus paint an initial overall picture of the party according to Gramsci. Given such premises – and given the assumption that the historical actors are now collective organisms rather than individuals – Gramsci can imagine the party as the modern Prince, in reference once again to Machiavelli's work.

MACHIAVELLI AND THE MODERN PRINCE

With the exception of Benedetto Croce, Niccolò Machiavelli is the Italian most frequently mentioned in the *Prison Notebooks*,[76] despite the fact that four centuries of history, innumerable institutional forms and diverse systems of political power separate the age of Machiavelli from that of Gramsci. This objective gap notwithstanding, there is one specific element that permits not only communication, but also a political dialogue between the two writers and their respective conditions. This element is, in fact, the particular form that modern politics has taken in Italy, a place that is fully integrated into Western modernity – in a Europe where the bourgeoisie have triumphed and where first liberal, then democratic conceptions have come to the fore – but that continues to preserve its own specific backwardness, as a result of which each innovation that emerges is of a dubious, mediated, 'corrupt' form compared to the ideal (and idealized) model of development. This backwardness is in turn the product of a gap that is, paradoxically, due to the precocity of certain developments – such as economic growth, the history of Italy's Communes, the Renaissance – that has destroyed the possibility of any political development in the 'classical' sense such as that seen in France and Britain. This backwardness/precocity has conditioned Italy's entire political history (and that of the dominions prior to Unification), thus providing a unique field of application for concepts that lie *within* the bounds of modern development, but are *decentralized* in relation to its principal axis. Machiavelli and Gramsci thus formulated a politics that could be said to lie *at the edge* of modernity, forced by history, as Althusser puts it, 'to think the conditions of possibility of an impossible task, to think the unthinkable',[77] by elaborating the conceptual instruments of modern politics within a terrain that lies outside the traditional sphere of European modernity.

Machiavelli and Gramsci can also be perceived as sharing a common ground in terms of their respective conditions for potential political action: Gramsci wrote the *Prison Notebooks* at a time when he could no longer be a 'politician in action',[78] finding himself in a Fascist prison following an epochal defeat, that of the working class in the face of Fascism; Machiavelli wrote his most important works after having been expelled from the Florentine Republic's political sphere. This potential identification with Machiavelli, together with the recouping of a politics aimed at the mobilization of the popular strata, establishes Machiavelli as a benchmark over and beyond his classical status as a political thinker. In fact, in the *Prison Notebooks* Machiavelli is first a heading title grouping together a series of notes on political matters, and then the name of an entire notebook[79] in which Gramsci collects and reformulates many of his previous notes; finally, Machiavelli is the inspiration for Gramsci's proposed solution to the problem of the relationship between individuals and collective organisms in the age of mass politics, with the formulation of a conception of the party as the modern Prince.

The interpretation of Machiavelli over the course of centuries has constituted the focal point of a genuine political challenge, ranging from the inclusion of *The Prince* in the Catholic Church's *Index Librorum Prohibitorum* (List of Prohibited Books) to Frederick II's *Anti-Machiavel*, up to its 'republican' re-reading in recent times.[80] Gramsci mentions the liberal-romantic interpretation of *The Prince* offered by Ugo Foscolo in his work *Sepulchres*, in which Foscolo perceived *The Prince*'s main aim as being that of exposing the secrets (*arcana*) of power: 'that great man, who even as he tempers the sceptre of the rulers, strips them of their laurels, and lets the people see how it drips with tears and blood'.[81] Machiavelli was thus deemed to have spoken to the people and to have taught them not to fall into the trap of the powers that be, thus implementing a form of negative education whilst falling short of dealing with the problem of the positive organization of political power by the emerging classes. Gramsci likened this reading of Machiavelli to the one offered by Rousseau:

> Rousseau saw in Machiavelli a 'great republican', who was forced by circumstances – without his moral dignity suffering as a consequence – to '*déguiser son amour pour la liberté*' [disguise his love of liberty], but while feigning to give lessons to monarchs, he had really given

them to the people. Filippo Burzio has noted that such an interpretation, rather than morally justifying Machiavellianism, in truth foresaw a 'Machiavellianism to the n-th power': since the author of *The Prince* not only gave advice on fraud, but also fraudulent advice, to the detriment of those at whom such advice was aimed.[82]

These interpretations, although having the merit of reassessing Machiavelli after centuries of oblivion, during which the Florentine secretary had been perceived exclusively as an extoller of the Princes' unscrupulousness and ferocity, in Gramsci's view fail to give due credit to Machiavelli's position. While it was true that Machiavelli spoke on the people's behalf, he did not do so in a negative manner. On the contrary, he alluded to the potentially positive form that a 'people's politics' could take:

> One may therefore suppose that Machiavelli had in mind 'those who are not in the know', and that it was they whom he intended to educate politically. This was no negative political education – of tyrant-haters – as Foscolo seems to have understood it; but a positive education – of those who have to recognise certain means as necessary, even if they are the means of tyrants, because they desire certain ends. Anyone born into the traditional governing stratum acquires almost automatically the characteristics of the political realist, as a result of the entire educational complex which he absorbs from his family milieu, in which dynastic or patrimonial interests predominate. Who therefore is 'not in the know'? The revolutionary class of the time, the Italian 'people' or 'nation', the citizen democracy which gave birth to men like Savonarola and Pier Soderini, rather than to a Castruccio or a Valentino.[83]

Savonarola was, for Machiavelli, a model of political abstraction, whereas Pier Soderini had come to symbolize the Florentine Republic, that is, its first incarnation, a 'son of the people' who as such lacked the 'characteristics of the political realist'; as was seen at the siege of Prato in 1512, where he failed to take advantage of a possible agreement with the Spanish troops who were threatening the town, thus exacerbating matters and provoking the ransacking of Prato. This, in turn, was to lead to the fall of the Florentine Republic and the return of the Medici.[84]

Machiavelli thus wished to teach the people about the reality of modern politics, not in order to warn it of the injustices of tyrants, but to educate the emerging classes, and in particular their leaders, in the use of such politics. In Machiavelli's mind, this was the only way of fighting the all-important battle for political power and for an organization of society that was in keeping with the interests of the emerging classes. In this regard, Gramsci wrote:

> For Machiavelli 'educating the people' could only have meant convincing it, and making it aware, that there can only be one politics, realistic politics, to achieve the desired end, and thus it is necessary to gather around, and obey, that very Prince who uses such methods to achieve the end, because only he who wants the end wants the means required to reach that end.[85]

The Prince, Gramsci continues, 'is written for a hypothetical "Man of Providence"' who is capable of understanding people's demands; it is written for the people, as is manifested in the final part thereof: 'The conclusion of *The Prince* justifies the whole book, also in the view of the popular masses who in reality forget the means employed to achieve an end if this end is historically progressive'.[86] Thus, Machiavellianism may be valuable both for the emerging classes and for the ruling classes. However, in its disenchantment with the mechanisms of modern politics, it acts as a driver to the emerging classes, who of course do not acquire, through the continuity of the ruling classes, the knowledge required to govern.

Gramsci continues by arguing that 'This position in which Machiavelli found himself politically is repeated today for the philosophy of praxis', which develops 'a theory and technique of politics which – however strong the belief that they will in the final resort be especially useful to the side which was "not in the know", since that is where the historically progressive force is to be found – might be useful to both sides in the struggle'.[87] Machiavelli thus becomes the forerunner of the philosophy of praxis as far as regards the emerging classes' means of political education, and also the source, rediscovered by Gramsci, by which new instruments can be conceived that are capable of fighting the political battle to govern society.

The theorists of the philosophy of praxis, just like Machiavelli, 'have tried to construct and divulge a popular, mass "realism"',[88] as a living force for a new type of Prince. Thus, Gramsci believed that the time was due for

> a study of the real connections between the two [Marx and Machiavelli] as theoreticians of militant politics, of action; and a book that extracts from Marxist thought an orderly system of actual politics along the lines of *The Prince*. The topic would be the political party in its relations with the classes and with the state – not the party as a sociological category but the party that wants to establish the state.[89]

While the new twentieth-century Prince's task remains the same, namely, to embody the political aspirations of an emerging class, this new Prince can no longer be the charismatic figure portrayed in Machiavelli's writings. Mazzini was no such Prince, nor could Marx himself play such a role:

> The modern Prince, the myth-Prince, cannot be a real person, a concrete individual. It can only be an organism, a social component [...]. Historical development has already produced this organism, and it is the political party – the modern formation that contains the partial collective wills with a propensity to become universal and total.[90]

Thus, if the "'Prince" could be translated in modern terms as "political party"',[91] in Gramsci's view a new *The Prince* needed to be written as a basis for Marxism. Such a study 'must have a section devoted to *Jacobinism* [...], as an example of how a concrete and operative collective will is formed'.[92] The Jacobins, in fact, 'were a "categorical" "incarnation" of Machiavelli's *Prince*'.[93] They were capable of creating a collective will that worked, that was politically effective; they were realists, political militants, partisans with weighty passions, just as the leadership of the working-class 'modern Prince' party should be. Here, Machiavelli is once again, in Gramsci's view, the symbol of modern politics, of that leadership of an emerging class that on the contrary, by its very nature, should not be a leading class.

4

Society

But society, like Man himself, always remains an irreducible historical and ideal entity which develops by continually contradicting itself and surpassing itself. Politics and the economy, the human environment and the social organism are one and the same thing, and always will be.

Antonio Gramsci
9 February 1918

THE ORGANICITY OF SOCIETY

Along the path we have traced from the individual to the collective organism and the State, the key role that Gramsci sees society playing in an age of mass politics has clearly emerged. From the social characteristics of individuality, to the social features of the 'expanded' State, society thus becomes the subject of enquiry of Gramscian analysis. Gramsci does not see society as a 'middle' ground between the aforesaid levels, but the place where the principles of order, as well as the revolutionary potential of these levels, are created. To understand the structure and operation of society's various different aspects, Gramsci thus analyses diverse terrains – the new type of Man of mass society, the rationalization introduced by Taylorism and Fordism, the increasingly important role played by collective organisms – mainly through a classical metaphor of political thought, namely, the biological reference to the organism. He does so mainly through the use of the adjectival form, that is, by characterizing a series of relations existing within society as 'organic'.

Thus, the linking up of the references to organicity to be found in the *Prison Notebooks* is not only a question of philological reconstruction, but it also has a specific meaning for the interpretation of the entire body of Gramsci's thoughts. In fact, it is also the metaphor of the organism, and the adjectival form of the term, that represents the starting point for Gramsci's rethinking of society, and therefore of the theory of revolution 'in the West'.

There are numerous examples in the *Prison Notebooks* of the use of terms associated with the concept of organicity. All of such terms reintroduce the opposition between a positive pole, represented by the term 'organic', and a negative pole identified with all that is disorganic. The first group contains terms such as 'coherent and co-ordinated'[1] or 'conscious and critical'[2] Likewise, the 'semantic field' of organicity includes those concepts expressing the organizational and constructive level of politics. First and foremost, the concept of 'conformism', given that the 'organic development' of a group necessarily encounters the problem of the '"conformation" [of the masses] according to the exigencies of the end pursued'[3] Then there is the concept of the State, which in Gramsci's view 'permits a certain organic equilibrium in the development of the intellectual group'[4] The concept of hegemony itself is defined by a close relationship with the strategies of preservation of organicity (cf. Chapter 1, section 'The conceptual constellation of ideology including hegemony').

At the opposing end of the semantic spectrum we encounter expressions linked to disorganicity: 'incoherent'[5] – with regard to language –, but also '"paternalistic", formalistic, mechanistic' in regard to a 'non organic, non systematic' political position.[6] Twice disorganicity is linked to a *pulviscolo* ('an unstable scattering' and 'specks of dust' in the English translation)[7] and to a 'formless state'.[8] The lack of organicity is, finally, a characteristic of the 'sporadic and disorganic rebelliousness of the popular masses'.[9]

Such adjectivizations contribute towards our understanding of Gramsci's use of the specific sociological opposition between organic and disorganic. In fact, the latter term does not appear in these cases to express the 'inorganic character' of a relationship, its structurally 'non-organic' essence, but rather a critical situation of a given organicity, or a hint of an alternative organicity that while possible, is not yet real. Thus, social relations are always organic, and their disorganicity is only visible as a result of a crisis in a *given* organic entity, or due to the incapacity of *another* organic entity to develop.[10] Gramsci thus seems to support a model of historical evolution based on the co-existence of moments of disintegration and moments of organic recomposition, during which the two phases – the revolutionary phase (during an 'organic crisis'[11]) and the ethical-political phase (the 'moment of "hegemony"'[12]) – must occur together in order to undermine a system of power.

Thus, the new order may only emerge from an objective state of disintegration of a society in crisis, such as that of a war, which is combined with a subjective state of systematic organization of a new social structure, supported by a new historical bloc capable of organically recomposing the fragmented elements.[13] The continual references in the *Prison Notebooks* to the concept of organicity may thus be interpreted as a sign of the need to build the initial elements of a new society and of a new organic relationship[14] within the context of the organic crisis of the liberal order, which may be identified as a crisis of a *given* organic structure. In this case, Gramsci's references to the war of position and to the importance of the hegemonic struggle,[15] both genuine strategies aimed at the recomposition of society marked by a different hegemony, prove useful. In analysing the sphere of political struggle, of the stability or crisis of the State, Gramsci thus adopts the 'semantic field' of organicity, and reformulates it in revolutionary terms in the attempt to describe the social level of mass politics.

ORGANIC INTELLECTUALS AND MASS INTELLECTUALITY

The most famous use of the adjective 'organic' in the *Prison Notebooks*, however, is probably the one referring to intellectuals when Gramsci discusses the distinction between organic intellectuals and traditional intellectuals in a long note from Notebook 4, later reformulated with certain modifications at the start of Notebook 12. The intellectual is organic, according to Gramsci, insofar as he links a 'social group'[16] to society, and through the latter to the State. The series of intellectuals organic to a social group thus constitute an intermediate body with a 'function [that] is precisely "organizational" or connective'.[17]

Whilst at first reading this distinction may appear to be that between a new class of intellectuals – organic intellectuals – linked to a social group in the ascendancy – the proletariat – and a series of old intellectual groups – traditional intellectuals – linked to social groups in decline – the bourgeoisie and the clergy, first and foremost –, upon closer examination one sees that this division refers to the distinction between the political function of intellectuals and their technical (that is, cultural, intellectual, specialist, scientific and organizational) functions. This also introduces the question of their problematic composition.

Proceeding in an orderly fashion, first we shall examine those passages in the *Prison Notebooks* that reveal the key problem Gramsci raises:

Are intellectuals an autonomous and independent social group, or does every social group have its own particular specialised category of intellectuals? The problem is a complex one, because of the variety of forms assumed to date by the real historical process of formation of the different categories of intellectuals.[18]

During the same period, this question was answered by Karl Mannheim, who considered intellectuals as, at one and the same time, *both* bearers of the demands of a given social group *and* as a relatively independent group committed to the reproduction of social norms. Thus, Mannheim saw them as both representatives of the intellectual functions of a specific social group and as a function of the social system as a whole. A group that ultimately performs the task of preserving the social order: 'it subsumes in itself all those interests with which social life is permeated [...] for the fulfilment of their [the intellectuals] mission as the predestined advocate of the intellectual interests of the whole'.[19]

Gramsci could be said to have analysed this same dual function of the intellectuals, but to have historicized it and divided it in two, in the attempt to break up its recomposing mechanism:

1) Every social group, coming into existence on the original terrain of an essential function in the world of economic production, creates together with itself, organically, one or more strata of intellectuals which give it homogeneity and an awareness of its own function not only in the economic but also in the social and political fields. [...] 2) However, every 'essential' social group which emerges into history out of the preceding economic structure, and as an expression of a development of this structure, has found (at least in all of history up to the present) categories of intellectuals already in existence and which seemed indeed to represent an historical continuity uninterrupted even by the most complicated and radical changes in political and social forms.[20]

Therefore, Gramsci's problem does not seem to be that of the estab-lishment of a group of intellectuals that is organic to the working class, a process that occurs for all emerging groups. The problem appears to be that of the relationship between the intellectuals from this new group and the pre-existing categories of intellectuals who are no longer the direct expression of the interests of given social groups, but represent the historical sedimentation of political and social transformations of the past. Thus, the latter groups of intellectuals are not completely organic to the interests of the governing class, which they may even find themselves challenging,[21] but could be considered organic to society in general, which they help reproduce through their mediation.

Traditional intellectuals, through Gramsci's separation of the two functions (in Mannheim's view, on the contrary, the two are connected), thus represent the function of the general reproduction of the system, in the form of an autonomous, independent group that perceives its own 'uninterrupted […] historical continuity'[22] that mirrors the continuity of the existing social order.

This leads Gramsci to state that 'The formation of traditional intellectuals is the most interesting problem historically',[23] because both during the pre-revolutionary phase and during the initial governance of the new social order, albeit in different ways, the problem of the reproduction of society, which regards intellectual mediation, has to be resolved, and the solution cannot be immediately provided by the emergence of the new social group. The mediation of traditional intellectuals, their role in the reproduction of the system, is in fact partially independent from the mediated object, that is, from society's internal relations. This relative independence permits their specific persistence vis-à-vis any changes, even sudden ones, of the object of their own mediation. This is why, in Gramsci's view, the existing links between traditional intellectuals and the dominant group need to be broken 'before attaining power'.[24] At the same time, this terrain needs to be garrisoned after power has been conquered, since the objective continuity of such mediation requires that a relationship be established, at least provisionally, with these classes 'reproducing' the social order.

It is the party, conceived as the seed of the organicity of the new order, that is to perform both such duties:

> The political party, for all groups, is precisely the mechanism which carries out in civil society the same function as the State carries out, more synthetically and over a larger scale, in political society. In other words it is responsible for welding together the organic intellectuals of a given group – the dominant one – and the traditional intellectuals.[25]

The emergent social group is thus called upon to link with a part of the pre-existing society, namely, that part entrusted with the function of intellectual mediation, in order to break its remaining organicity and create the conditions under which said emergent group may independently take over this very function. This is why one of the most important indicators of the crisis of the liberal order is the behaviour of the traditional intellectuals who 'detaching themselves from the social grouping to which they have hitherto given the highest, most comprehensive form [...] [perform] an act of incalculable historical significance; they are signalling and sanctioning the crisis of the state in its decisive form'.[26] Gramsci also describes this process in a note regarding the category of officials, endorsing an analogy between intellectuals and officials that is reiterated on several occasions in the *Prison Notebooks*:

> Each new property relationship has needed a new type of official, that is, each new ruling class has formulated its problems of officials in a new way, but for a certain period has not managed to disregard tradition and vested interests, that is, the group of officials already in place on its arrival [...]. This problem partly overlaps with the problem of the intellectuals.[27]

The reference is clearly being made here to the Soviet situation, where following their coming to power, the Bolsheviks had to deal with the problem of having to rely on 'bourgeois technicians and specialists' to maintain the bureaucratic, economic and scientific apparatuses in working order.[28] In addition to the problem of stripping society's organicity of part of that society (cf. Chapter 2, section 'The social production of the individual: Gramsci and Durkheim'), there is now also the problem of the technical aspect of the reproduction of the new order. The importance of intellectual mediation, which is identified as the key terrain in the age of mass politics, is thus made clear in the difficult mixture of the organic/political element with the traditional/technical element, until the emerging class has attained its own complete, independent technical capacity.

Thus, the problem that Gramsci poses here – as we have already seen in the case of the political class that the modern Prince has to build – is not that of a new group of intellectuals linked to an emergent social class, but rather that of the environment that this group finds itself in, that is, its relationship, on the one hand, with the need to foresee in current society those elements that are to be part of the new order, and, on the other hand, with the 'viscous parasitic sedimentations left behind by past phases of history'.[29] Therefore, the focus is placed on the transformation of the historical conditions in which 'the theoretical aspect of the theory-practice nexus'[30] finds itself – the intellectuals in other words – operates. This transformation starts from a given premise of Gramsci's analysis: the dominance or centrality of one social group in the world of production is not enough to establish the necessary preconditions for the overthrowing of social relations, nor for what is the most important and difficult task, namely, that of exercising and maintaining power.[31] The development of a group of organic intellectuals – that social stratum that gives a given group 'homogeneity and an awareness of its own function'[32] prior to the heads-on clash with the dominant group – is not sufficient either. In order to run the entire course of the mediations starting from the social group in question through to society and ultimately to the State, there is also a need to strike the organicity of society itself, which is innervated by various groups of traditional intellectuals who must be countered, on the one hand, and won over to the new hegemony, on the other, otherwise the organic process leading from the emergent social group to the State will be interrupted. The class struggle thus also includes this endeavour to destroy and conquer, which in Gramsci's vocabulary is also known as the 'war of position' of an increasing duration and intensity.

Therefore, Gramsci's innovative understanding is that a revolution is inconceivable without the mediation of the intellectuals that are organic to the emergent social group, and is likewise inconceivable without seizing the function of general mediation, which is provisionally identified with the groups of (traditional) intellectuals who are already organic to society. Traditional intellectuals, in fact, represent the technical capacity to maintain the formal structure of society's dominance, and in doing so they perform the political function of maintaining order. Organic intellectuals, on the other hand, emerge as a political element of an ascendant social group, but they are also characterized by the technical specialization of that group (industrial labour). The innovative aspect of Gramsci's analysis thus lies in this dual identification of the political role and the technical capacity of both figures, particularly in view of the 'education' of the new intellectuals of the ascendant group, who in addition to their political function deriving from their association with the emergent group must also perform the technical function of preserving the (new) order, and ultimately become the means driving the power that flows through the new society. This technical function must be linked to industrial labour, in Gramsci's view:

> The traditional and vulgarised type of the intellectual is given by the man of letters, the philosopher, the artist [...]. In the modern world, technical education, closely bound to industrial labour even at the most primitive and unqualified level, must form the basis of the new type of intellectual. On this basis the weekly *Ordine Nuovo* worked.[33]

The insistence on the productive sphere in Gramsci's definition of the new intellectual in this case shows the consequences of the political and social importance, as well as the economic significance, of the growth of material production in the USSR at that time. Therefore, Gramsci's new 'mass' intellectual – an amplified version of the soviet 'new Man' in a certain sense – is to be found and constructed within the universe revealed by the industrial model:

> The mode of being of the new intellectual can no longer consist in eloquence, which is an exterior and momentary mover of feelings and passions, but in active participation in practical life, as constructor, organiser, 'permanent persuader' and not just a simple orator (but superior at the same time to the abstract mathematical spirit); from technique-as-work one proceeds to technique-as-science and to the humanistic conception of history, without which one remains a 'specialist' and does not become a 'leader' (specialist + political).[34]

Thus, the horizons opened up by Gramsci – for a revolutionary strategy in the West, on the one hand, and for the emergence in the USSR of figures capable of reproducing the new order, on the other hand – were those of an intellectual combining the characteristics of the specialist with those of the politician: the former derives from industrial labour, while the latter originates from the organic link with the intellectual's own group.[35] However, this horizon is not only characterized by the transition from the status of intellectual based on eloquence and on the function of preserving the liberal order, to that based on the technical education implicit in labour and designed to construct a new order. It also implies a tendency to broaden the category of intellectual itself, in a historical, truly revolutionary transition away from single individuals towards an intellectual function of the masses as a whole:

the nature of the philosophy of praxis is in particular that of being a mass conception, a mass culture, that of a mass which operates in a unitary fashion, i.e. one that has norms of conduct that are not only universal in idea but 'generalized' in social reality. And the activity of the 'individual' philosopher cannot therefore be conceived except in terms of this social unit, i.e. also as political activity, in terms of political leadership.[36]

Thus, in addition to the central function of social mediation performed by intellectuals/officers, which is a key aspect of the *Prison Notebooks*, there is also the potential dissolution, within the revolutionary process, of the 'rank' of specialists performing this specific function. In fact, the masses now become the key players in their own movement, given that their norms of conduct are already foreseen in existing social reality, as the result of their practical activity: 'The problem of creating a new stratum of intellectuals consists therefore in the critical elaboration of the intellectual activity that exists in everyone at a certain degree of development'.[37]

This oscillation between the disenchanted analysis of the division leaders/led, which also emerges within a homogeneous social group, and the need to overcome such a division during the course of the revolutionary process is what characterizes Gramsci's rethinking of the figure of the intellectual.

HOW SOCIETY WORKS

Gramsci's use of expressions that refer to the semantic field of the social sciences is extended further if we take into consideration two specific terms that are frequently encountered in the *Prison Notebooks*, and are employed when examining the forms of integration within society: these two terms are 'coercion' and 'conformism'.

The term 'coercion' generally takes on a negative meaning in Gramsci's writings, when it represents the violent, mechanical element accompanying the State's actions, defined firstly as 'hegemony protected by the armor of coercion', or 'political society + civil society'.[38] If we consider this division in the narrow sense (however, as we have seen, the relationship between the two concepts is much more complex than that of a simply dichotomy), then political society comprises all State institutions and organizations exercising coercion directly, namely, the bureaucracy, the armed forces, schools, prisons and so on. Within this context, social organicity is guaranteed by procedures manifesting themselves in administrative decisions implemented by the State in its capacity as sole guarantor of legitimacy through force. However, alongside this definition, as we have already seen in the case of the term 'environment', Gramsci uses 'coercion' in another sense, that of an environmental force that imposes itself indirectly, that is, a characterizing, inescapable aspect of every social relation: 'As if there has not always been some form of coercion! Just because it is exerted unconsciously by the environment and by single individuals, and not by a central power or a centralized force, does it cease to be coercion?'[39]

Once again, it is useful to identify the presence in Gramsci's discourse of a similar evolution to that to be found in Durkheim, namely, that endorsing the independence of social facts, which thus represent a separate field of study.[40] In fact, in Durkheim's view, social facts require causal explanations that remain within the social field, and in order to do so coercion must be identified as a distinguishing characteristic of such facts: 'A social fact is identifiable through the power of external coercion which it exerts or is capable of exerting upon individuals.'[41] Society, the source of this coercive power, is thus a historically produced, unnatural 'fact', but is not isomorphic to the individual, upon whom it imposes itself through coercion: facts are considered to be social when they are 'capable of exercising a coercive influence on the consciousness of individuals'.[42] The theoretical steps that Durkheim takes are thus: the autonomization of the field of social facts, the recognition of coercion as a characteristic of their identification and the acknowledgement that society is an autonomous source of this coercion.[43]

In point of fact, Gramsci extends the meaning of the term in this very direction, shifting the emphasis from the State/governmental context to the social context. Consequently, he formulates a notion of coercion that is not immediately ascribable to political power, since such coercion is exercised through dynamics of society as a whole, as the result of the random interaction of individual wills through reciprocal behaviour and adaptation. However, this coercion, expressed 'by the environment and by single individuals',[44] remains in Gramsci's view, contrary to what Durkheim believes, ultimately the expression of the ruling class. In fact, it is a form of coercion that is not neutral and refers to a single entity such as society, but is always an expression of the power of a historical bloc representing specific interests which in turn organize an organic system, or of a new organic system that wishes to break up and replace the previous system. This is another reason why the concept of coercion in Gramsci does not necessarily carry a negative connotation. It may serve not only to maintain a given order, but also to rationalize a social grouping that wishes to defeat and replace the existing historical bloc.

Once again Gramsci places the focus – like the social sciences of his time, and in particular Durkheim's sociology – on new and decisive relevance of social facts.[45] And once again, using the language of the social sciences and dealing with the problems raised by those same sciences, Gramsci moves away from them, reformulating the (revolutionary) political theory that not only the crisis of the liberal order, but also the by now clearly evident inadequacies of orthodox Marxism call for.

The second term adopted by Gramsci from sociology is that of 'conformism': the 'tendency toward conformism in the contemporary world', he writes, 'is more widespread and deeper than in the past'.[46] This expansion of conformism, in Gramsci's view, is. on the one hand, horizontal since it 'extends across nations and even continents',[47] as shown by the American-style rationalization of production that was creating 'a new type of worker and of Man'[48] and was to spread right across Europe. On the other hand, it is of a vertical nature, that is, it deepens because the 'collective man'[49] produced by this conformism is different from the type that had existed up until then: initially this collective man 'was produced by extraneous factors and once formed would disintegrate, repeatedly', whereas now he 'is formed essentially from the bottom up, on the basis of the position that the collectivity occupies in the world of production',[50] through lengthy processes stabilizing forms of behaviour and guaranteeing a previously unheard of efficiency of that political power capable of governing such behaviour.

The conformism that Gramsci focuses on must therefore be interpreted as an attempt to open political theory up to an idea that the more aware of the social science scholars of the time had already elaborated. This concerned the fact that the turn of the century, as previously mentioned, marked the advent of mass politics. This important change in the political scenario led Gramsci to reflect on the types of social action exercised by social classes and groups; in doing so, he took account of Durkheim's model of social coercion, probably through the mediation of Sorel who, at the end of the nineteenth century, had introduced Durkheim's theories into Marxist debate.[51] For example, Gramsci reiterates the fact that 'conformism [...] means nothing other than "sociality"',[52] in a process of identification that appears to follow that between coercion and social fact established by Durkheim in *The Rules of Sociological Method*. In Gramsci's view, the only expression of sociality is that of a certain degree of conformism, and it is only created as a result of the coercive thrust of a certain force external to the individual. The difference lies in the degree of conscious elaboration of the conformism with which one is imbued, and in particular in the actual nature of this conformism: 'We are all conformists of some conformism or other, always mass-men or collective men. The question is this: of what historical type is the conformism, the mass-man to which one belongs?'[53]

Besides constituting a means with which to investigate society, conformism is thus also the means by which 'new possibilities for freedom, including individual freedom'[54] ought to be imagined. Thus, the interpretative approach already proposed for coercion also holds for conformism. This approach involves the Gramscian use of the term that, on the one hand, is analytic, and is to be used to investigate the form of current society; and, on the other hand, it is programmatic and is to be employed to deal with the problem of the constitution of a new sociality within the new order.

Relations between conformism and socialism, and between coercion and socialism, are however some of the questions that Gramsci was not able to develop in full, as they are necessarily linked to the practical processes of the construction of socialism that the Bolshevik leadership was tackling during the years of Gramsci's imprisonment. Nevertheless, the *Prison Notebooks* set out the problem of their possible development within the context of the new order, not in the brief critical remarks on Trotsky's 'coercive' positions,[55] but in the analysis of the law, understood as an instrument with which the ruling group rationalized itself while at the same time getting as much of society as possible to 'conform' to a model designed to achieve the interests of that ruling group.

In Gramsci's view, by analysing the law one can identify both the genealogy of the ruling class and its ambition, expressed through the legal system, to 'conform' society.[56] To do so, the focus must be shifted from the 'negative or repressive aspect of this activity [which] is, precisely, penal justice, criminal law', to the positive aspect, that is, to law as a 'meritorious activity'.[57] Gramsci writes:

If every State tends to create and maintain a certain type of civilisation and of citizen (and hence of collective life and of individual relations), and to eliminate certain customs and attitudes and to disseminate others, then the Law will be its instrument for this purpose (together with the school system, and other institutions and activities).[58]

It was Durkheim, once again, who identified 'restitutory law' – 'that it is not expiatory, but comes down to a mere *restoration of the "status quo ante"*'[59] – as the very heart of the social integration of a society characterized by the advanced division of labour. In fact, while at first sight 'domestic law, contractual law, commercial law, procedural law, and administrative and constitutional law'[60] all appear to go towards loosening society's coercive pressure on individuals, not establishing offences punishable with criminal penalties, in practice the very exercise of such personal rights is connected to the pre-eminent role played by society in regard to such: 'it is far from the case that society is absent from this sphere of legal activity [...], its intervention is none the less the essential cog in the mechanism', given that 'if a contract has binding force, it is society which confers that force'.[61]

Gramsci and Durkheim thus share the belief in the importance of law in the definition of 'society's power', in regard to the 'free' acceptance of conformism as expressed in the rules of law. However, while in regard to the transition from a punitive form of law to a strictly regulatory form, Durkheim places the emphasis on the importance of restitutory law compared to criminal law, Gramsci, on the other hand, appears to go beyond this. In fact, in confirming the transition of coercion from a forced and centralized element to a widespread element in society, and thus one that individuals increasingly introject, and that is imposed by the threat of punishment increasingly less frequently, Gramsci further expands his notion of law to include

> those activities which are at present classified as 'legally neutral', and which belong to the domain of civil society; the latter operates without 'sanctions' or compulsory 'obligations', but nevertheless exerts a collective pressure and obtains objective results in the form of an evolution of customs, ways of thinking and acting, morality, etc.[62]

Therefore, the concept of law 'will have to be extended'[63] to comprise not only those spheres where the penalty is restitutory rather than criminal, but also those in which by not intervening, the State devolves the task of getting society to conform to civil society (which, it should not be forgotten, is a constituent part of the State), thus implementing the 'soft' side of the disciplining process.[64]

Gramsci's divergence from Durkheim's analysis regards the ultimate aim of law as conceived above, which clearly shows its relationship with class rule:

> The law does not express the whole of society (if it did, those who break the law would have to be considered antisocial beings by nature or mentally deficient); the law, rather, is an expression of the ruling class, which 'imposes' on the whole of society those norms of conduct that are most tightly connected to its own raison d'être and expansion. The greatest function of the law is the following: to presuppose that insofar as all citizens can become members of the ruling class, all of them must freely accept the conformity set down by the law.[65]

The forms of law that Gramsci takes into consideration thus reflect the various means by which the ruling class gets society to conform. These means vary depending, on the one hand, on diverse contingencies, such that direct coercion is used more often in periods of organic crisis, and coercion mediated by society during phases of ruling class expansion. On the other hand, they depend on the subject that needs to be made to conform: so that 'A social group dominates antagonistic groups, which it tends to "liquidate", or to subjugate perhaps even by armed force; it leads kindred and allied groups'.[66] Within this framework, with its unavoidable duplicity, the characteristic feature of mass politics appears to be that of a gradual transition from 'brute coercion'[67] to 'Social coercion',[68] and thus to an accentuation of the mediated forms of coercion, which remain the focal point of Gramsci's interest, particularly with regard to the manner in which they spread.

GRAMSCI'S 'SOCIOLOGICAL OPERATORS'

Alongside the notions of coercion, conformism and the new understanding of law in the analysis of society and its movement, Gramsci also utilizes more specific terms, which in the *Prison Notebooks* emerge as genuine 'sociological operators'. The first of these is the term 'regularity'.

The note introducing the question is entitled *Regularity and Necessity*, and is to be found in Section VI (*Miscellaneous notes*) of Notebook 11, which is the same one that contain the criticism of Bukharin's

Historical Materialism. Gramsci starts by wondering where Marx's ideas of 'regularity and necessity in historical development'[69] originated from, deeming that such a source was more likely to have been political economics rather than the natural sciences. More specifically, Gramsci focuses on the concept of 'determined market', which he defines as:

> the scientific discovery that specific decisive and permanent forces have risen historically and that the operation of these forces presents itself with a certain 'automatism' which allows a measure of 'predictability' and certainty for the future of those individual initiatives which accept these forces after having discerned and scientifically established their nature.[70]

Thus, one could say that Gramsci sees the concept of the determined market as the theoretical framework within which the social sciences operate in relation to capitalist society. This framework includes not only a "determined relation of social forces in a determined structure of the productive apparatus", but also 'a determined political, moral and juridical superstructure'.[71] Within these coordinates, it is therefore possible, thanks to the repetitive nature of social phenomena and to 'their relative independence from individual choices and from arbitrary government interventions',[72] to identify certain regularities that enable events to be foreseen to a noticeable degree.

The mistake made by classical economics is to naturalize these elements and consider the regularities of *one* determined market to be natural, eternal features of the phenomena themselves. Gramsci, instead, places the conditions of such regularities within their historical context:

> It is from these considerations that one must start in order to establish what is meant by 'regularity', 'law', 'automatism' in historical facts. It is not a question of 'discovering' a metaphysical law of 'determinism', or even of establishing a 'general' law of causality. It is a question of bringing out how in historical evolution relatively permanent forces are constituted which operate with a certain regularity and automatism.[73]

The determined market thus describes the same object and the same dynamics that were seen at work in regard to the concept of the historical bloc and to the analysis of competing organic systems: regularity in a determined context and discontinuity among diverse contexts; uniformity of phenomena and internal contradiction among competing organic systems. If 'the law of causality and the search for regularity, normality and uniformity'[74] is taken without any reference to this contextual framework, which in the *Prison Notebooks* is formulated in diverse ways but which always has the same meaning, then as far as Gramsci is concerned, one either commits the mistake of the 'pure economists [that] conceive of these elements as "eternal" and "natural"',[75] or that of naive mechanicism resulting in 'the flat vulgar development of evolutionism'.[76] In both cases 'the "overthrow" of praxis' becomes impossible, since 'In mechanical terms, the effect can never transcend the cause or the system of causes'.[77]

The problem of how praxis is to be overthrown, however, is only partly resolved in Gramsci's writings through the theory of organic crises perceived as moments when contradictions defy the balance of society (cf. Chapter 5, section 'The political science of crisis'). However, it is clear that there is a thorny question here that Gramscian analysis fails to completely resolve. While, on the one hand, Gramsci reformulates the concept of revolution in correspondence to the advent of mass politics, as a process rather than an event, he nevertheless fails to clearly specify the forms that the overthrowing of the existing order is to take during a war of position in the West.[78] This impasse is ingrained in the reflections laid out in the *Prison Notebooks*, which can no longer take the form of youthful subjectivism, and which therefore have to deal with the tangled question of revolution in an age of mass politics.

In this case, one can only allude to a possible direction that is not further developed in the *Prison Notebooks*, but which takes into consideration the fact that at times of the organic crisis, disequilibrium and disintegration of the system, genuine opportunities may be created for the disorganiza-tion and reorganization of forces, of historical blocs, of different power relations, and thus of a new equilibrium, a new organicity that replaces the old one. However, this is still to happen through a traditionally insur-rectional phase, because the 'war of manoeuvre', 'which before used to be "the whole" of war', is not entirely replaced by the 'war of position', but is rendered 'merely "partial"'.[79] The study of regularities, starting from this scenario, is clearly an integral part of this theory of revolution.

In analysing the term 'regularity', we have already seen a second sociological operator being used by Gramsci in the *Prison Notebooks*, namely, 'automatism'. Once again there is a note dedicated entirely to the topic, which starts by pondering the question: 'Is freedom in conflict with so-called automatism?'[80] Gramsci's reply is that 'Automatism is in conflict with free will, not with freedom. Automatism is a group freedom, in opposition to individualistic free will.'[81] This understanding of the term reveals a link with the concepts of coercion and conformism, specific phenomena of mass politics that the construction of the first workers' State must necessarily have to deal with. With regard to automatism, however, Gramsci analysed the question in greater detail:

> given the collaborative and co-ordinated activity of a social group that, following certain principles accepted (freely) out of conviction, works towards certain goals, a development then occurs which may be called automatic and which may be considered as the development of certain recognizable laws that can be isolated using the methods of exact sciences. At any moment a free choice is made according to certain basic orientations that are identical for a great mass of individuals or single wills, in so far as these latter have become homogeneous in a determined ethico-political climate. Nor is it the case that everyone acts in the same way; individual free wills are, rather, manifold, but the homogeneous part predominates and 'dictates law'.[82]

Automatism, understood not as the result of any external, coercive imposition, but as a homogeneity achieved politically through hegemony, creates identifiable laws that acquire scientific value. The final reference to the group that 'dictates law', not coincidentally placed in inverted commas, clearly points to the dual nature of this automatism: it is a law insofar as it creates an automatism that can be scientifically studied, and it is a law insofar as it is 'dictated' by one group, as a result of its successful political activity vis-à-vis society. The intentional activity of this organized section of society is in fact the precondition for the establishment of the automatism; and this is why there can be no universally valid automatism, since 'regularity or automatism can be of different types at different times'.[83]

The third 'sociological operator' taken into consideration is 'predictability', and this is linked to regularity and automatism. Once again, the provisional nature of the notes in the *Prison Notebooks* should be borne in mind here: in this case, this provisional nature emerges in the form of the ambivalent character of the formulations marking a still incomplete thought process. What Gramsci attempts to do, therefore, is to formulate a concept of predictability permitting political action within an organic system, without slipping into the teleologism of a prognosis conceived on the basis of the natural sciences.[84] In fact, on the one hand, he criticizes Croce's argument that social facts cannot be predicted: 'If social facts cannot be predicted, and the very concept of prediction is meaningless, then the irrational cannot but be dominant, and any organisation of men must be anti-historical, a "prejudice".'[85] On the other hand, he challenges the claim of positivist sociology 'to derive "experimentally" the laws of evolution of human society in such a way as to "predict" that the oak tree will develop out of the acorn'.[86] Gramsci reiterates, on the contrary, the teachings of the *Theses on Feuerbach*, according to which 'one can "scientifically" foresee only the struggle, but not the concrete moments of the struggle, which cannot but be the results of opposing forces in continuous movement, which are never reducible to fixed quantities since within them quantity is continually becoming quality'.[87]

Following the competing 'organic systems' model, the aforementioned stances can only be considered consistent with one another when considered characteristics of two different phases: a period of relative stability of an organic system whereby a certain predictability of social facts may be observed and studied; and a period of organic crisis, which on the contrary is characterized by contrasting forces that constantly change quantity into quality, and do not permit any homogeneous behaviour to be established. The crucial point of both concepts in Gramsci is thus a notion of predictability linked to the material forces competing within society in an attempt to impose their own regularities and their own automatisms, and thus together with these the predictability of social facts. When one of these forces wins the hegemonic battle – at least temporarily – and establishes its own organic system, then by doing so it creates an automatism, that is, a certain, objective predictability of social facts. At this point such facts may be studied by a science that, however, is tied to the organic system created: 'science is the union of the objective fact with a hypothesis or system of hypotheses which go beyond the mere objective fact'.[88] If, on the other hand, the situation is one where the forces in play are still competing with one another, in a period of organic crisis in which the old system is breaking up – that is, it loses its regularity and predictability – but the new system has yet to be organically created, then 'Prediction reveals itself […] not as a scientific act of knowledge, but as the abstract expression of the effort made'.[89] The prediction in this case is nothing more than the will of the historical actor who wishes to impose its own regularity: 'one can "foresee" to the extent that one acts, to the extent that one applies a voluntary effort and therefore contributes concretely to creating the result "foreseen"'.[90]

Summing up then, account has to be taken of two considerations that Gramsci makes in an effort to relativize the field of study of the regularities of social phenomena, and these concern the validity of such regularities under a specific condition, 'an historical fact, corresponding to certain conditions',[91] that he deems to be historically determined and surmountable: the condition whereby 'the great masses of the population remain (or at least are reputed to remain) essentially passive'.[92] In this note, Gramsci is historicizing statistics as one branch of social science, noting two aspects of historical development that seem to confirm the need to make critical use of it, avoiding considering it 'as an essential law operating of necessity'.[93] The first aspect is the advent of an age in which planned policies replace those based on free, conflicting individual initiative: 'even the demand for a planned, i.e. guided, economy is destined to break down the statistical law understood in a mechanical sense'.[94] The second aspect, directly connected to the first, is 'the replacement by political organisms (parties) of single individuals and individual (or charismatic, as Michels calls them) leaders', hence 'the process whereby popular feeling is standardized ceases to be mechanical and casual (that is produced by the conditioning of environmental factors and the like) and becomes conscious and critical'.[95] These two historically important phenomena, which appear to sweep across both the USSR and the rest of the capitalist world, are in Gramsci's view an expression of an ongoing development in which 'Human awareness replaces naturalistic "spontaneity"'.[96]

So while, on the one hand, Gramsci warns against the universal, dogmatic use of the social sciences, in an age of collective organization in the forms of both State and political party, with the advent of mass politics, on the other hand, he points to the utility of these sciences within the context of a given organic order, which in this case appears to be of a medium-term nature. Within this context, the study of the regularity of social facts is not only theoretically plausible, but also politically useful. In fact, the note from which numerous quotes have been taken also contains the following:

If philology is the methodological expression of the importance of ascertaining and precising particular fact in their unique and unrepeatable individuality, one cannot however exclude the practical utility of isolating certain more general 'laws of tendency' corresponding in the political field to the laws of statistics or to the law of large numbers which have helped to advance various of the natural sciences.[97]

Likewise, the statement that the 'planned economy' should 'break down the statistical law understood in a mechanical sense' is immediately followed by the warning: 'although such an economy will have to be based on statistics, it does not, however, mean the same thing'.[98]

Ultimately, considering sociological laws as a surrogate of the collective will in historical development, as the Marxism of the Second International had done – which is probably the real target for Gramsci's criticisms –, does not necessarily mean ignoring the practical utility and predictive capacity of such laws. Moreover, 'the process whereby popular feeling is standardized'[99] in modern political parties, which is the second historical development perceived by Gramsci as moving towards a non-mechanical application of the laws of sociology, provides for its own laws of tendency, and Gramsci's interest in the study of elitism is proof of the cogency of such historical development.[100]

This analysis of what we have termed the 'sociological operators' used and reformulated in the *Prison Notebooks* clearly reveals Gramsci's interest in the political value of social relations. This interest, which remains a fundamental characteristic of all Gramsci's writings, constitutes a novel feature of contemporary political and sociological thought, representing not so much a shift 'from the political to the social', as what may be termed a repositioning of the political within a social context. Gramsci follows this direction when he adopts a broader notion of causality of social phenomena than the one adopted by the Marxism of his time. In this regard, Gramsci moves closer to the more visionary sociological tradition that, particularly with Weber, takes the concept of cause beyond the *homo oeconomicus*, that is, beyond the confines of the calculation of economic interest and the constriction of economic laws, to also include the ethics corresponding to a given conduct of life.

The problem that a philosophy of praxis has to deal with is therefore that of the mechanisms controlling the transition from a philosophy conception of the world to its praxis, conceived, however, in at least two partially different ways: as the subjective capacity to implement a political-philosophical programme, and in this case the main point of reference is the party-Prince; but also as the identification of the ethics corresponding to the human type that one wishes to transform, and the ethics that is created in the new order. An ethics that is not subjectively imposed (whereas the order in question is subjectively determined to a certain extent), but that derives from the transformations of society. This is why the reflection on the overcoming of the separation of the rulers from the ruled, that is, on a cultural revolution of the same importance as the Renaissance, the Reformation or the Enlightenment, is accompanied by a disenchanted analysis of the effects on the new human type of the objective phenomena of Taylorism and bureaucratization. This interweaving of a subjective, albeit not singular force (the political party) and an objective force, the outcome of which, however, is not fully determined (Taylorism-Fordism and bureaucracy), was to form the backdrop to Gramsci's entire reflections in the *Prison Notebooks*.

5

The crisis

The crisis currently besetting Italy can only be resolved by the Workers' State.

Antonio Gramsci
30 May 1920

A NEW UNDERSTANDING OF THE CRISIS

Gramsci's political education, his coming round to socialist ideals, and his early experience as a journalist and political leader, all occurred during the period of the greatest crisis that Italy's liberal order had ever experienced: the crisis stretching from the First World War to the advent of Fascism.[1] During this period, the classical economic definition of 'crisis' was no longer capable of accounting for the series of political and social upheavals that together seemed to point to a genuine 'systemic crisis', that is, a 'catastrophic crisis besetting European civilization'.[2]

The crisis of authority of the leading classes, the crisis of legitimacy of State institutions, the crisis of parliamentarianism, the international crisis triggered by the October Revolution, all condition the use of the concept in Gramsci's writings of that period. In this specific case, Gramsci's analysis perceives crisis as an exceptional, unique and in some way definitive event. An event that can certainly not be foreseen – and the outcome of which cannot be guaranteed, contrary to what a certain economistic Marxism believed – but one that is certainly exceptional compared to the normal, albeit contradictory, development of the capitalistic system. The perception of an 'epochal systemic crisis' was thus very much present in Gramsci's writings during, and at the end of, the First World War, and his reflections on the construction of a new order is the natural consequence thereof: 'There can be no doubt that the bourgeois State will not survive the crisis. In its present condition, the crisis will shatter it.'[3]

The subsequent phases of stabilization of Fascism – from that of 1921 when the movement organized to form a party, until the end of the crisis triggered by the assassination of Italian socialist politician Giacomo Matteotti in 1924 – saw Gramsci's understanding of crisis lose some of the 'epochal' characteristics that had distinguished it during the turbulent years of the delegitimization of the liberal order at the end of the war. In fact, the crisis was portrayed increasingly less as a historical watershed. The concept of crisis appeared to Gramsci less capable of accounting for a whole series of heterogeneous phenomena contributing towards the dissolution of the existing social order. Indeed, the concept began to be seen as an attribute of given elements identified as being 'in crisis'. Such elements included the Fascist Party, the middle classes, industrial production, the People's Party and so on.

The first observations challenging the understanding of crisis as an irreversible event already began to appear in the mid-1920s:

At this moment in time, the country is going through a crisis that is undermining the entire State apparatus from its very roots upwards. This crisis may be decisive, although any hypothesis of this kind is hazarded in view of the fact that this is the bourgeois State that has achieved the greatest organization and power ever achieved, during the course of human history, by any form of State.[4]

There is a gradual semantic shift here, one full of overlapping elements. However, during the early 1920s the concept of crisis in Gramsci's writings slowly lost not only its irreversible character, but also its specificity, that is, its reference to an event triggered by a specific circumstance: 'Italian society is afflicted by a crisis, a crisis rooted in the inherent characteristics of that society, and in the irreconcilable conflict between such characteristics: there is a crisis that the war has precipitated, exacerbated and rendered insuperable.'[5] War is no longer the event triggering this crisis of hegemony (as it was later to be called in the *Prison Notebooks*) of the leading classes, but merely a factor accelerating an ongoing process.

The period between the end of the 1920s and the mid-1930s, at a time when Gramsci was reflecting once again on this matter in the *Prison Notebooks*, saw the stabilization not only of Italy through Fascism, but also of the international system that revolved around Nazism in Germany, around Stalinism in Russia and around the New Deal in the USA. The latter nation in particular was offering an effective political response to an extremely damaging economic crisis, through the creation of a specific series of 'fortresses and emplacements' that the

USA did not originally possess (and which had not been necessary up until then), thanks to their 'rational demographic composition', that is, to the absence of 'numerous classes with no essential function in the world of production'.[6] Gramsci completely rethinks the concept of crisis in this context. Crisis is no longer a specific, definitive historical fact, but a given dynamic of the capitalist system. So what Gramsci creates in his *Prison Notebooks* is a genuine dynamic theory of crisis that perceives it as a process rather than as an event, more as a contradictory development of the system than as an aspect of that system's breakdown.

In the *Prison Notebooks* this dynamic theory of crisis is accompanied by a mapping of the forms that crises take within specific contexts. Thus, crises are analysed within economic, political and social contexts, and also from the generational and gender points of view. The concept of crisis therefore changes substantially, and can no longer be employed in a teleological sense within a definitive, immutable theoretical framework. On the contrary, thanks to its dynamic characteristics, its polysemic quality, it permits the identification of an open field of inquiry, of a materialistic interpretative framework, by means of which the capitalistic system as a whole may be studied and challenged.[7]

In the majority of cases, Gramsci's use of the concept of crisis in the *Prison Notebooks* is therefore not the canonical form adopted by the Marxism of his time, which on the contrary is based on the sequence: the emergence of a social class –> the development of a social order –> the emergence of contradictions –> the separation of structure and superstructure –> the crisis of this social order and the establishment of a new order. In Gramsci, on the other hand, crisis is a more or less evident condition of capitalist development, embraced by the two principles that Marx sets out in his 'Preface' to *A Contribution to the Critique of Political Economy* (1859):

(1) the principle that 'no society sets itself tasks for the accomplishment of which the necessary and sufficient conditions do not already exist' <or are not in the course of emerging and developing>; and (2) that 'no society perishes until it has first developed all the forms of life implicit in its internal relations'.[8]

What is represented within the confines of these two principles, however, is no linear development constituted by the accumulation of those contradictions that find their revolutionary outlet in the crisis.

The space circumscribed by the aforesaid principles opens up a field of possibilities having both a temporal extension (the war of position) and a spatial dimension (the expanded notion of the State), within which capitalist dynamics may either continue to develop – overcoming the crisis as in the case of 'The passage of the troops of many different parties under the banner of a single party'[9] – or be replaced by a new social organization. For this very reason, according to the famous Gramscian adage, 'The crisis consists precisely in the fact that the old is dying and the new cannot be Born'.[10] The oscillation between the old and the new that Gramsci refers to is therefore not relegated to transitional status, but is a constant factor that opens up possibilities for the political action of an organized body. The further observation that 'one can "scientifically" foresee only the struggle, but not the concrete moments of the struggle'[11] expresses this very meaning of crisis as an opportunity for political struggle, rather than as a given point at which existing contradictions erupt.

The perception of crisis as the non-correspondence of structure and superstructure – as has already been seen with regard to the concept of ideology – thus fails to take account of the richness of the concept of crisis to be found in the *Prison Notebooks*. It is in this very relationship, or rather within the force field generated by the clash between different competing historical blocs, that the crisis is played out each time. It is no coincidence that having expounded the limits within which the moments of transition may be conceived (those of Marx's 'Preface'), Gramsci then introduces the very question of the relations of forces, that is, of the political battle to be fought *within* the crisis, in the genuinely political space created by Marx's two principles.

Thus, what is not present in Gramsci's writings is the 'model of collapse', or a conception of crisis as the culminating point at which 'the contradictions come to a head'. On the contrary, in anticipation of what could be considered the definitive note on the question to be found in the *Prison Notebooks*, Gramsci does not believe the crisis to be the end point of capitalism, but rather that 'the development of capitalism has been a "continual crisis"'.[12]

The fact that in the *Prison Notebooks*, the concept of crisis makes no reference to a definitive, general event at this point permits it to be utilized differently, in the form of more precise references describing the crisis as the 'crisis of a particular element'. In fact, in Gramsci the crisis is always a crisis 'of authority', 'of hegemony', 'organic', 'generational', 'of *libertinism*', and is never a 'crisis of the capitalist social order' in general. The only note in the *Prison Notebooks* in which the concept of crisis and that of capitalism are brought together is in fact that of the quote regarding capitalism as a 'continual crisis'.

Gramsci never refers to capitalism when dealing with the question of crisis, almost as if it were superfluous to mention that the object of the crisis, and not its subject, is represented by the dynamics of the capitalist social order itself. The various types of crisis, on the other hand, all refer to, and are dependent on, the type of development of society imposed by the capitalist system, and for this reason their underlying causes are to be found in the mechanisms governing that system, that is, in their object. However, this is no reason to consider the capitalist system, in its entirety and as a subjective element, as being 'in crisis'. In Gramsci's view, the object of the crisis, its contents and its causes are all to be found in capitalist development, whereas economistic Marxism had always perceived capitalism as the subject of the crisis, that is, as the element which at that given moment in time was 'in crisis'. The difference between the two interpretations of crisis – between Gramsci and economistic Marxism – is of fundamental importance to understand the entire *Prison Notebooks*. In the 1930s, Gramsci appears to have raised the question of why, after more than fifty years of organic crisis, the capitalist system continued to be so strong; of why that system's internal contradictions had not led to its collapse, but on the contrary had indeed strengthened it; and finally, of how to reformulate the concept of crisis, and thus of struggle, in keeping with this acknowledgement of capitalism's strength.[13]

THE MULTIPLE MEANINGS OF 'CRISIS'

The concept of crisis takes on various meanings in the *Prison Notebooks*. In order to substantiate this reading of the nebula of meanings that the concept of crisis is given, we can start by examining the only note that deals with the question directly. This consists in a writing drafted just once (b), dating from mid-1933, of note number 5 of Notebook 15, entitled *Past and present. The crisis*. Gramsci immediately specifies that 'Whoever wants to give one sole definition of these events [...] must be rebutted', and then states that 'We are dealing with a process that shows itself in many ways, and in which causes and effects become intertwined and mutually entangled. To simplify means to misrepresent and falsify.'[14] The crisis is thus presented as a 'complex process [...], and not a unique "fact" repeated in various forms through a cause having one single origin'.[15]

The central topic of the note in question is clearly the 'crisis of '29', the effects of which, following its onset in the USA, had already been felt throughout Europe. When interpreting this event, Gramsci was concerned with avoiding taking the obvious shortcut consisting in the identification of a starting point, a specific event that triggers, and therefore accounts for, the crisis: 'We may say that there is no starting date as such to the crisis, but simply the date of certain of the more striking "manifestations"'.[16] Gramsci continues by arguing that in fact 'The whole post-war period is one of crisis', before proceeding to claim that 'For some (and perhaps they are not mistaken) the war itself is a manifestation of the crisis', and concluding that the crisis 'began at least with the war, even if this was not its first manifestations'.[17]

The search for the origin or triggering cause of the crisis is thus represented as necessarily misleading. On the contrary, the phenomenon of crisis needed to be analysed starting from these elements: '1) [...] the crisis is a complicated process, 2) [...] it began at least with the war, [...] 3) [...] [it] has internal origins, in the modes of production and thus of exchange'.[18] Thus, Gramsci formulates a theory of crisis based around the following ideas: 1) a crisis is a process rather than an event; 2) a crisis always has remote origins that, however, do not alone explain its subsequent development; 3) crisis is an inherent feature of the capitalist mode of production.

In the second section of the note, Gramsci further deepens the divide between himself and his Marxist contemporaries:

We might, then, say – and this would be more exact – that the 'crisis' is none other than the quantitative intensification of certain elements, neither new nor original, but in particular the intensification of certain phenomena, while others that were there before and operated simultaneously with the first, sterilizing them, have now become inoperative or have completely disappeared. In brief, the development of capitalism has been a 'continual crisis', if one can say that, i.e. an extremely rapid movement of elements that mutually balanced and sterilized one another. At a certain point in this movement, some elements have gained predominance and others have disappeared or have become irrelevant within the general framework. Events that go under the specific name of 'crisis' have then burst onto the scene, events that are more or less serious according to whether more or less important elements of equilibrium come into play.[19]

The passage in question is highly suggestive and permits a more precise reformulation of the concept Gramsci was in the process of developing at that time. The crisis, in fact, is described through the 'language of disequilibrium', as a form of an imbalance caused by the intensification of certain existing phenomena that fail to find a counterparty capable of 'immunizing them' or of counterbalancing them.[20] According to this view, it could be said that crisis is ever-present – in a latent or explicit form – within the context of a balancing game played out between conflicting forces. In the former case in particular – that of a latent form of crisis – it is continuously neutralized by the advent of opposing forces that rebalance the system and permit it to develop. On the other hand, a crisis becomes explicit when certain elements become more intense or others suddenly fall dormant. Thus, the unbalancing of the capitalist order's 'zero sum game' reveals the existence of a crisis, albeit one that is inherent to the functioning of that system as it is constantly rebalanced.

The dynamics of this balancing movement entail long periods during which the crisis is not immediately visible, but nevertheless remains a fundamental element underlying the functioning of the capitalist system. The 'passive revolution' – a transformation that, as we have seen (Chapter 3, section 'Bureaucracy and officials: Gramsci and Weber'), arises in the absence of any strong popular action and is controlled by the classes already in power – is the term that Gramsci uses to describe this 'critical' balancing game when it proves successful, that is, when equilibrium is re-established by the dominant class. To put it briefly, the passive revolution is the form taken by the process of transformation when the crisis is played out through the leading class actions, in the absence of any competing subjective elements that upset said equilibrium, or in their presence but accompanied by their continual rebalancing: 'Hence theory of the "passive revolution" not as a programme, as it was for the Italian liberals of the Risorgimento, but as a criterion of interpretation, in the absence of other active elements to a dominant extent.'[21]

The emphasis placed on the problem of equilibrium and on the forces guaranteeing it leads to an analysis of the real nature of these forces in the historical period of the post-war years. In fact, what does Gramsci mean when he talks of the 'intensification of certain phenomena'?[22] It is at this point that he begins to specify the nature of the crisis:

At a certain point in their historical lives, social groups become detached from their traditional parties [...]. In every country the process is different, although the content is the same. And the content is the crisis of the ruling class's hegemony, which occurs either because the ruling class has failed in some major political undertaking for which it has requested, or forcibly extracted, the consent of the broad masses (war, for example), or because huge masses (especially of peasants and petit-bourgeois intellectuals) have passed suddenly from a state of political passivity to a certain activity, and put forward demands which taken together, albeit not organically formulated, add up to a revolution. A 'crisis of authority' is spoken of: this is precisely the crisis of hegemony, or general crisis of the State.[23]

The concept of crisis is specified in this political context as a 'crisis of hegemony' or a 'crisis of authority'. As already mentioned, two phenomena may cause such a crisis: 1) the 'passivity' of certain forces, that is, the historical absence of the rebalancing role that the leading classes should have exercised and that, given the defeat in the war, are no longer capable of exercising; 2) the intensification of opposing forces, that is, the advent of mass politics witnessing 'huge masses [...] [that] have passed suddenly from a state of political passivity to a certain activity'.[24] In both cases, the existing equilibrium is at risk. In the post-war period the two phenomena arose concurrently, whereby Gramsci formulated a concept of 'definitive' crisis. The contradictions inherent in the capitalist system were not balanced and enhanced, but became merely destructive, and in this situation – we are still dealing with the historical analysis of Italy during the immediate post-war years – two possible solutions were envisaged within this impasse characterized, among other things, by the absence of any strong organization of the subaltern classes (the Italian Communist Party was only founded in 1921): 'The passage of the troops of many different parties under the banner of a single party', or the 'solution [...] of the charismatic leader'.[25]

Both solutions raised the same problem in Gramsci's eyes, namely, the use of such time of acute crisis to advance the struggle of the working class and its allies. In this context the crisis does not become the event marking the death of capitalism and the birth of a new order, but the field of political battle on which the working class and its allies have to be capable of playing. At this point the discourse regarding the concept of crisis becomes a genuine 'political science of crisis', thanks to which the dynamics of the periods of crisis can be established, together with the role of the economic element and the diverse forms this takes in different contexts, the dangers inherent in times of imbalance and the political force required to shatter the contradictory dynamics of social relations. A political science of crisis, therefore, that describes the conditions and rules of development of the crisis, but which also alludes to the requirements to be met in order to take action within the context of such crisis.[26]

THE POLITICAL SCIENCE OF CRISIS

To define a political science of crisis, Gramsci needs to extend his analytical scope beyond the historical experience from which the problem emerged – the years immediately after the First World War – in order to identify the political regularities and constants of times of crisis also by comparing the various different historical developments following such times:

> the modern world is currently experiencing a phenomenon similar to the split between the 'spiritual' and the 'temporal' in the Middle Ages [...]. Regressive and conservative social groupings are shrinking back more and more to their initial economic-corporative phase, while progressive and innovative groupings are still in their initial phase – which is, precisely, the economic-corporative phase.[27]

Considered in relation to the Middle Ages, the reflection Gramsci makes is once again derived from the two principles stated in Marx's 'Preface' to *A Contribution to the Critique of Political Economy* (1859). This is thus a recurrent characteristic of the large-scale transitions between organic systems, which rarely witness the players in the new order as already established and ready to take on the role of leading a new society when the preceding order has been delegitimized. The construction of the revolutionary subject, although carefully prepared, therefore seems to require experience of the crisis,[28] either when it is latent or during periods in which the contradictions in question surface.

Thus, at this point Gramsci formulates a number of general principles characteristic of these times of acute crisis, the first of which has to provide the coordinates of the phenomenon in question:

When studying a structure one must distinguish the permanent from the occasional. The occasional gives rise to political criticism, the permanent gives rise to sociohistorical criticism; the occasional helps one assess political groups and personalities, the permanent helps one assess large social groupings.[29]

Gramsci thus makes a distinction here that at first sight appears to refer to an understanding of crisis as an exceptional event, one that sweeps over the system when the equilibrium between its fundamental components – seen as of a 'permanent' nature – is altered, but which does not arise when the 'occasional' aspects of the system clash. However, upon closer examination this distinction does not appear so clear-cut. In fact, the permanent level remains such as long as the old social structure preserves a certain unity and strength, that is, as long as 'regularities' and 'automatisms' subsist in the majority of cases. (cf. Chapter 4, section 'Gramsci's "sociological operators"'). As long as this unity is preserved, even if only to a partial degree – and it only ceases to exist when the social order collapses altogether – the opposing forces necessarily only ever operate at the 'occasional' level – or rather, at that level that is occasional when seen from the point of view of the existing system – even when faced with a crisis of legitimacy. Only the victory of those forces opposing the system seals the definitive transformation thereof, thus permitting the actions and deeds of those forces to acquire, in practice and not a priori, permanent status:

> The great importance of this distinction becomes clear when a historical period is studied. A crisis exists, sometimes lasting for decades. This means that incurable contradictions have come to light within the structure and that the political forces positively working to preserve the structure itself are nevertheless striving to heal these contradictions, within certain limits. These insistent and persistent efforts (since no social formation ever wants to admit that it has been superseded) form the terrain of the 'occasional', wherein one gets the organization of those forces that 'strive' to demonstrate (in the final analysis through their own triumph, but in immediate terms through ideological, religious, philosophical, political, juridical, etc., polemics) that 'the necessary and sufficient conditions already exist to render the accomplishment of certain tasks historically possible and therefore obligatory'.[30]

Thus, the immediate field of battle is that of the 'occasional', where the various forces in play organize themselves and a 'superstructural' battle – in the broad, non-peripheral sense of the term illustrated in Chapter 1 – is fought that, nevertheless, is also an integral part of the battle being fought at the permanent level. So the distinction between occasional and permanent does not appear to refer to any ranking of the importance of the levels at which the political battle is fought, or to any time sequence to be followed in order to be able to identify the system's 'key' elements. By renouncing any linear reading of the crisis, it could be said, on the other hand, that Gramsci perceived the two moments in time as coessential, that is, that no distinction can be made – this is vitally important – between the moment at which a given social order plunges into 'permanent crisis' from the 'occasional' level of struggle where crisis manifests itself as a surmountable contradiction. The transition from the occasional to the permanent, therefore, is not dictated by the gravity of the contradictions in question, or even by the importance of the various areas affected by the crisis (the economic, political or social fields), but by the strength of the alternative subjective forces that challenge the established order, and which demonstrate 'in the final analysis through their own triumph'[31] their capacity to impose the permanent level within the crisis. Gramsci then states that:

> A frequent error in historical analysis consists in the inability to find the relation between the 'permanent' and the 'occasional'; as a result, remote causes are presented as if they were the direct causes, or else direct causes are said to be the only efficient causes. On the one hand there is an excess of 'economism', on the other an excess of 'ideologism'; one side overrates mechanical causes, and the other overrates the 'voluntary' and individual element.[32]

If the contrast between economism and voluntarism is put in such terms, it appears clear that Gramsci's recommended direction cannot be any mere mediation between the two. The search for the causes of a historical upheaval is in fact strictly bound, also from the historiographical viewpoint, to the subsequent development of the subjective force dictating change. Thus, if it is not to take the form of a 'passive revolution' – that is, a programme for change formulated by the classes holding power – a revolutionary event needs, at least in part, to set in place its own conditions within a situation of crisis that permits modification of the relationship between the occasional and the permanent.

Having formulated these two general principles – the principle of political action within the context of the transition between organic systems and that of the coessential character of permanent and occasional in such transition – Gramsci can then analyse the role that the economic element plays both within and outside such coordinates. Giving Rosa Luxemburg's work *The Mass Strike, the Political Party and the Trade Unions*[33] as an example, Gramsci notes that within this work 'The immediate economic factor (crisis, etc.) is seen as the field artillery employed in war to open a breach in the enemy's defences'.[34] Luxemburg's book assigns a key role in the revolutionary process to the economic crisis, and as such it represents 'the most significant theory of the war of manoeuver applied to the study of history and to the art of politics'.[35] According to Gramsci's reading of Luxemburg's work, as well as 'open[ing] a breach' in the enemy lines, the economic crisis also managed to 'organize in a flash one's own troops',[36] thus operating as the aggregator and organizer of the antagonistic subject.

In Gramsci's view this interpretation is flawed by a certain economistic prejudice since, on the one hand, it transposes, in an excessively mechanical manner, a military technical principle to the sphere of politics,[37] while, on the other hand, it makes reference to a type of conflict that the advent of the First World War, with its lengthy trench warfare, had radically challenged. The immediate efficacy of the economic element, in fact, is 'much more complex than the impact of field artillery in a war of manoeuver'.[38] At the same time, the advent of the war of position cannot be ignored, given that 'one cannot choose the form of war one wants', but one must accept the form that is '"imposed" by the overall relation of the forces in conflict'.[39]

Despite criticizing this 'rigid form of economic determinism',[40] Gramsci, on the other hand, expands on the analogy between the art of politics and military techniques:

In my view, Ilyich [Lenin] understood the need for a shift from the war of manoeuver that had been applied victoriously in the East in 1917, to a war of position, which was the only viable possibility in the West [...]. In the East, the state was everything, civil society was primordial and gelatinous; in the West, there was a proper relation between state and civil society, and when the state tottered, a sturdy structure of civil society was immediately revealed. The state was just a forward trench; behind it stood a succession of sturdy fortresses and emplacements.[41]

In this reformulation of military strategy, and by analogy of political strategy, the element 'of manoeuver' does not disappear altogether, but 'must be seen to have a reduced tactical function rather than a strategic function'.[42] Rosa Luxemburg – like Trotsky, who with his 'permanent revolution' is the target of this latter citation – ultimately expresses a position that takes no account of the growing importance of the war of position, which in political terms takes the form of mass politics. One corollary of this element, which Gramsci adopts following Lenin's example, is the question of 'whether the fundamental historical crises are directly determined by economic crises'.[43] Gramsci responds unequivocally: 'It may be ruled out that immediate economic crises of themselves produce fundamental historical events'.[44]

By defining the place reserved for the economic element in this manner, the concept of crisis may thus be specified by different adjectives, the most important of which is undoubtedly that of 'organic crisis'. The organicity of a crisis is confirmed by the fact that 'quantity becomes quality',[45] when an increase in the points of conflict and in 'disintegrating' subjective actions begin to challenge the system's general equilibrium, its regularities and its automatisms, and consequently rearranges the relationship between the occasional and the permanent. In this case, 'the crisis is now *organic* and no longer *conjunctural*',[46] since it challenges what is considered the 'naturalness', and thus the 'insuperability', of that specific social system, of that specific 'determined market', of that specific relationship between what is permanent and what is occasional:

> But what is the 'determinate market', and what is it in fact determined by? It will be determined by the fundamental structure of the society under consideration; one must therefore analyse this structure and identify within it those elements that are <relatively> constant, determine the market, etc., as well as those other 'variable and developing' elements that determine conjunctural crises up to a point when even the <relatively> constant elements get modified and the crisis becomes organic.[47]

Before an organic crisis is reached, the leading class must necessarily experience a specific political crisis that Gramsci refers to as the 'crisis of authority' or 'crisis of hegemony'.[48] In particular, this concerns the leading class's loss of ideological domination, which happens when 'the ruling class has lost consensus, that is, if it no longer 'leads' but only "rules"'.[49] The unbalancing of the leading function, in favour of the repressive function marks, albeit not definitively, the start of a clear process of crisis. The crisis of hegemony, perceived in this sense as a political crisis, a crisis of legitimacy and consensus, represents one of the most important specifications of the concept of crisis made by Gramsci, which within the framework of his discourse takes the place that had been reserved for economic crisis in almost all of the analyses produced by the Marxism of the Second International. The importance of the crisis of hegemony in the *Prison Notebooks* is also dictated by the fact that it marks a structural change of that time, with the emergence of the masses in the political sphere, and the impossibility of preserving domination, on the one hand, through coercion alone, and, on the other hand, through a group of basically self-referential intellectuals who remain distinctly removed from all practical matters.

The last two Gramscian definitions of crisis – the 'crisis of generations' and the 'crisis of *libertinism*'[50] – represent two 'cyclical' moments of the phases of crisis. In fact, the 'crisis of generations' is that process whereby 'in the struggle between generations, the young get closer to the people, but when crisis reach the turning point, the young people return to their class'.[51] Gramsci's political experience during the immediate post-war years had seen this very transition in the younger generations of Italy's bourgeoisie, from enthusiasm for the political potential of the working classes, to the sudden 'realignment' among the Fascist ranks. The 'crises of *libertinism*', on the other hand, are phenomena that derive from changes in the world of labour:

> In order to achieve a new adaptation to the new mode of work, pressure is exerted over the whole social sphere, a puritan ideology develops which gives to the intrinsic brutal coercion the external form of persuasion and consent. Once the result has been to some extent achieved, the pressure breaks up [...] and is followed by the crisis of *libertinism* [...]. This crisis, however, has no more than a superficial effect on the working masses [...]; these masses, in fact, have already

acquired the new ways of life and remain subjected to the pressure because of the basic necessities of life.[52]

The crises of libertinism thus concern adaptation to the new mode of work, although they principally characterize the upper classes who do not materially require to follow this new 'conformism' that the productive apparatus calls for, and which, not having to deal with the changed conditions, can afford to have a '"libertarian" conception associated with the classes which are not engaged in manual production'.[53] The '"Puritanical" initiatives' promoted by American industrialists in relation to the imposition of Fordist-Taylorist methods of production, for example, had 'the purpose of preserving, outside of work, a certain psycho-physical equilibrium which prevents the physiological collapse of the worker, exhausted by the new method of production'.[54] The prohibition of alcohol and the regulation of sexual conduct, which Gramsci discusses at length in the famous notebook on *Americanism and Fordism*, are just two examples of this need to rationalize the after-work conduct of workers. However, in this regard the conflicting response of the workers did not materialize through the development of a 'libertarian' conception, but, on the contrary, through the revolutionary struggle for political control over this transformation, to 'find for themselves an "original", and not Americanised, system of living, to turn into "freedom" what today is "necessity"'.[55] The crises of libertinism, despite being the sign of an ongoing 'critical' change, did not lay the way for any revolutionary struggle.

CRISIS AND ORGANIZATION

Within the various different forms that the concept of crisis takes in the *Prison Notebooks*, Gramsci identified one element that he believed to be key to allowing an antagonistic subject to develop and impose itself in a crisis. The element in question is organization, the most important weapon an antagonistic force may deploy when the equilibrium is constantly oscillating. What is it that proves decisive 'in the last instance' in situations of organic crisis, when the existing equilibrium is disrupted and the struggle between the old and the new intensifies?

the decisive element in every situation is the permanently organised and long-prepared force which can be put into the field when it is judged that a situation is favourable (and it can be favourable only in so far as such a force exists, and is full of fighting spirit). Therefore the essential task is that of systematically and patiently ensuring that this force is formed, developed, and rendered ever more homogeneous, compact, and self-aware.[56]

This organized force, however, should not be conceived and used simply as a battering ram – an idea more suited to the war of manoeuvre – but also as a 'counterweight' (in keeping with the language of equilibrium theory) that may be moved and repositioned depending on how the crisis develops. This organized force must be used intelligently and 'expended' politically where it is most effective, within the context of a conflict that has expanded over the course of time, and is characterized by different levels of engagement and phases of differing intensity. In order to manage this force efficiently – following Machiavelli in wishing to shape the side that was 'not in the know' – in note 17 of Notebook 13 Gramsci formulates a theory of the 'relations of forces' capable of indicating 'the points of least resistance, at which the force of will can be most fruitfully applied'.[57]

This note is entitled *Analysis of situations: relations of forces*, and is the redrafted writing (c) of part of note 38 of Notebook 4 (a). This latter, the rough writing, before dealing with the question of relations of force, had already framed the question within the two principles of Marx's 'Preface' to *A Contribution to the Critique of Political Economy* (1859) and reviewed the observations on the difference between the occasional and permanent features of the development of a system of power. Thus, Gramsci's intention was to formulate one single argument delineating the field of possibility (the two principles), then to establish the specific conditions of the ages of crisis (the occasional/permanent relationship), and finally to provide, with his theory of the relations of forces, a revolutionary political science permitting the most beneficial use of the organized force.

In regard to these relations of forces, Gramsci thus distinguishes between an initial phase when the relations of forces are objectively determined and two further phases – the political phase and the military phase – which depend on the organizational forms achieved and on the hegemonic elements present. The first phase is 'closely linked to the structure [...]. This relation is what it is, a refractory reality: nobody can alter the number of firms or their employees, the number of cities or the given urban population, etc.'[58] Thus, this is a given fact that merely gives us to understand whether in society 'there exist the necessary and sufficient conditions for its transformation'.[59] The other two phases – the political and the military – on the other hand, establish the space within which 'the decisive passage from the structure to the sphere of the complex superstructures'[60] is revealed. The second, political phase in particular represents the moment at which, given the relation of social forces and the relation of military forces, 'an evaluation of the degree of homogeneity, self-awareness, and organization attained by the various social classes',[61] that is, the result achieved by organizational endeavours over time, becomes of decisive importance.

This model of the relations of forces thus constitutes the embryo of a revolutionary political science laying out the construction of an organized force both before and during the phases of the system's acute crisis. However, Gramsci's political experience had led him to a very different situation, that of the post-war years characterized by an Italian Socialist Party insufficiently organized along revolutionary lines, and by an Italian Communist Party that had only seen the light of day in 1921, at the very beginning of the Fascists taking over power in Italy. What happens, therefore, when an acute crisis arises but the organized force is incapable of directing the spontaneous forces present within society? In such a case, the crisis is transformed from an opportunity to a situation of great danger for the subaltern classes:

> Ignoring and, even worse, disdaining so-called 'spontaneous' movements – that is, declining to give them a conscious leadership and raise them to a higher level by inserting them into politics – may often have very bad and serious consequences. It is almost always the case that a 'spontaneous' movement of the subaltern classes is matched by a reactionary movement of the right wing of the dominant class, for concomitant reasons.[62]

There is a clear historical reference to the Fascist regime here, although it should be noted that the player in Gramsci's writings remains the subaltern classes and their (more or less effective) leadership. In fact, it is this absence of any connection between spontaneous movements and a conscious leadership that is responsible for the emergence of a right-wing movement of the leading classes, rather than any random cause or historical necessity. The 'failure of the responsible groups to give conscious leadership to spontaneous rebellions and thus enable them to become a positive political factor'[63] is the principal reason for the failure of the second phase of the relations of forces.

The movement always arises spontaneously from the masses, in fact, when the equilibrium is unbalanced and the crisis emerges into the open. The leadership of this movement, however, depends on the degree of organization and consciousness that has been established before the crisis, on the one hand, and during the process of crisis itself, on the other. At this point, Gramsci's political science does not claim to establish any 'scholastic and academic' canons, whereby 'the only authentic and worthy movement is one that is one hundred percent conscious'.[64] On the contrary, it is precisely because 'reality is teeming with the most bizarre coincidences' that a revolutionary political science must be capable of creating a framework within which it is possible 'to "translate" the elements of historical life into theoretical language, but not vice versa, making reality conform to an abstract scheme'.[65]

Thus, while the crisis has been, and continues to be, the backdrop to the history of capitalism, it is also, at the same time, the constant scenario in which the class struggle is played out: a scenario in which the effort of 'translating' society's spontaneous movements into political practice is offensive and defensive at the same time, because in any political struggle one is never completely on the defensive against the reaction, just as one is never in a purely revolutionary attacking position: 'In politics, the siege is reciprocal'.[66] In certain moments, however, the struggle intensifies, the crisis deepens and the occasional level at which the competing forces had previously battled against one another is slowly transformed into a permanent level. The post-war period was an example of this, when the situation arose of a 'struggle between "two conformisms", that is, a struggle for hegemony, and a crisis of civil society'.[67] In that particular case, the possibility of fighting at the level of the crisis depended on the political and organizational strength that the competing forces had been capable of establishing. While the 'quiescence' of the balancing elements is in fact a prerequisite for the emergence of a revolutionary process, the inescapable factor remains that of the 'intensification' of those forces pressing for the breaking of the existing equilibrium. In the post-war period, this organizational level was absent.

Ultimately, economic crises, despite making any rebalancing more difficult, do not actually produce any fundamentally important effects, but 'they can simply create a terrain more favourable to the dissemination of certain modes of thought, and certain ways of posing and resolving questions involving the entire subsequent development of national life'.[68] The economic crisis creates at least a terrain more favourable to a change in mentality, and it is just the detachment of the intellectuals from the dominant group that endorses the acute phase of the crisis: in doing so 'traditional intellectuals [...] [perform] an act of incalculable historical significance; they are signalling and sanctioning the crisis of the state in its decisive form'[69] (cf. Chapter 4, section 'Organic intellectuals and mass intellectuality').

In the same note containing this passage, one encounters once again the comparison between the medieval crisis and the crisis experienced during the transition to mass politics. The difference noted between the two situations of crisis once again highlights the importance of class organization within the crisis. In fact, contemporary traditional intellectuals, despite detaching themselves from the dominant social group,

> have neither the kind of organization possessed by the church nor anything comparable to it; that is what makes the modern crisis more severe than the medieval crisis. The medieval crisis lasted for several centuries, until the French Revolution, when the social grouping that had become the economic driving force in Europe after the year 1000 was able to present itself as an integral 'state' with all the intellectual and moral forces that were necessary and adequate to the task of organizing a complete and perfect society.[70]

The contemporary crisis is thus aggravated by the fact that traditional intellectuals do not have a solid 'shore' to land on, given that the new order, despite having to test the seeds of its organizational forms within existing society, is still not able, with its organic intellectuals, to allude to any new, alternative hegemony capable of recouping, at the level of its own hegemony, those traditional intellectuals freed by the crisis of the old system. Once again the difficulty of conceiving the forms of the 'organic recombination', that is, the rearticulation of society's different elements to form a new order, comes to the fore. This is the fulcrum that all of the *Prison Notebooks* revolve around: the analysis of the transition from one organic system to another that is not seen simply as a process of destruction and reconstruction, as it was in accordance with an 'Eastern' scheme of things that is no longer workable with the advent of mass politics.

6

Temporality

'Current events' lead us to relive the last and the psychology of our predecessors. And it helps us clarify our ideas, and forces us to transform our vocabulary.

Antonio Gramsci
5 February 1918

THE DUAL CHARACTER OF GRAMSCIAN TIME

The *Prison Notebooks*, for the best part of their existence as a political work, have regularly been interpreted in the same way with regard to their alleged temporal structure. In fact, Western Marxism's use of Gramsci's work has been heavily conditioned by the Italian Communist Party's political use of the notebooks, at least up until the 1970s.[1] Gramsci's thoughts were classified as part of the historicist school of thought, on the basis of the presumed continuity with an Italian tradition that, starting with Francesco De Sanctis, was later developed by Antonio Labriola, and ultimately by Benedetto Croce, and is thus also considered to take in Antonio Gramsci. This historicist school of thought implied a linear, progressive conception of time, in which each historical moment could be broken down and comprehended on the basis of the relationship between its component parts.[2] In addition to the political consequences of the aforementioned classification, which was so often reiterated that it became a cliché difficult to negate, the conception of time inherent in these interpretations concealed, for a long time, the much more complex temporal structure of Gramsci's work. Interest in this topic has re-emerged in recent years, even though it has not been fully formulated as yet.[3] The emphasis on the 'multiple temporal levels' present in the *Prison Notebooks*, on the other hand, has often led to the work's interpretation tending in the opposite direction, that is, towards the unreserved valorization of the temporal pluralities present in Gramsci's works, thus offering an intriguing reading of the notebooks, but possibly one that is a little too audacious given the real content of the work.[4]

Thus, whosoever wishes to analyse the question of the structure of time in Gramsci must first acknowledge that it is not an easy thing to identify. Together with an understanding of temporality as a plural entity – as in the case of the theory of personality, of linguistic phenomena and of considerations regarding common sense, all questions that will be shortly dealt with here – there is, in fact, a 'hegemonic temporality' in the *Prison Notebooks* that determines these relations in more ways than one, and acts as a type of 'temporal unifying device'.[5] This is not a case *merely* of one of the many temporal layers that, within a 'presumed' unit such as the individual or a language, carries on its battle by trying to impose its own course. In fact, this is *also* a case of the temporality of that force that, temporarily and not 'naturally' of course, prevails over others despite not managing to, or being able to, assimilate them completely. This force not only endeavours to get time to conform to it, as a specific mode if its own prevalence over other temporalities, but at least in part it also over-determines the rules of this struggle. These two forms of temporality – plural temporality that is always struggling to prevail and singular temporality represented by the hegemonic force at the time – are simultaneously and constantly at play in Gramsci's analysis. In the case of plural temporality, the outcome of the struggle is different each time, from one case to the next; within singular temporality, the upheaval occurs at the beginning of every new age, when the 'temporal line' changes and points in another direction.

This dual character of time inherent in the *Prison Notebooks* reflects the dynamic character of the historical blocs, of the determined market and of the competing organic systems. The dominant bloc that, as we saw when analysing the concept of 'automatism' (Chapter 4, section 'Gramsci's "sociological operators"'), 'predominates and "dictates law"',[6] in practice also dictates time. The over-determination of this 'temporal force' in relation to the plurality of conflicting times thus needs to be taken into account: the groups governing society fight their war of position with the benefit of this force that over-determines the conflict. This plurality does not therefore occur in neutral territory, but in a context partially structured by hegemonic time, and this privileged position of the dominant bloc is merely the thing that is at stake here, that is, hegemony: and the establishment of one given time structure is a specific development of this hegemony.

In this regard, Alberto Burgio was the first to point out the difference between the Gramscian concepts of 'duration' and of 'constituting an epoch'. Burgio identified the dual structure of historical temporality in Gramsci, which sees the continuity of duration interrupted by the intervention of an epoch-making phenomenon.[7] However, Burgio appears to situate these two temporalities in succession, on the basis of a linear model that, rather paradoxically, seems to reassemble historical development. The only possible asynchronous movement in this model is represented by the geographical differences that stagger the levels of linear temporality, producing the effect of a 'contemporaneity of the non-contemporaneous', as in the case of French history compared to the histories of the other European nations fighting a battle that had already been won in France by the Revolution.[8] However, the dual structure of Gramscian time that we are trying to reconstruct here is based in the *Prison Notebooks* on the consubstantiality of these temporalities rather than on their consecutiveness, following that relationship between the permanent and the occasional that we have already analysed (Chapter 5, section 'The political science of crisis'), whereby the two terms are not determined a priori, but are dependent upon the organic system of which they are part.

Duration and epoch thus co-exist as temporal courses. The former is the stage for the imminent struggle between social forces within a system of hegemonic power. The latter is the unequal background in which this struggle is played out. In regard to duration, there are no novelties at the level of overall social organization, but only diverse forms of organization of the system. Constituting an epoch, on the other hand, entails establishing a new civilization, destroying the old automatisms and creating new ones, and modifying the relationship between the occasional and the permanent. However, if the event that constitutes an epoch arises only rarely, this does not mean that the temporality inscribed in an epoch is not present and does not play a decisive role in the epoch's duration. On the contrary, an epoch manifests itself in every hegemonic conflict, both in the force that at that moment governs the process and in the structure of the battlefield that, at least in part, is determined by this same force. Likewise, while it is true that duration characterizes homogeneous, linear time, and any ripples in that time are relegated to the ranks of the accidental, it is also true that it is impossible to determine the precise moment at which duration becomes epoch; likewise, it is not possible to determine the moment at which the struggle at the occasional level becomes permanent struggle.[9]

There are four notes in the *Prison Notebooks* in which the concept of 'constituting an epoch' emerges. These four notes refer, respectively, to four movements: 1) the idea of progress; 2) what Gramsci termed the 'Dreyfus movement'; 3) Fascism; and 4) Americanism. In Gramsci's view, only the first of these constitutes an epoch, while the other three are expressions: 2) of 'movements [that] can have a relatively "progressive" content' but are not epoch-making in that 'They are rendered historically effective by their adversary's inability to construct, not by an inherent force of their own';[10] 3) of political phenomena that seem to take society backwards to an absolutist form, but in reality are only of a '"transitory" character';[11] 4) of reorganizations that fail to create a new civilization but simply 'remasticate the old European culture'.[12] While Dreyfusism, Fascism and Americanism do not constitute an epoch but are simply 'transitory' moments within the capitalistic epoch, the idea of progress, on the other hand, is epoch-making since it marks the emergence of a new 'mentality', of a new 'relationship [...] between society and nature' that may be rationally interpreted, which means that 'mankind as a whole is more sure of its future and can conceive "rationally" of plans through which to govern its entire life'.[13] This is a revolution in mentality comparable solely with Soviet efforts to construct a 'new Man' for a new epoch-making transition.

Adopting a less theoretical, more analytical approach, we shall now render this analysis of Gramsci's writings concrete by retracing the path followed by this book up to now, this time in regard to the question of temporality: from the theory of personality (the individual) to common sense and language (collective organisms), and the distinction between East and West (society). In this way we can analyse the question of the temporal nature of epochal change, armed with the appropriate tools.

SIGNS OF TIME: THE THEORY OF PERSONALITY, COMMON SENSE, LANGUAGE, EAST AND WEST

How can we incorporate the question of temporality in the reconstruction formulated in Chapter 2 regarding the theory of personality? The key element to be borne in mind is the individual as a stratified being composed of strictly individual elements together with others that are socially determined. The conflict between these two components is summed here with the conflict inherent in the social elements of individuality, which reproduce in the individual those conflicts that characterize a society divided into different social classes. The individual is thus the object of different, competing temporalities that express present and past conflicts:

> it contains Stone Age elements and principles of a more advanced science, prejudices from all past phases of history at the local level and intuitions of a future philosophy which will be that of a human race united the world over.[14]

This temporal plurality is the point of departure for each individual, who experiences his own life according to the different times – just for the sake of example – of folklore and of 'disenchantment' of the world,[15] of dedication to one's work and of Taylorist-Fordist rationality, of superstition and of science. This temporal plurality should not be confused, however, with an objective, eternal condition that sees fragmentariness as a value in itself, and which consequently expresses a politics that tends to incorporate these diverse temporalities into one 'harmonious plurality'.[16] The Gramscian approach, linked to a progressive, unifying vision of emancipation – whether this is to be considered an advantage or a limitation makes little difference here – on the other hand, is characterized by the acknowledgement of a struggle aimed at temporal uniformity:

> Having established that the contradictory nature of the system of social relations implies that people's consciousness is inevitably contradictory, the question arises as to the manner in which this contradiction manifests itself, and how unification can be gradually achieved.[17]

This urge for temporal unity is characteristic of all the forces at play within the hegemonic struggle, each of which tries to bring its adversaries into its 'own temporality'. Even the working class has to move in this direction, through individual coherence, control over its own actions, the systematic and organic development of a 'new Man', and consequently of a new order. The October Revolution was greeted by Gramsci as an epoch-making event also because it laid the basis for such possible unity:

> For a mass of people to be led to think coherently and in the same coherent fashion about the real present world, is a 'philosophical' event far more important and 'original' than the discovery by some

philosophical 'genius' of a truth which remains the property of small groups of intellectuals.[18]

In this case, coherence is the result of that action designed to encompass the diverse temporalities within the temporality of revolution.

Of course, one should not underestimate the importance of Gramsci's willingness to accept plurality, compared to the monistic view of the working class in vogue during his time. One should not forget that Gramsci's innovation was radical, not only in considering the struggle within each formally perceived political unit (including the individual) to be fundamental, but also in valorizing this plurality in the phases of transition to the new order. The revolutionary process, as we have seen, is for this reason among others rethought on a longer timescale and in terms of its 'consensual' characteristics. However, the ultimate purpose of Gramsci's politics remains that of social unity and individual coherency, to be achieved through a process that unfolds parallel to transformation.

The two types of temporality therefore manifest themselves through the co-existence of: 1) diverse temporal layers and 2) a strained tendency towards unity, or rather, towards diverse, diverging unities. If one moves from the individual level to that of collective phenomena, this dual temporal structure emerges with equal force. Common sense, on the one hand, and language, on the other, in fact represent the collective forms of this temporal plurality that must tend towards unification.

Common sense is the plural 'residue' that the intellectual history of humanity has rooted in popular consciousness, and it thus manifests itself as the incoherent stratification of worldviews, prejudices and beliefs. It contains all and everything, from the most conservative and reactionary elements to the 'intuitions of a future philosophy'.[19] This latter aspect, identified as 'good sense', is what interests Gramsci: 'This is the healthy nucleus that exists in "common sense", the part of it which can be called "good sense" and which deserves to be made more unitary and coherent'.[20] The plurality and incoherence of common sense contribute towards reproducing domination, because they fragment individual wills and prevent the formation of collective wills as an alternative to the dominant one. Such alternative collective wills, on the other hand, may emerge from the combination of the development of good sense and of criticism of common sense: 'At those times in history when a homogeneous social group is brought into being, there comes into being also, in opposition to common sense, a homogeneous – in other words coherent and systematic – philosophy.'[21] The time of common sense is of a plural character because it is within that time that a hegemonic struggle is fought; however, the time of the dominant group over-determines this plurality because it forces it in a certain direction, at least until an opposing homogeneous social group forms.

Gramsci's writings in his Notebook 29 reflect this same temporal structure in regard to the question of language. Language is also plural on two different levels: the internal level of the individual's linguistic capacity, which sees the individual sharing a dialect and the national language (if not more than one language); and on the level of the national and international communities, which sees dialects and languages take their respective shares of the territory, but also sees them superimposed to a certain extent. It has been repeatedly pointed out, and rightly so, that in Gramsci the dynamics of divulgation, struggle and contamination of language reflect the dynamics of power relations. Thus, 'linguistic power' possesses the same features, and operates in the same ways, as political power.[22] Following this isomorphism, what Gramsci calls 'immanent or spontaneous grammars' correspond to individual consciousness, to the extent that 'one can say that each person has a grammar of his own'.[23] '"Normative" grammar', on the other hand, is that process that tends to standardize language, and may take two different forms: the first is through the prestige of a language deriving from its expression of a progressive force, which gains hegemonic supremacy through the '"spontaneous" expression of grammatical conformity'.[24] This process is not coercive but 'imitative' and evolves through 'reciprocal monitoring, reciprocal teaching';[25] the second is the form dictated by the State's action in imposing a national language through the educational/coercive force of its institutions.[26]

The choice therefore is not between conserving a plurality of languages and imposing a single language, but between two different ways of achieving unity. The opportunity to master a national language, in fact, is in Gramsci's view an essential prerequisite for the emancipation of the subalterns. It is something that cannot be sacrificed in the name of linguistic plurality.[27] Temporality comes to the fore once again here: this is a question of standardizing languages at a national level – because only languages possess the instruments with which modern thought can be expressed in full[28] – rendering them translatable and thus getting away from the myth of the universality of language (Esperanto) in order to synchronize different national linguistic structures to the same (revolutionary) time. The temporality of duration, linguistically represented by the plurality of dialects and languages competing for prestige, is superimposed by the epochal temporality of national languages, which are the only ones that can enable a strong link to be established between popular culture and national politics, between the people and the leading groups.

One final consideration regarding the dual temporal nature of the *Prison Notebooks* concerns one of the most famous Gramscian distinctions, the one that makes reference to the diverse relationship between State and civil society in the East and in the West. In the East, Gramsci writes, society was 'primordial and gelatinous', whereas in the West it was 'a succession of sturdy fortresses and emplacements'.[29] In reality, this spatial division refers to a temporal division, that is, it points to the development of Western societies. In the West, power cannot be taken by attacking the 'places' of power, because power has been disseminated throughout society, rendering society a conservative inertial force within which the revolutionary use of the war of manoeuvre is no longer sufficient. Often scholars have insisted on this idea of the contemporaneity of the non-contemporary, that is, on the multiplicity of temporal levels in the diverse functional spaces globally dominated by capitalism, in particular in relation to theories of uneven development.[30] There are undoubtedly good reasons in support of this interpretation, and the identification of plural temporalities remains, even within the context of our insistence on the duality of Gramscian time, a significant feature of Gramscian analysis. However, in analysing this distinction, perhaps too much attention has been paid to the 'Western' side of the process, that is, to the changes displayed by Western societies having resisted the challenge of revolution in the West. Nevertheless, in keeping with Gramsci's work, the focus should also be in the other direction, that of the East described in this famous quotation.

In Gramsci's analysis, 'Eastern' civil society was certainly considered more primordial and gelatinous at the end of the war, when the Bolsheviks dealt the fatal blow to Russia's Tsarist regime. However, the advent of the Worker's State, with the intense period of politicization of the masses right through the 1920s, had radically changed the political panorama. There is substantial evidence of this. For example, the revolutionary event itself had already established the basis for the possible unification of the contrasting temporalities within individuals, creating a 'densification' of social life. Then during the 1920s, the attempt to stabilize relations between factory workers and peasants through the New Economic Policy (NEP) had created that social fabric subject to the hegemony of the workers that had been missing before. It was this very process that led Gramsci to use the concept of hegemony, and to consider Lenin as its precursor, being the first person to put it into practice:

> the theoretical-practical principle of hegemony has also epistemological significance, and it is here that Ilich's [Lenin] greatest theoretical contribution to the philosophy of praxis should be sought [...]. The realisation of a hegemonic apparatus, in so far as it creates a new ideological terrain, determines a reform of consciousness and of methods of knowledge: it is a fact of knowledge, a philosophical fact.[31]

Gramsci was thus aware that the transition to mass politics had changed the scenario not only in the West, in relation to the liberal order, but also in the East in relation to the forms through which the revolution had been achieved. The post-revolutionary era in the USSR, just like mass politics in the West (Fascism and Americanism), thus both presented the scenario of a war of position in which neither side was any longer characterized by a primordial and gelatinous civil society. For this reason, Gramsci was able to translate the social bloc from the economic terms of the USSR at the time of the NEP to superstructural terms, that is, of the intellectual blocs of the capitalistically stabilized western countries. While in the writings of Bukharin – the greatest theoretician of the NEP – the formation of the bloc is driven first and foremost by the economic forces politically manoeuvred by the Workers' State, in Gramsci it is hegemony, specifically that of an intellectual and cultural nature, that underlies the formation of that bloc.[32] In this case, it was the 'economically backward' Soviet Russia (albeit more advanced politically, as the first experimental Workers' State) that dictated the guiding principles and the theoretical-political problems to the international communist movement.

Thus, the global scenario is one of diverse, competing hegemonic times that massively effect the synchronization of the plural temporalities to be found within each of the blocs. Planism,[33] Corporatism and Soviet planning all represent different, competing 'temporal rhythms' whereby States endeavour to hegemonically (but also coercively) unify their respective societies.

THE SHAPE OF DURATION: THE PASSIVE REVOLUTION

Having thus illustrated the bases for the dual structure of time in the *Prison Notebooks*, we can now turn to the concept that Gramsci uses to analyse the temporal nature of duration as characterized by the hegemonic force that prevails, operating as a 'temporal unifying device'. The concept in question is that of passive revolution. As often is the case in the *Prison Notebooks*, Gramsci does not coin a new word out of nothing. Instead, he utilizes a concept previously formulated by others and shifts its meaning,[34] thus formulating a new concept in practice (a process in keeping with the linguistic observations on the historicity of language and against its artificiality).

As previously mentioned (Chapter 3, section 'Bureaucracy and officials: Gramsci and Weber'), Gramsci takes the term from the *Historical Essay on the Neapolitan Revolution of 1799* by Vincenzo Cuoco, where the expression indicated the absence of popular involvement in the revolution due to the gap between the leaders and the people. Italy's political 'moderates' – as Gramsci calls the diverse members of the ranks of Italian liberalism who were behind the unification of Italy – based a precise political programme around the concept of passive revolution, transforming it into a political strategy, into their hegemonic and pedagogic action vis-à-vis the other forces of the Risorgimento.

By taking a broader view, Gramsci pointed out that Cuoco used this expression to indicate the development of 'countries that modernize the State through a series of reforms or national wars without undergoing a political revolution of a radical-Jacobin type'.[35] Thus, the French Revolution, which established a clean break with the feudal past, was compared with the passive revolutions witnessed in the other European States, in which:

> the needs that found a Jacobin-Napoleonic expression in France were satisfied in small doses, legally, in a reformist manner, thereby managing to safeguard the political and economic positions of the old feudal classes, avoiding agrarian reform and making especially sure that the popular masses did not go through a period of political experience such as occurred in France in the Jacobin era.[36]

The absence of the masses' political involvement, together with the slow, partial acceptance of certain revolutionary demands on the part of the leading groups, may be considered those features of the hegemonic programme known as passive revolution.

According to Gramsci, this manner of historical development, characterized by the temporality of duration, conceals a 'domesticated dialectic because it "mechanically" presupposes that the antithesis should be preserved by the thesis in order not to destroy the dialectical process'.[37] The thesis (the hegemonic group) determines the antithesis (the subaltern group) and guides the actions, and eventually incorporates the demands, of such. Thus, the situation that arises is that of 'historical inertia', where time flows homogeneously and politics is transformed from subjective action aimed at changing the world to the administration of the existing power structure. The only undisciplined movement that remains in society is the inconsequential (in terms of power) 'sporadic and incoherent rebelliousness of the popular masses'.[38]

The unification of Italy is the historical example of this flowing of time. In his notes on the Risorgimento, Gramsci pointed out the limitations of the Italian democrats (the Action Party) when it came to bringing the masses to the centre of the political stage. These limits were due to the decision to secretly organize groups of 'Carbonari', which did not permit the masses to get involved. In doing so, the democrats placed their faith in the episodic temporality of conspirational action. However, Gramsci was also interested in grasping those mechanisms by which the Moderates managed to produce a 'centripetal hegemonic field' capable of engulfing the rival leading group, and with it the possibility of a possible alternative unity:

> Out of the Action Party and the Moderates, which represented the real 'subjective forces' of the Risorgimento? Without a shadow of doubt it was the Moderates, precisely because they were also aware of the role of the Action Party: thanks to this awareness, their 'subjectivity' was of a superior and more decisive quality.[39]

Gramsci continues by arguing that 'the Action Party was led historically by the Moderates', who proved ideologically appealing to the Party, and succeeded in controlling, and taking advantage of, the fragmented nature of the Party's political action. The Moderates managed to impose a unitary temporality because: 1) they 'represented a relatively homogeneous social group, and hence their leadership underwent relatively limited oscillation';[40] 2) they were 'intellectuals already naturally "condensed" by the organic nature of their relation to the social groups whose expression they were' and consequently 3) they 'exercised a powerful attraction "spontaneously", on the whole mass of intellectuals of every degree who existed in the peninsula'.[41] The unity of intentions, a close relationship with the social group they represented, and the 'ideological' appeal they had for traditional intellectuals: these were the three key characteristics in Gramsci's view. Only an equally coherent force of the same kind could have struggled in the hegemonic field, contending the position of leading group and establishing a different temporality. This counterforce was resoundingly absent: the Action Party 1) 'did not base itself specifically on any historical class, and the oscillations which its leading organs underwent were resolved, in the last analysis, according to the interests of the Moderates';[42] 2) was composed of characters 'steeped in the traditional rhetoric of Italian literature',[43] who 'only offered woolly statements, and philosophical allusions'[44] to 'popular masses who were foreign to that cultural tradition';[45] and finally 3) 'was itself attracted and influenced' by the Moderate Party, 'on the one hand, as a result of the atmosphere of intimidation [...] and, on the other, because certain of its leading personalities (Garibaldi) had, even if only desultorily (they wavered), a relationship of personal subordination to the Moderate leaders'.[46] The Action Party 'considered as "national" the aristocracy and the landowners, and not the millions of peasants',[47] whereas the French Jacobins, who proved capable of imposing their own temporality on the revolutionary process, 'strove with determination to ensure a bond between town and country',[48] promoting an agrarian reform that in rural areas permitted the synchronization of two different times: 'Rural France accepted the hegemony of Paris; in other words, it understood that in order definitively to destroy the old regime it had to make a bloc with the most advanced elements of the Third Estate, and not with the Girondin moderates.'[49] The exclusion of the great peasant masses from the newly founded Italian State resulted instead in a territorial and social divide between a South that created savings from the exploitation of the peasants and North that drained these resources to finance industrial development. This is how Gramsci interpreted the onset of the 'Southern question': he saw it basically as the failure to synchronize revolutionary developments, thus leaving a contradictory temporal plurality in place within the framework of the dominance of the Moderates.[50] This was the time of duration and of passive revolution.

Once the nation had been unified, the process of 'gradual but continuous absorption' of democratic leaders was to continue in the form of 'transformism', which in this case consisted in 'the parliamentary expression of this action of intellectual, moral and political hegemony'.[51] Transformism operated in this manner not only as the leading classes' attempt to defend the power structure that had been consolidated with the unification of Italy, but also as a (passive) political dynamic that slowly led to the gradual expansion of the State's foundations. Thus, transformism became a genuine 'form of historical development',[52] a form of historical time. Seeing transformism purely as a conservative response, in fact, does not help us grasp Gramsci's intuition whereby transformism is the parliamentary expression of hegemonic action. In fact, by preserving power relations and the specific interests on the basis of which national unity had been built, transformism also operates as a filter for the new demands of a changing society. The new industrial and financial bourgeoisie is in this way gradually included in the mechanisms of representation of interests within the political system, through the dynamics of inclusion 'from above'. Thus, transformism renews the basis of the State's consensus without compromising its power structure, and therefore avoids involving the masses – 'simultaneously'[53] in Gramsci's words – in the reorganization of the State. The 1882 electoral reform, which extended voting rights on the basis of individuals' education rather than wealth, may be interpreted in this way.

The school system was also part of the hegemonic project of Italy's leading classes, through implementation of the only educational plan capable of challenging the '"Jesuitical" school',[54] by means of which the Moderates were able to present themselves as the only 'effective collective force in operation' during the Risorgimento, thereby limiting the contribution of the Action Party to 'individual figures [...] tendentiously exalted in order to incorporate them', thus breaking their 'collective ties'.[55] Thus, the historical reconstruction of the Risorgimento in schools – its temporal rhythm once again – will aid the construction of a possible national history rooted in moderate values, that will disrupt the formulation of any alternative historical accounts. The historical truth of the Risorgimento was to be that of the Moderates, helped by the fact that the Action Party 'was incapable of offering any effective alternative to this propaganda which, through the schools, became the official version taught'.[56]

THE FORM OF EPOCH: HOW NOVELTY EMERGES

We have seen how Gramsci views the passive revolution as representing the bourgeois model of the 'historical management' of development and change: a model that was implemented immediately after the French Revolution, with the formation of the Nation States in Europe in reaction to these upheavals. The characteristic temporality of this development is that of the passive revolution, which unfolds across a linear timescale, the development of which is controlled by a 'false' dialectic in which the thesis presupposes the antithesis prior to conflicting with it.

Just a few years after Gramsci had formulated these reflections, Walter Benjamin wrote his theses *On the Concept of History*, containing a similar criticism of bourgeois time:

> The concept of mankind's historical progress cannot be sundered from the concept of its progression through a homogeneous, empty time. A critique of the concept of such a progression must underlie any criticism of the concept of progress itself.[57] (Thesis XIII)

The homogeneous, empty time described by Benjamin seems to copy that of the passive revolution described by Gramsci: homogeneity entails conformism, just as emptiness precludes any chance of an alternative subjective construction. This comparison, in addition to being fascinating due to the fact that the two writers did not know each other's work,[58] could be useful in particular when investigating the features of the second temporality that Gramsci alludes to: 'epochal time'. However, it should be said that this is an aspect that is not specifically dealt with in the *Prison Notebooks*, but one that emerges every now and then without being formulated in full. The problem of how the 'time of revolution' emerges in Gramsci's writings, and in particular how it is to be triggered – apart from its phenomenology, which as we have seen is characterized by the synchronization of different times – remains unresolved (cf. note 78 to Chapter 4). Certain cues for a reflection on the question – which do not purport to include Gramsci in present-day discussions regarding immanence/transcendence or articulation/event – may be found, nevertheless, when comparing the notebooks with Benjamin's *Theses*. In Thesis XIV, Benjamin states that:

History is the subject of a construction whose site is not homogeneous, empty time, but time filled full by now-time [*Jetztzeit*]. Thus, to Robespierre ancient Rome was a past charged with now-time, a past which he blasted out of the continuum of history.[59] (Thesis XIV)

The first thing to be said here is that for Benjamin, 'epochal' time – his *Jetztzeit*, the messianic now-time introducing the novelty – is the time that makes history. History that sees a subject refer to fragments of the past in order to break the continuity of bourgeois time: the Jacobins could thus trace themselves back to the ancient Romans in order to break the homogeneous, empty time of the feudal system. Materialist historiography is thus called upon to oppose historicism (that of the Second International) that culminates in universal history, and whose 'procedure is additive: it musters a mass of data to fill the homogeneous, empty time'.[60] Historical materialism, on the contrary, develops a historiography contemplating radical interruptions in the temporal linearity of a dominion: 'Thinking involves not only the movement of thoughts, but their arrest as well.'[61] For materialists, historical time is that full of *Jetztzeit*, in which the present recalls fragments of the past in order to redeem and revive them. The link between two moments in time thus disrupts the linearity of bourgeois time and reveals a different movement.

This image of non-linear temporality constituted by historical highs and lows of particular intensity appears to be present in the *Prison Notebooks* as well: for example, in the relationship that Gramsci portrays between Machiavelli and the French Jacobins. Both are treated as 'fragments' of the past that may be reactivated within the context of a history that proceeds with an oscillating intensity rather than through any process of accumulation. Along this new temporality, even the historical sequence is questioned. With regard to the need for a simultaneous incursion of the peasant masses into political life, Gramsci wrote:

> That was Machiavelli's intention through the reform of the militia, and it was achieved by the Jacobins in the French Revolution. That Machiavelli understood it *reveals a precocious Jacobinism* that is the (more or less fertile) germ of his conception of national revolution.[62]

Thus, in Gramsci's writings the relationship between the Jacobins and Machiavelli marks a break in the linearity of bourgeois time. Not only did the Jacobins evoke Machiavelli, but the reference also holds if the normal sequence of time is inverted: while the 'Jacobins [...] were certainly a "categorical embodiment" of Machiavelli's Prince', Machiavelli also shared a 'precocious Jacobinism'.[63] Their destinies were also similar from the historiographical point of view: both were 'used' by the history of the victors – Machiavelli becoming a symbol of political cynicism, imprisoned in a political science synonymous with the administration of power, while the Jacobins were reduced to symbolizing extremism and fanaticism – but both could also live on in the temporality of a revolutionary force capable of identifying itself with them.[64] Gramsci's references to the Jacobins and to Machiavelli thus served the following purpose in the *Prison Notebooks*: to force the present to identify itself with their actions, thus offering the working class the key to an alternative historical time to that of passive revolutions.

A further example of this 'intense' non-linear temporality is regards the problem of the relationship between town and countryside, between factory workers and peasants. Besides, this was the point on which the Workers' State that emerged from the October Revolution hinged. In criticizing the Action Party's indifference towards the peasant masses – unlike the Jacobins, who had imposed a radical agrarian reform[65] –, Gramsci pointed out how it also possessed a specific historical 'tradition to which it could go back and attach itself' in order to promote this synchronization. This was the medieval tradition of the Communes that bore witness to a 'nascent bourgeoisie [that] seeks allies among the peasants against the Empire and against the local feudalism'.[66] The historical bloc of town and countryside, the synchronization of these two times to revolutionary time, was already the key to democratic revolution at the time, and this is one of those aspects of 'epochal time' that chronologically links distant events on the basis of their intensity:

> the most classic master of the art of politics for the Italian ruling classes, Machiavelli, had also posed the problem – naturally in the terms and with the preoccupations of his time. In his politico-military writings, the need to subordinate the popular masses organically to the ruling strata, so as to create a national militia capable of eliminating the companies of fortune, was quite well understood.[67]

In Gramsci's view, an alternative historical time to that of passive revolution is thus potentially ever-present, even within the context of the linear development of a time that is over-determined by the practice of the hegemonic subject. It is up to the revolutionary subject that wishes to establish hegemony to be able to reconnect with those moments in history that have expressed such intensity, and to bring to contemporaneity those attempts made to overturn the old organic system in order to create a new one. The hegemony of an emergent subject thus always presupposes the urge to synchronize the diverse temporalities of the subaltern groups. This is the only way that the latter may get free from the depoliticizing uniformity of bourgeois time. In this sense, Gramsci views contemporariness as the product of political endeavour: it does not exist originally, but needs to be created.

How such a process is to be started, that is, how the synchronization of the times of the subaltern groups is to disrupt the unity of homogenous, empty time, is a question that is destined to remain unanswered in the *Prison Notebooks*. Gramsci does not manage to (or perhaps cannot) illustrate the forms by means of which 'novelty' is to be produced within an organic system. The only epoch-making event that had seen the working class as protagonist had been triggered, in fact, by a war of manoeuvre (the October Revolution), within the context of a weak civil society that no longer existed following the advent of mass politics. It is likely that this 'unspoken aspect' of Gramsci's work corresponds to an 'unspoken' structural aspect of political theory, an aspect that remains unspeakable for the simple reason that it cannot be rationalized within the categories of politics. It comes as no surprise that all of the classical dichotomies of Marxist thought – theory and practice, structure and superstructure, ideology and class consciousness – bear witness to the impossibility of rationally defining the transition from the one to the other. At this point, the fact that Gramsci's writings permit a reflection on this question without forcing a solution is a strength, and not a weakness, for all those who wish to utilize his open Marxism to interpret and change contemporary society.

Conclusion

The path followed in this volume is one of the possible paths that may be taken within the *Prison Notebooks*, but certainly not the only one. The rich, complex structure of the notebooks, in fact, is open to various, not necessarily convergent, readings guided in the main by the type of interest the work elicits in the reader: that of historical-political reconstruction, or of philosophical reflection, or of literary or political criticism and so on. However, it is also true that Gramsci has not left the reader with a hotchpotch of random reflections, to be assembled as one likes in order to support one theory or another. In fact, his thought is constantly situated, never generic; it is always historical, never absolute; and rooted in a specific circumstance such as that of the prison, which did not allow for any immediate, more direct transfer to the sphere of political practice. His imprisonment, in fact, defines the form of Gramsci's work, at least in part, through those restrictions resulting from the lack of contact with the outside world; from the impossibility of having the materials he required in order to study more systematically; from the necessarily precarious, contracted, allusive character of his brief notes. This form of writing, which in prison became a form of thinking, forced Gramsci to channel his thought through constant marginal notes to a 'diverse' thought which at that moment in time is, explicitly or implicitly, the subject of study or interpretation. This way of proceeding, which constantly forced Gramsci's arguments, rather than impoverishing his reasoning, produced a series of deviations, reformulations and openings that would be unthinkable under different conditions of 'theoretical production'.

Gramsci therefore constantly reformulated and reutilized the vocabulary of other theoretical traditions different from Marxism – such as sociology, anthropology and linguistics – which today, 80 years after his death, has been revived in contemporary debates. It is no coincidence that many of the themes dealt with in this volume have had a direct influence on social and political studies over the last decade. These intellectual terrains have seen part of what we may call the 'Gramscian challenges' being played out, namely, the study of the ideological levels of modern capitalism, the critique of methodological individualism, the general crisis of the 'intermediate bodies', the new form of global society, the analysis of the economic crisis and the nature of time in a globalized world. Thus, Gramscian tools may be fruitfully employed on such terrains, without any 'Gramscianism' – as a political programme, or worse as a 'worldview' of a non-existent political subject – polluting the wells of scientific curiosity in order to provide sustenance to small-scale political experiments.

So we need to proceed along that narrow path permitting us to maintain a broad view of the text together with the interpretative accuracy required in order to avoid simple generalizations. Thus, specification of the viewpoint from which the interpretation of the writings proceeds not only clarifies the adopted approach, but is also a sign of scientific seriousness. My interpretation of the *Prison Notebooks* is characterized by the attempt to emphasize the explicit and implicit fundamental theoretical articulations of Gramsci's thought within a given historical framework, but in the absence of any precise prescriptive pointers. In fact, Gramsci's reflections are situated at a time of epochal transformation – a period that marks the transition from 'free-market competitive' capitalism to 'organized-monopoly' capitalism, from bourgeois society to mass society, from the 'liberal' nineteenth century to the 'political' twentieth century – and he constantly endeavours to regulate and calibrate his own theoretical tools in order to take on this new reality. This is another reason why one century later, within the context of similarly epochal changes, there is renewed interest in Gramsci's writings.

Notes

INTRODUCTION

1. Eric J. Hobsbawm, 'Per capire le classi subalterne [Understanding the Subaltern Classes]', *Rinascita – Il contemporaneo*, special issue 'Gramsci nel mondo [Gramsci in the World]', 8, 28 February 1987: 15–34. For 'The 250 most cited authors in the Arts and Humanities Citations Index 1976–1983' cf. Eugene Garfield, Institute for Scientific Information, *Current Comments*, 48, 1986.
2. This first edition of the *Prison Notebooks* comprised six volumes in which the notes were arranged on a subject basis. These volumes were published between 1948 and 1951, edited by F. Platone and P. Togliatti (*Il materialismo storico e la filosofia di Benedetto Croce* [Historical Materialism and the Philosophy of Benedetto Croce]; *Gli intellettuali e l'organizzazione della cultura* [The Intellectuals and the Organization of Culture]; *Il Risorgimento* [The Risorgimento]; *Note sul Machiavelli, sulla politica e sullo Stato moderno* [Notes on Machiavelli, Politics and the Modern State]; *Letteratura e vita nazionale* [Literature and National Life]; *Passato e presente* [Past and Present]). Just a very few passages, considered politically 'inappropriate', had been eliminated from this edition, together with all the rough writings (a) that Gramsci subsequently redrafted.
3. In 1947 Togliatti, the true promoter of Gramsci's posthumous success, had already warned: 'We Communists should be very careful not to believe that the work of Antonio Gramsci is ours alone. No, this is the heritage of everyone, of all Sardinians, of all Italians, of all workers fighting for their freedom, regardless of their religious or political beliefs', Palmiro Togliatti, 'Gramsci, la Sardegna, l'Italia (1947) [Gramsci, Sardinia, Italy]', in Togliatti, *Scritti su Gramsci* [Writings on Gramsci], edited by G. Liguori, Rome: Editori Riuniti, 2001: 128.
4. See the graph of the recurrence of the name 'Gramsci' in English-language books over the last 60 years, to be found at books.google.com/ngrams. In 2008 (the last figure available), following twenty years of stagnation, the peak achieved in the 1970s was almost reached, and it is likely that said peak has since been easily surpassed.
5. Q16§2, in SPN: 383–4.
6. Alberto Burgio, *Gramsci: il sistema in movimento* [Gramsci: The Moving System], Rome: DeriveApprodi, 2014: 107.

CHAPTER 1

1. Michael Freeden, *Ideology: A Very Short Introduction*, Oxford: Oxford University Press, 2003: 12. Freeden makes reference to the famous metaphor of the *camera obscura* present in *The German Ideology*: 'If in all ideology men and their circumstances appear upside-down as in a *camera obscura*, this phenomenon arises just as much from their historical life-process as the inversion of objects on

the retina does from their physical life-process', Karl Marx, Friedrich Engels, *The German Ideology*, translated by C. Dutt, 1845 (www.marxists.org/archive/marx/works/1845/german-ideology). This passage was to have a substantial impact on the Marxist theory of ideology after Marx: cf. Terry Eagleton, *Ideology: An Introduction*, London-New York: Verso, 1991: 70–84; Jan Rehmann, *Theories of Ideology: The Powers of Alienation and Subjection*, Leiden-Boston: Brill, 2013. However, Marx's analysis of this 'appearance' tends to underline its necessary role as a constituent part of capital relations more than its being as the mystification of reality; cf. Maurizio Ricciardi, 'L'ideologia come scienza politica del sociale (Ideology as a Political Science of the Social)', *Scienza & Politica*, 52, 2015: 179 (http://scienzaepolitica.unibo.it/article/view/5282). Gramsci himself underlined this same point in Q7§21, in PN3: 171–2.

2. Cf. Karl Mannheim, *Ideology and Utopia: An Introduction to the Sociology of Knowledge*, translated by L. Wirth and E. Shils, London-Henley: Routledge & Kegan Paul, 1998 (1st ed. 1929); Mannheim, *Essays on the Sociology of Knowledge*, translated by P. Kecskemeti, London: Routledge, 1998 (1st ed. 1952).

3. Cf. Louis Althusser, *On the Reproduction of Capitalism: Ideology and Ideological State Apparatuses*, translated by G.M. Goshgarian, London-New York: Verso, 2014 (1st ed. 1970); Althusser, *For Marx*, translated by B. Brewster, London-New York: Verso, 2005 (1st ed. 1965). In Althusser's view, the dominant class itself is forced to participate in the totality that it has created, and its relationship with ideology 'can never be purely *instrumental*; the men who would use an ideology purely as a means of action, as a tool, find that they have been caught by it, implicated by it, just when they are using it and believe themselves to be absolute masters of it. [...] the ruling class does not maintain with the ruling ideology, which is its own ideology, an external and lucid relation of pure utility and cunning', Althusser, *For Marx*: 234.

4. Cf. the use made of such by Stuart Hall, in the field of cultural studies, in 'Politics and Ideology: Gramsci', in S. Hall, B. Lumley and G. McLennan (eds), *On Ideology. Working Papers in Cultural Studies*, Birmingham: Centre for Contemporary Cultural Studies, 1977: 45–76; Hall, 'Gramsci's Relevance for the Study of Race and Ethnicity', *Journal of Communication Inquiry*, 10(2), 1986: 5–27. A different, but nonetheless interesting, use has been made by Ernesto Laclau and Chantal Mouffe in *Hegemony and Socialist Strategy: Towards a Radical Democratic Politics*, London-New York: Verso, 2011 (1st ed. 1985); cf. also Laclau, *New Reflections on the Revolution of our Time*, New York: Verso, 1990: 193–5; Mouffe, 'Hegemony and Ideology in Gramsci', in Mouffe (ed.), *Gramsci and Marxist Theory*, London: Routledge & Kegan Paul, 1979: 168–204.

5. It should be pointed out that there is no precise correspondence between the Italian term *senso comune* and its common English translation 'common sense'. The English term, in fact, is strongly characterized by its reference to the individual capacity to evaluate matters and act rightly on the basis of a common sense of judgement, and thus is identifiable as a 'positive' quality that is not necessarily conservative from the political point of view (take, for example, the revolutionary work *Common Sense* by Thomas Paine [*Rights of Man, Common Sense and Other Political Writings*, Oxford: Oxford University Press, 1998: 1–59]). The Italian term, on the other hand, generally indicates the conformism of individuals in relation to the communities to which they belong, and as such its conservative

connotations are often accentuated. This distinction is important since, among other things, in his *Prison Notebooks*, Gramsci distinguishes between *senso comune* and *buon senso* (the latter translating as 'good sense' in English); the latter term, with its positive connotations rendering it much closer to the English term 'common sense', represents 'the healthy nucleus that exists in "common sense"', Q11§12, in SPN: 328.

6. Q4§35, in PN2: 174–5.

7. *Ibid.*: 175.

8. Ricciardi, 'L'ideologia come scienza politica del sociale [Ideology as a Political Science of the Social]'.

9. Q4§35, in PN2: 175. Cf. Emmet Kennedy, '"Ideology" from Tracy to Marx', *Journal of the History of Ideas*, 3, 1979: 353–68.

10. As Ricciardi and Scuccimarra point out: 'Napoleon basically accused the *Idéologues* of incompetence with regard to the material exercise of power, that is, the incompetence of those who only deal with ideas and ignore organisational restrictions. The new science of ideas and its supporters would not manage to grasp power as a different, separate institutional practice from society's movements', Maurizio Ricciardi and Luca Scuccimarra, 'L'ideologia e la sua critica [Ideology and its Critique]', *Scienza & Politica*, 47, 2012: 5–9 (http://scienzaepolitica.unibo.it/article/view/3835).

11. Q4§35, in PN2: 175.

12. *Ibid.*

13. 'At the end of my logic I have traced the plan of the elements of ideology, such as I conceived they ought to be, to give a complete knowledge of our intellectual faculties, and to deduce from that knowledge the first principles of all the other branches of our knowledge, which can never be founded on any other solid base', A.L.C. Destutt De Tracy, *A Treatise on Political Economy (To Which is Prefixed a Supplement to a Preceding Work on the Understanding or Elements of Ideology)*, translated by T. Jefferson, Auburn, Alabama: The Ludwig Von Mises Institute, 2009 (1st ed. 1822): xx.

14. This construction proceeds also by means of a series of expressions deriving from the term 'ideology', such as 'political-ideological apparatus', Q19§3 (QC: 1967, author's translation), 'ideological structure', Q3§51 (PN2: 53), 'ideological superstructure', Q8§171 (PN3: 332) and 'ideological bloc', Q1§44 (PN1: 138). Gramsci also makes use more than 100 times of the term 'conception of the world' (the translation of the German term *Weltanschauung*), together with a series of derivatives of such term, such as 'view of the world', Q4§3 (PN2: 141), Q4§55 (PN2: 226), Q10§11 (QC: 1249); 'general conception of life', Q1§28 (PN1: 117), Q1§46 (PN1: 153), Q19§2 (QC: 1961), Q19§27 (SPN: 103); 'conception of the world and of life', Q8§204 (PN3: 352), Q9§64 (QC: 1134), Q10II§52 (SPN: 347); Q11§62 (SPN: 406), Q13§33 (SPN: 150), Q15§50 (SPN: 171), Q27§1 (CW: 189), Q27§2 (CW: 192); and 'conception of reality', Q10I§5 (FSPN: 338), Q10II§1 (FSPN: 369), Q10II§31 (FSPN: 386), also formulated as 'conception of the objective reality' in his critique of Bukharin in Q11§17 (SPN: 444).

15. Cf. Nikolai Bukharin, *Historical Materialism: A System of Sociology*, 1921 (www.marxists.org/archive/bukharin/works/1921/histmat). While, on the one hand, Gramsci's criticism of Bukharin's 'casual' use of common sense clearly hits the mark, on the other hand, the influence that this work had on the writing of the

Prison Notebooks is a complex matter that goes beyond the scathing judgements contained in the notes referring explicitly to the question (see Michele Filippini, *Una politica di massa. Antonio Gramsci e la rivoluzione della società* [Mass Politics: Antonio Gramsci and the Revolution of Society], Rome: Carocci, 2015: 103–49).

16. Q7§29, in PN3: 179.

17. Q4§35, in PN2: 175.

18. In regard to the 'scientism' of the Marxism of the Second International, see Hans-Josef Steinberg, *Sozialismus und deutsche Sozialdemokratie: zur Ideologie der Partei vor dem 1. Weltkrieg* [*Socialism and German Social Democracy: The Ideology of the Party before the First World War*], Hannover: Verlag für Literatur und Zeitgeschehen, 1967.

19. Q4§15, in PN2: 157.

20. Gramsci retrieves his conception of ideology from the following passage in Marx's 'Preface' to *A Contribution to the Critique of Political Economy*, 1859 (www.marxists.org/archive/marx/works/1859/critique-pol-economy/preface. htm), which makes mention of the concept of 'ideological forms'. Gramsci translated the German original into Italian as follows: 'nell'osservazione di tali sovvertimenti bisogna sempre far distinzione tra il sovvertimento materiale nelle condizioni della produzione economica, che deve essere constatato fedelmente col metodo delle scienze naturali, e le forme giuridiche, politiche, religiose, artistiche o filosofiche, in una parola: le forme ideologiche, nel cui terreno gli uomini diventano consapevoli di questo conflitto e lo risolvono' [In studying such transformations it is always necessary to distinguish between the material transformation in the economic conditions of production, which can be determined with the precision of natural science, and the legal, political, religious, artistic or philosophic – in short, ideological forms in which men become conscious of this conflict and fight it out], QT: 746.

21. Q12§1, in SPN: 12 (we have replaced 'deputies' with 'underlings', a better translation of the Italian word *commessi* offered by Buttigieg and that can be inferred from Q4§49, in PN2: 199).

22. Q8§169, in PN3: 330.

23. Q1§65, in PN1: 173.

24. A reading of Gramsci's hegemony through the concept of articulation has been offered by Laclau and Mouffe in *Hegemony and Socialist Strategy*.

25. Q8§169, in PN3: 330.

26. Q1§43, in PN1: 129.

27. Q13§17, in SPN: 175–85.

28. *Ibid.*: 177. When drafting his notes in the *Prison Notebooks*, Gramsci often underlines the initial words of each note to form a title. Often the title is preceded, or replaced, by another recurrent title that is generally called the 'heading title' (*Past and present, Father Bresciani's progeny, Reformation and Renaissance, Popular literature, History of the subaltern classes, Lorianism* etc.). This fact indicates the subject-by-subject layout of the Notebooks, which was probably designed to facilitate the organization of the material for the purposes of its future publication.

29. Q13§17, in SPN: 177. This is the reference in Marx: 'No social order is ever destroyed before all the productive forces for which it is sufficient have been developed, and new superior relations of production never replace older ones

before the material conditions for their existence have matured within the framework of the old society', Marx, 'Preface' to *A Contribution to the Critique of Political Economy*.

30. Q13§17, in SPN: 179.

31. *Ibid.*: 185.

32. This was the opening article in the one-off publication *La città futura* [The City of the Future] published on 11 February 1917, a four-page newsletter published by the Piedmont Youth Federation of the Italian Socialist Party, addressing socialist youth with the aim of providing young people with a framework with which to interpret reality in accordance with socialist principles, and to encourage action and organization. The Federation had initially entrusted the editing of this publication to Andrea Viglongo, who in turn passed the task on to Gramsci upon specific request from the latter. The newsletter contains, among other things, articles by Gaetano Salvemini ('Cosa è la cultura [What is Culture]'), Benedetto Croce ('La religione [Religion]') and Armando Carlini ('Che cosè la vita [What is Life]'). The remaining articles were all written by Gramsci (cf. HPC: 28–9, 40–3, 49–50, 50, 64–6, 70–5; also in PPW: 19–26).

33. 'Tre principii, tre ordini [Three Principles, Three Orders]', *La città futura* [The City of the Future], 17 February 1917 (PPW: 24).

34. *Ibid.*: 25.

35. Gramsci often uses this term in the articles published in *L'Ordine Nuovo* [The New Order] in 1919–21, whereas he rarely uses the term 'capitalistic class' or 'class of capitalists'.

36. Marx and Engels, *The German Ideology*.

37. Ferruccio Rossi-Landi, *Marxism and Ideology*, translated by R. Griffin, Oxford: Clarendon Press, 1990 (1st ed. 1978).

38. Cf. Marx and Engels, *The German Ideology*; Vladimir Ilyich Lenin, *What is to be Done?*, translated by J. Fineberg and G. Hanna, 1901 (www.marxists.org/archive/lenin/works/1901/witbd). The opposition of truth and falsehood expressed using the metaphor of the *camera oscura* is developed in a complex manner (which nevertheless maintains the duality of such) in the concepts of alienation and of the fetishism of goods to be found in *Capital*, where the 'ideological effect' is created by the goods themselves and their circulation (cf. György Lukács, *History and Class Consciousness: Studies in Marxist Dialectics*, translated by R. Livingstone, Cambridge, MA: MIT Press, 1971 (1st ed. 1923).

39. Q10II§41, in FSPN: 395.

40. *Ibid.*: 396.

41. Q7§19, in PN3: 171.

42. Q11§12, in SPN: 333

43. Cf. Q11§17, in SPN: 441, 444.

44. *Ibid.*: 445.

45. Q7§19, in PN3: 171.

46. *Ibid.*

47. As we have already argued, Gramsci is a deeply realistic politician, and in this is the heir to a long Italian tradition that unsurprisingly sees Machiavelli, a key figure in the *Prison Notebooks*, as its forerunner. Indeed, it was Machiavelli himself who insisted on 'the effectual truth of the matter' in a sense very close to that used here (Niccolò Machiavelli, *The Prince*, translated by P. Bondanella, Oxford:

Oxford University Press, 2005: 53). Gramsci submitted that 'the perishable nature of all ideological systems, side by side with the assertion that all systems have a historical validity, and are necessary' (Q13§10, in SPN: 138) must be maintained.

48. This was the case, as we have seen, of the constant criticism in the *Prison Notebooks* of the sociological simplifications inherent in Bukharin's materialism.

49. Q7§16, in PN3: 169.

50. Cf. Filippini, *Una politica di massa* [Mass Politics]: 103–50.

51. Q4§61, in QC: 507, author's translation (we are not happy with the translation in PN2: 235, in this case by J. Buttigieg, because besides making the mistake of confusing 'history' with 'science' at the end of the quote, it also loses certain essential references. Original: 'L'ideologia = ipotesi scientifica di carattere educativo energetico, verificata <e criticata> dallo sviluppo reale della storia, cioè fatta diventare scienza (ipotesi reale), sistematizzata'; Buttigieg translation: 'Ideology = scientific hypothesis that has the power to educate and is verified <and criticized> – i.e., transformed into science (real hypothesis), systematized – by the real development of science [sic!]'). The italics are also ours, and are designed to emphasize the constitutive role that the struggle and victory play in the battle of ideas, endowing ideology with scientific status, and thus with the status of truth.

52. I deliberately use an expression taken from Badiou, which expresses a concept of truth connected to practice (and to fidelity to an event) that clearly reveals its procedural and conflictual character: Alain Badiou, *Manifesto for Philosophy*, New York: State University of New York Press, 1999 (1st ed. 1989).

53. *The German Ideology*, written between 1845 and 1846, was not published until 1932, when Gramsci was already in prison. The majority of the notes in the *Prison Notebooks* had already been written by then, and in any case it is almost certain that Gramsci had never read the manuscript of Marx's work.

54. Q10I§12, in SPN: 56.

55. *Ibid.*

56. Q13§5, in QC: 1564, author's translation.

57. Q13§17, in QC: 1584, author's translation (SPN: 182 contains a translation of this passage, but it wrongly uses the term 'organ' instead of 'organism').

58. Q7§99, in PN3: 223.

59. Q4§61, in QC: 507, author's translation.

60. Q10II,§12, in SPN: 365–6.

61. Q12§1, in QC: 1520, author's translation (there is a translation in SPN, on p. 13, but it loses the 'social' attribute that Gramsci assigns to the term 'system'). Cf. Walter L. Adamson, *Hegemony and Revolution: A Study of Antonio Gramsci's Political and Cultural Theory*, Berkeley: University of California Press, 1980: 170 ff.

62. Q7§16, in PN3: 169.

63. Giovanni Malagodi, *Le ideologie politiche* [Political Ideologies], Bari: Laterza, 1928: 95. Reading Malagodi's reference, Sorel's *Reflections on Violence* (Cambridge: Cambridge University Press, 1999 [1st ed. 1908]), Gramsci probably coins the expression following his reflections on the impressions the book had made on him prior to his arrest, attributing it directly to Sorel. Malagodi's book is also an important source for Gramsci's concept of ideology, seen as a 'conception of the world' and not only as a 'false consciousness' (Malagodi, *Le ideologie*

politiche: 59–60). See the note by V. Gerratana in QC: 2632, together with Marco Gervasoni, *Antonio Gramsci e la Francia. Dal mito della modernità alla 'scienza della politica'* [Antonio Gramsci and France: From the Myth of Modernity to the 'Science of Politics'], Milan: Unicopli, 1998: 169–70. Malagodi's book is also mentioned in Q4§15 (PN2: 157), where the importance of the notion of historical bloc is mentioned for the first time.

64. 'Inorganic' in Q5§105 (PN2: 355); 'not organic' in Q13§29 (SPN: 204).

65. Q13§23, in SPN: 210–18.

66. Q10I§7, in FSPN: 343.

67. Q1§65, in PN1: 173.

68. Hence, Gramsci has the following to say in his Notebook number 27 dedicated to the notes on the question of folklore: 'One can say that until now folklore has been studied primarily as a "picturesque" element [....]. Folklore should instead be studied as a "conception of the world and life" implicit to a large extent in determinate (in time and space) strata of society and in opposition (also for the most part implicit, mechanical and objective) to "official" conceptions of the world (or in a broader sense, the conceptions of the cultured parts of historically determinate societies) that have succeeded one another in the historical process', Q27§1, in CW: 188–9.

69. Q8§173, in PN3: 333.

70. Q4§41, in PN2: 189.

71. Q11§38, in FSPN: 293.

72. Q11§15, in SPN: 437–8. Gramsci follows this path when he goes as far as arguing that, as a consequence, 'one social group can appropriate the science of another group without accepting its ideology', Q11§38, in FSPN: 293.

73. Bukharin's *Historical Materialism* (which in the *Prison Notebooks* Gramsci refers to as the *Saggio popolare* [Popular Manual]) in Gramsci's view assumes this notion of pure objectivity taken from positivism: 'it is the concept itself of "science", as it emerges from the *Popular Manual*, which requires to be critically destroyed. It is taken root and branch from the natural sciences, as if these were the only sciences or science par excellence, as decreed by positivism [...]. To think that one can advance the progress of a work of scientific research by applying to it a standard method, chosen because it has given good results in another field of research to which it was naturally suited, is a strange delusion which has little to do with science', Q11§15, in SPN: 438–9.

74. Q11§37, in FSPN: 291.

75. Cf. Q11§34, in SPN: 446, where Gramsci deals with the problem of the objectivity of the external world, and thus of the relationship between Man and Nature, tackling the theories of Engels and Lukács (the part on Lukács has not been translated in SPN, cf. QC: 1449). With regard to Gramsci's comments on the early theoretical acquisitions of quantum mechanics and of the physics of indeterminacy, see Marina Paladini Musitelli (ed.), *Gramsci e la scienza. Storicità e attualità delle note gramsciane sulla scienza* [Gramsci and Science: The Historicity and Actuality of Gramsci's Notes on Science], Trieste: Istituto Gramsci del Friuli Venezia Giulia, 2008.

76. See Gramsci's criticism of G.A. Borgese's observations regarding the statements made by the astrophysicist Arthur Eddington in Q11§36 (FSPN: 286–7) and Q11§68 (QC: 1506).

77. Q11§38, in FSPN: 293. Gramsci also warns against the exaggerated expectations that science engenders if it is perceived as the solution to all problems, to the extent that it creates 'Scientific superstition: it brings with it ridiculous illusions and notions that are even more infantile than those of religion. People start to expect something like the Land of Cockaigne where the forces of nature, without much need of human labour, will provide society with abundance of all that is required to satisfy its needs. This infatuation, the ideological dangers of which are obvious (superstitious faith in the power of man, paradoxically, leads to the impotence of the very bases of their power), must be opposed in diverse ways, and the most important of these has to be a better understanding of the basic principles of science. Science should be disseminated by scientists and serious scholars and no longer by omniscient journalists and know-it-all autodidacts. People expect "too much" from science, and therefore they are unable to appreciate what science really has to offer', Q4§71, in PN2: 242.

78. Q11§37, in FSPN: 291–2.

79. Q11§27, in SPN: 465.

80. Q11§37, in FSPN: 292.

81. Q11§12, in SPN: 326.

82. *Ibid.*

83. The first Italian translation, by P. Burresi, was published in instalments in the journal *Nuovi studi di diritto, economia e politica* [New Studies in Law, Economics and Politics], 3–4, May–August 1931: 176–223; 5, September–October 1931: 284–311; 6, November–December 1931: 369–96; 1, January–February 1932: 58–72; 3-4-5, May–October 1932: 179–231. Weber's essay had originally appeared in German in 1904–05 in the 'Archiv für Sozial Wissenschaft und Sozial Politik' [Archive for Social Science and Social Policy], while an extended version appeared in 1920 inside the first volume of Weber's *Sociology of Religion* (Max Weber, *The Protestant Ethic and the Spirit of Capitalism*, London-New York: Routledge, 2001 [1st ed. 1905]).

84. Q4§3, in PN2: 142.

CHAPTER 2

1. Emilio Santoro, *Autonomy, Freedom and Rights: A Critique of Liberal Subjectivity*, Dordrecht: Kluwer Academic, 2003 (1st ed. 1999).

2. Q11§12, in QC: 1376, author's translation (SPN translates 'man-in-the-mass': 324, 333); Q13§7, in SPN: 242.

3. Q8§130, in PN3: 310; Q15§74, in QC: 1833-4, author's translation; Q22§2, in SPN: 286.

4. Cf. Howard Moss, *Gramsci and the Idea of Human Nature*, Farnham: Ashgate, 1997; Peter D. Thomas, *The Gramscian Moment: Philosophy, Hegemony, and Marxism*, Leiden: Brill, 2009: 386–405.

5. Q10II§48, in SPN: 360. Gramsci thus starts from the materialist premise that no concept of 'Man in general' may be defined based on any biological or spiritual element: 'Human nature is the ensemble of social relations that determines a historically defined consciousness, and this consciousness indicates what is "natural" and what is not <and human nature is contradictory because it is the ensemble of social relations>', Q8§151, in PN3: 321.

6. Q10II§54, in QC: 1345, author's translation (SPN translates Gramsci's term *centro di annodamento* simply as 'hub': 352).

7. Q10II§54, in SPN: 352.

8. *Ibid.*

9. *Ibid.*

10. With regard to one of the two principles of civil society, Hegel writes: 'this particular person stands essentially in relation [*Beziehung*] to other similar particulars, and their relation is such that each asserts itself and gains satisfaction through the others, and thus at the same time through the exclusive mediation of the form of universality', George Wilhelm Friedrich Hegel, *Elements of the Philosophy of Right*, translated by H.B. Nisbet, Cambridge: Cambridge University Press, 1991 (1st ed. 1820): 220.

11. Q7§35, in PN3: 185. The Gramscian argument is clearly part of the critique of methodological individualism, which has taken a succession of diverse forms (see Charles Taylor, *The Malaise of Modernity*, Toronto: House of Anansi Press, 1991; Michel Foucault, *The Order of Things: An Archaeology of the Human Sciences*, New York: Pantheon Books, 1970 [1st ed. 1966]), some of which indeed originate from Gramsci: see Laclau and Mouffe: *Hegemony and Socialist Strategy*; Laclau, *On Populist Reason*, London: Pluto Press, 2005.

12. Q10II§54, in SPN: 352.

13. Marx and Engels, *The German Ideology*.

14. Q10II§54, in SPN: 352.

15. *Ibid.*

16. *Ibid.*

17. Q9§90, in QC: 1161, author's translation.

18. Q6§87, in PN3: 74-5.

19. Karl Marx, *Theses on Feuerbach*, translated by C. Smith, 1845 (www.marxists. org/archive/marx/works/1845/theses). Whilst in prison, Gramsci had a German copy of the Theses contained in an anthology of Marxian writings, and he took on the task of translating the Theses during his early years of imprisonment: Karl Marx, *Lohnarbeit und Kapital. Zur Judenfrage und andere Schriften aus des Frühzeit* [Wage Labour and Capital. The Jewish Question, and Other Early Writings], Leipzig: Philipp Reclam, 1920. For Gramsci's translation into Italian of the aforementioned work, see *Quaderno 7[a] (1930-31)* in QT: 743-5.

20. 'The premises from which we begin are not arbitrary ones, not dogmas, but real premises from which abstraction can only be made in the imagination. They are the real individuals, their activity and the material conditions under which they live, both those which they find already existing and those produced by their activity'. Marx and Engels, *The German Ideology*.

21. For example, see the analyses of Caesarism (Q13§27, in SPN: 219-22), his interest in French literature (see the comparison with Italian literature in CW: 196-286) and his interpretation of Jacobinism (Q19§24, translated in part in SPN: 55-84).

22. Q3§47, in PN2: 48. See also Q5§44, in PN2: 302-4.

23. Cf. Q1§48, in PN1: 155-61; Q1§106, in PN1: 194-5 and the notes with the heading title *Cattolici integrali, gesuiti, modernisti* [Catholic integralists, Jesuits, modernists] (Q5§14, in PN2: 277-81; Q5§141, in PN2: 391-4; Q6§195, in PN3: 139-41; Q14§52, in FSPN: 97-9; Q20§4, in FSPN: 76-92).

24. Cf. Q1§78, in PN1: 183; Q4§3, in PN2: 140-4; Q5§29, in PN2: 294.

25. 'Bergsoniano! [Bergsonian!]', *L'Ordine nuovo* [The New Order], 2 January 1921, author's translation (SF: 13). In the *Prison Notebooks*, Gramsci points out that 'The Turin movement was accused simultaneously of being "spontaneist" and "voluntarist", or Bergsonian (!)', Q3§48, in PN2: 50. Also see the reference to the 'vital impulse' in Q13§1 (SPN: 127, the expression is rendered by the French 'élan vital', but in the *Prison Notebooks* it is given in Italian as *impulso vitale*), and the reference to *Creative Evolution* in the article 'Merce [Commodities]', *Avanti!* [Forward!], 6 June 1918 (NM: 87).

26. The main intellectual school of thought examining such questions, both prior to and at the same time as the social sciences, was that of conservative liberalism: cf. Hippolyte Taine, *The Origins of Contemporary France*, translated by J. Durand, New York: P. Smith, 1931 (1st ed. 1875–93) and Gramsci's interest in the author in Q2§91 (PN1: 334–5), but in particular Ernest Renan, *La réforme intellectuelle et morale* [Intellectual and Moral Reform], Paris: Michel Lévyfrères, 1871. The title of Renan's work is also a 'formula' that Gramsci often utilized in the *Prison Notebooks* (Q14§26, in FSPN: 25–8), as mediated by the work of Sorel ('Germanesimo e storicismo di Ernesto Renan. Saggio inedito di Georges Sorel [The Germanism and Historicism of Ernesto Renan: An Unpublished Essay by Georges Sorel]', *Critica sociale* [Social Critique], 1932, instalments II, III, IV, V: 110–44, 139–207, 358–67, 430–44).

27. This is a reference to the definition of nineteenth-century Germany coined by Pierangelo Schiera, to underline a different, yet symmetrical attempt at governing society in a different context: Pierangelo Schiera, *Il laboratorio borghese. Scienza e politica nella Germania dell'Ottocento* [The Bourgeois Laboratory: Science and Politics in 19th Century Germany], Bologna: Il Mulino, 1987.

28. Q11§12, author's translation (SPN: 324, wrongly translated with 'man').

29. Émile Durkheim, *The Division of Labour in Society*, translated by W.D. Halls, London: Macmillan, 1984 (1st ed. 1893). We do not know whether Gramsci read this work or not; however, what we do know is that he lent great importance to the literature constituting the cultural background to Durkheim's book. It should be noted that the work was cited and discussed in Bukharin's *Historical Materialism*, expressly so in Chapter 4 (*Society*) and implicitly in other parts of the book. At the end of the century, two of Durkheim's essays were published in Italian by *Rivista italiana di sociologia* [Italian Journal of Sociology] and by *Riforma sociale* [Social Reform], together with two excerpts from *On suicide* (translated by R. Buss, London: Penguin Books, 2006 [1st ed. 1897]): 'Lo stato attuale degli studi sociologici in Francia [The Present State of Sociological Studies in France]', *Riforma sociale* [Social Reform], 2, 1895: 607–22, 691–707; 'La sociologia e il suo dominio scientifico [Sociology and its Scientific Field]', *Rivista italiana di sociologia* [Italian Journal of Sociology], 4, 1900: 127–48; 'Il suicidio dal punto di vista sociologico [Suicide from a Sociological Viewpoint]', *Rivista italiana di sociologia* [Italian Journal of Sociology], 1, 1897: 17–27; 'Il suicidio e l'instabilità economica [Suicide and Economic Instability]', *Riforma sociale* [Social Reform], 7, 1897: 529–57.

30. Cf. Bruno Karsenti, *La société en personnes: études durkheimiennes* [Society in Person: Durkheimian Studies], Paris: Economica, 2006.

31. Durkheim, *The Division of Labour in Society*: 84.

32. *Ibid.*

33. *Ibid.*: 85.
34. 'We can therefore formulate the following proposition: *The division of labour varies in direct proportion to the volume and density of societies and if it progresses in a continuous manner over the course of social development it is because societies become regularly more dense and generally more voluminous*', ibid.: 205, emphasis in the original.
35. Going back to a concept underlying the work of Gilbert Simondon, who centres his analysis around a critique of liberal anthropology that assumes individuals to be given entities instead of placing the emphasis on the process of the creation of individuality: *L'individuation psychique et collective* [Psychic and Collective Individuation], Paris: Aubier, 2007; David Scott, *Gilbert Simondon's Psychic and Collective Individuation: A Critical Introduction and Guide*, Edinburgh: Edinburgh University Press, 2014.
36. Q10II§54, in SPN: 352 (the translation of *centro di annodamento* has been modified from 'hub' to 'centre of interaction').
37. Q10II§48, in SPN: 360. It is interesting to note that the expression Gramsci uses, 'social circles', is once again an expression taken from sociological terminology. In particular, Georg Simmel used this expression in a chapter of his work, *Sociology: Inquiries into the Construction of Social Forms* (translated by A.J. Blasi, A.K. Jacobs and M. Kanjirathinkal, vol. 2, Leiden: Brill, 2009 [1st ed. 1908]: 363–408) entitled, in fact, *The Intersection of Social Circles*. The chapter in question was contained in an anthology that Gramsci possessed in prison (Robert Michels [ed.], *Politica ed economia* [Politics and Economics], Turin: Utet, 1934: 263–306), albeit after Gramsci had drafted the note in question. As we have seen, Gramsci without doubt read Bukharin's *Historical Materialism* that mentions Simmel and 'the circle of mutually interacting persons' (Chapter 4, *Society*).
38. Georges Sorel, 'Letter to Daniel Halévy', in *Reflections on Violence*: 28–9.
39. *Ibid.*: 17–18.
40. Enrico Augelli and Craig N. Murphy, 'Consciousness, Myth and Collective Action: Gramsci, Sorel and the Ethical State', in S. Gill and J.H. Mittelman (eds), *Innovation and Transformation in International Studies*, Cambridge: Cambridge University Press, 1997: 25–38; Darrow Schecter, 'Two Views of the Revolution: Gramsci and Sorel, 1916-1920', *History of European Ideas*, 5, 1990: 637–53; Joseph V. Femia, *Gramsci's Political Thought: Hegemony, Consciousness, and the Revolutionary Process*, Oxford: Clarendon Press, 1981: 86–8, 124; Nicola Badaloni, 'Gramsci and the Problem of the Revolution', in Mouffe (ed.), *Gramsci and Marxist Theory*: 80–109.
41. During the 1890s, Sorel was among those European intellectuals who took part in the intense, productive period of revisionism of Marxism. A debate developed between France, Italy and Germany, involving a series of orthodox Marxists (Kautsky, Plekhanov), revisionists (Bernstein, Merlino), sociologists (Enrico Ferri, Émile Vandervelde) and other European intellectuals such as Benedetto Croce. The dispute started with the publication, in 1896, of a number of articles by Bernstein, in which the latter attacked the political strategy of German social democracy, challenging a series of concepts from Marxist doctrine such as revolution, and certain dogmas such as that of the growing polarization of social classes, which until then had been deemed undisputable (collected three years later in Eduard Bernstein, *The Precondition of Socialism*, Cambridge: Cambridge

University Press, 1993 [1st ed. 1899]). The debate over the revision of Marxism following the deaths of its founders (Engels had died in 1895) quickly involved political writers and philosophers from all over Europe, including Sorel himself.

42. Elements of this conservatism are evident in his early writings: Georges Sorel, *Le Procès de Socrate. Examen critique des thèses socratiques*, Paris: Alcan, 1889 (partial translation 'The Trial of Socrates', in J. Stanley (ed.), *From Georges Sorel: Essays in Socialism and Philosophy*, Oxford: Oxford University Press, 1976: 62–70) and *Contribution à l'étude profane de la Bible* [Contribution to a Secular Study of the Bible], Paris: A. Ghio, 1889.

43. Georges Sorel, 'L'Ancienne et la nouvelle métaphysique [The Old and the New Metaphysics]', Ère nouvelle [The New Era], March 1894: 329–51; April 1894: 461–82; May 1894: 51–87; June 1894: 180–205.

44. Georges Sorel, 'Les théories de M. Durkheim [*Mr. Durkheim's Theories*]', *Le Devenir social* [The Social Becoming], 1–2, 1895. Émile Durkheim, *The Rules of Sociological Method*, translated by W.D. Halls, New York-London-Toronto-Sydney: The Free Press, 1982 (1st ed. 1895).

45. Georges Sorel, 'Le teorie di Durkheim [*Mr. Durkheim's Theories*]', in Sorel, *Le teorie di Durkheim e altri scritti sociologici* [Durkheim's Theories and Other Sociological Writings], translated by P. Reale, Naples: Liguori, 1978: 93 (the Italian translation shall be used hereinafter for any citations).

46. *La Critica. Rivista di storia, letteratura e filosofia* [The Critique: Journal of History, Literature and Philosophy] is the journal founded and edited by Benedetto Croce in 1903. Initially Croce paid for its publication himself (the Italian publishing house Laterza was to subsequently publish it as of 1906), and gradually become a consolidated presence in the field of philosophical and literary studies. It was to become one of the few journals capable of maintaining a degree of independence from Fascism, and was not to follow the way of many other intellectual journals that were forcibly shut down by the regime. In fact, it was published right up to 1944. The correspondence between Sorel and Croce can now be found in Georges Sorel, *Lettere a un amico d'Italia* [Letters to an Italian Friend], Bologna: Cappelli, 1963.

47. Georges Sorel, 'L'antica e la nuova metafisica [The Old and the New Metaphysics]', in Sorel, *Scritti politici e filosofici*, Turin: Einaudi, 1975: 70 (the Italian translation shall be used hereinafter for any citations).

48. *Ibid.*: 76.

49. The centrality of the class struggle was only to be developed fully in his writings published shortly afterwards in the journals *Le Devenir social* [The Social Becoming] and *L'Ère nouvelle* [The New Era], but Sorel already realized that 'it would be a good idea, in fact, to show that moral concepts in each period of history depend on the class struggle', *ibid.*: 175.

50. *Ibid.*: 130.

51. *Ibid.*: 169, emphases in the original.

52. Q10II§48, in SPN: 360.

53. Q10II§9, in SPN: 401, our italics. In his Notebook number 8, Gramsci writes: 'Concept and fact of "determined market"; that is, the discovery that specific forces have risen historically and their operation manifests itself within a certain "automatism" that gives individual initiatives a certain degree of "predictability" and certainty. "Determined market" can therefore be said to be a "determined

relation of social forces in a determined structure of the productive apparatus" that is guaranteed by a determined juridical superstructure', Q8§128, in PN3: 308.

54. Q10II§54, in SPN: 352, our italics.

55. Q14§13, in SPN: 265, our italics.

56. Q14§65, in CW: 130, our italics.

57. In 1929 Gramsci began to translate from German and Russian, and to do a number of exercises in English (Cf. letter to Tania, 9 February 1929, in LP1: 245–6; letter to Giulia, 11 March 1929, in LP1: 253; letter to Tatiana, 18 November 1929, in LP1: 292–3). His commitment to such translation work gradually lessened as his notebooks began to take form, until in 1932 he stopped translating altogether. Gramsci's *Quaderni di traduzioni* [Translation Notebooks] (QT) were published as the initial volumes of the National edition of the works.

58. QT: 743.

59. 'Gramsci, not being a professional translator, made the same classical mistakes as anyone who tries his hand at such a job without possessing not only the required linguistic knowhow, but also the due specific skills: just like any translator when they first start, in fact, Gramsci tried to transpose the individual expressions from the source language to the target language in the most literal manner possible, with what appears to be, but in fact is not really, the paradoxical result – given moreover the considerable differences in syntax, grammar and vocabulary between on the one hand German and Russian, and on the other hand Italian – of a translation at one and the same time slavish to, and distant from, the original', Giuseppe Cospito and Gianni Francioni, *Introduzione* [Introduction] to QT, tome I: 30. These observations are particularly true of the translations from German and Russian of works that Gramsci was not familiar with; less so in the case of Marxian writings, which on the contrary Gramsci knew well. This is another reason why the slight deviations in the translation of such writings are useful when it comes to reconstructing the various different theoretical influences on Gramsci's work.

60. The German original reads as follows: 'Die materialistische Lehre von der Veränderung der Umstände und der Erziehung vergisst, dass die Umstände von den Menschen verändert und der Erzieher selbst erzogen werden muss', Karl Marx, *Thesen über Feuerbach*, 1845 (www.marxists.org/deutsch/archiv/marx-engels/1845/thesen/thesfeue-or.htm).

61. Sorel, 'L'antica e la nuova metafisica [The Old and the New Metaphysics]': 169.

62. Q7§12, in PN3: 165.

63. *Ibid.* This analysis was to be reiterated in the pages of *Americanismo e fordismo* [Americanism and Fordism], where Gramsci pointed out that in the USA – 'in which the "structure" dominates the superstructures more immediately and in which the latter are also "rationalised"' – 'Hegemony here is born in the factory', Q22§2, in SPN: 285–6.

64. Sorel, 'L'antica e la nuova metafisica [The Old and the New Metaphysics]': 169.

65. There are numerous passages in which Sorel reiterates the importance of the analysis of industrial development: 'in a certain sense we can say that they [the machines] are *devices that subject nature to experience*: however, this is not a case of an individual, temporary experience, but of a permanent, social experience', *ibid.*: 136. 'If we were to write a history of the spirit of Man, no distinctions should be made, as A. Comte did, starting from the predominance of theological,

metaphysical and positive concepts, but we should base our history on the type of industrial factories', *ibid.*: 152. 'In order to critically analyse our knowledge, we must turn to the machines; K. Marx, who had fully understood the importance of industrial machinery, had to search for the fundamental principle of ethics in those human phenomena that arise around machinery', *ibid.*: 174.

66. Cf. Dario Ragazzini, *Leonardo nella società di massa: teoria della personalità in Gramsci* [Leonardo in Mass Society: The Theory of Personality in Gramsci], Bergamo: Moretti & Vitali, 2002.

67. Q11§12, in SPN: 324.

68. Q11§13, in SPN: 419.

69. Q11§12, in SPN: 333 (the translation of the first part has been slightly modified. SPN translates it with: 'active man-in-the-mass has a practical activity').

70. Cf. Maurizio Ricciardi, *La società come ordine. Storia e teoria politica dei concetti sociali* [Society as Order: The History and Political Theory of Social Concepts], Macerata: Eum, 2010.

71. Letter to Tania, 5 October 1931, in LP2: 82.

72. Q16§12, in QC: 1875, author's translation.

73. Q15§74, in FSPN: 273–4.

74. Q15§9, in QC: 1762–4, author's translation.

75. Letter to Tania, 6 March 1933, in LP2: 279.

76. Q15§9, in QC: 1764, author's translation.

77. Q8§36, in PN3: 257 (cf. Chapter 6, section 'The shape of duration: the passive revolution').

78. Q22§2, in SPN: 286.

79. Q15§11, in SPN: 109. 'In proposing to apply to the concept of passive revolution "the interpretative principle of molecular changes [...]", Gramsci would seem to suggest that the analysis conducted in regard to the "catastrophes of character" also be applied to collective organisms', Valentino Gerratana, *Gramsci. Problemi di metodo* [Gramsci: Problems of Method], Rome: Editori Riuniti, 1997: 141.

80. Q15§9, in QC: 1764, author's translation.

81. Q8§195, in PN3: 346.

82. Q10§54, in SPN: 353.

CHAPTER 3

1. Maurizio Ricciardi, 'Il concetto di rivoluzione sul limite della modernità politica' [The Concept of Revolution at the Edge of Political Modernity], in Maurizio Ricciardi (ed.), *Ordine sovrano e rivoluzione in età moderna e contemporanea* [The Sovereign Order and Revolution in the Modern and Contemporary Ages], Bologna: Clueb, 2003: 18–19.

2. This expression is to be found both in Otto Bauer ('The Nation', in B. Anderson and G. Balakrishnan (eds), *Mapping the Nation*, London: Verso, 1996: 51) and in Max Weber ('Community of political destiny', in *Economy and Society: An Outline of Interpretive Sociology*, translated by E. Fischoff, H. Gerth, A.M. Henderson, F. Kolegar, C. Wright Mills, T. Parsons, M. Rheinstein, G. Roth, E. Shils and C. Wittich, 1968 [1st ed. 1922]: 903). Also see Ernest Renan's definition of the nation as 'everyday plebiscite' ('What is a Nation?', in G. Eley and R. Grigor Suny (eds), *Becoming National: A Reader*, New York: Oxford University Press, 1996: 17).

Gramsci knew all three authors, and he mentioned them all at various points in the *Prison Notebooks* (Bauer: Q11§27, in SPN: 463; Q11§70, in SPN: 387. Weber: Q2§75, in PN1: 318–19; Q3§119, in PN2: 106. Renan: Q14§26, in FSPN: 25–6).

3. Cf. Denis Mack Smith, *The Making of Italy, 1796–1866*, London: Macmillan, 1988; Clara Maria Lovett, *The Democratic Movement in Italy, 1830–1876*, Cambridge, MA: Harvard University Press, 1982.

4. Santi Romano, 'Lo Stato moderno e la sua crisi [The Modern State and its Crisis] (1909)', in Romano, *Lo Stato moderno e la sua crisi: saggi di diritto costituzionale* [The Modern State and its Crisis: Essays on Constitutional Law], Milan: Giuffrè, 1969: 14.

5. Q3§18, in PN2: 25.

6. *Ibid.*

7. Q25§4, in QC: 2287, author's translation.

8. Q8§187, in PN3: 343.

9. This concept was proposed by Christine Buci-Glucksmann in *Gramsci and the State*, translated by D. Fernbach, London: Lawrence & Wishart, 1980 (1st ed. 1975): 69–110. It was subsequently widely reutilized in the literature: cf. Carlos Nelson Coutinho, *Gramsci's Political Thought*, translated by P. Sette-Camara, Leiden: Brill, 2012 (1st ed. 1989): 77–92.

10. Q1§47, in PN1: 153.

11. Q8§130, in PN3: 311.

12. Q6§155, in QC: 810–11, author's translation. Buttigieg (PN3: 117) translates *nel suo significato integrale* with 'in the full sense', but in this way it loses the association between the adjective 'integral' and the verb 'integrate', that is, with the process whereby different elements combine to form a single whole.

13. The importance of these definitions is such in Gramsci that the relationship between civil society and political society (or State) becomes the central element of politics. 'In economics, the centre of unity is value […]. In philosophy – praxis, that is, the relation between human will (superstructure) and the economic structure. In politics – the relation between state and civil society, that is, the intervention of the state (centralized will) to educate the educator, the social milieu in general', Q7§18, in PN3: 170. The fact that civil society, in Gramsci's view, is not just the place of economic relations, but more strictly speaking that of social relations, is clear from his assertion that 'between the economic structure and the state with its legislation and its coercion stands civil society', Q10II§15, in FSPN: 208.

14. Perry Anderson accuses Gramsci of inconsistency and incoherence in 'The Antinomies of Antonio Gramsci', *New Left Review*, 100, 1976: 12–34; for a critique of Anderson's thesis, cf. Thomas, *The Gramscian Moment*: 93–5.

15. Gramsci writes that 'It is possible to imagine the state-coercion element withering away gradually, as the increasingly conspicuous elements of regulated society', Q6§88, in PN3: 75.

16. Q8§142, in PN3: 317. Gramsci utilizes a broad concept of 'official', assigning such a social meaning as well. So, hereinafter we shall translate the Italian *funzionario* with 'official' (as Buttigieg does in the PN, rather than using the term 'functionary' as is found in the SPN) bearing in mind Gramsci's own observation regarding the meaning of the term in English: 'The word "*ufficiale*" or "*officiale*". This word causes misunderstanding, or at the very least incomprehension and astonishment,

especially in translations from foreign languages (above all, English). "*Ufficiale*", in Italian, has increasingly narrowed its meaning, and now it is likely to refer only to military officers; it has retained its broader meaning only in some expressions that have become idiomatic or in expressions of bureaucratic origin: "*pubblico ufficiale*", "*ufficiale dello stato civile*", etc. In English, on the other hand, "official" refers in general to functionaries of all kinds (in the case of the army, "officer" is used, but that, too, denotes a "functionary", generally speaking), not just to functionaries of the State but also to all kinds of nongovernmental positions (a trade union functionary, etc.); it even refers to a simple "employee"', Q5§130, in PN2: 383.

17. Q8§142, in PN3: 317.

18. Durkheim, *The Division of Labour in Society*: 310.

19. Q8§142, in PN3: 317.

20. Cf., respectively, Q6§138 (PN3: 109), Q4§49 (PN2: 199–210), Q8§52 (PN3: 266–7).

21. While the origins of the concept of 'disciplining' can be traced back to Weber (*Economy and Society*: 1148–56), it was Gerhard Oestreich (*Neostoicism and Early Modern State*, translated by D. McLintock, Cambridge: Cambridge University Press, 2008 [1st ed. 1969]: 258–73) who specified the contents thereof in relation to the formation of the modern State.

22. Weber, *Economy and Society*: 54, emphases in the original.

23. Q13§36, in SPN: 185-6, emphasis in the original (translation amended from 'functionaries' to 'officials').

24. It is a certain fact that Gramsci had read at least the following two works by Weber: *Parliament and Government in Germany under a New Political Order* (in *Political Writings*, translated by R. Speirs, Cambridge: Cambridge University Press, 1994: 130–271) in the translation by E. Ruta published by Laterza in 1919, and *The Protestant Ethic and the Spirit of Capitalism* in the translation by P. Burresi (cf. note 83 to Chapter 1). Weber's major posthumous work *Economy and Society* was mentioned in Q2§75 (PN1: 318), but the note was taken from an article on the political party written by Robert Michels. Certain passages from the aforementioned work by Weber can be found, translated into Italian, in the anthology *Politica ed economia* [Politics and Economy] that Gramsci had whilst in prison (cf. note 37 to Chapter 2). The passages in question, translated from the first edition of the work edited in 1922 by Marianne Weber, bear the title *Carismatica* [Charismatic] (pp. 183–6), *Trasformazioni del charisma* [The Transformation of Charisma] (pp. 186–97) and *I tipi del Potere (Autorità)* [Types of Power (Authority)] (pp. 198–262). It should also be pointed out that Gramsci moved from Moscow to Vienna in November 1923, just one year after the publication of *Economy and Society*, where he remained until May 1924. Therefore, it is probable that on that occasion he examined the work in question, together with *Politics as a Vocation* and the essays written for *Verein für Sozialpolitik*. Another possible source of Gramsci's knowledge of Weber's theories is represented by the articles by Giovanni Ansaldo, a guest writer on Piero Gobetti's journal *Rivoluzione liberale* [Liberal Revolution]. These articles specifically include 'La democrazia tedesca nel pensiero di Max Weber [German Democracy in the Thought of Max Weber]', *Rivoluzione liberale* [Liberal Revolution], 4, 1923: 13–15), which gave rise to a debate between Gobetti and Ansaldo with regard to the applicability, in

Italy, of Weber's theories on the link between religious ethics and capitalism, and on the role of the bureaucracy.

25. Weber distinguishes between *Herrschaft* and *Macht*: 'A. "Power" (*Macht*) is the probability that one actor within a social relationship will be in a position to carry out his own will despite resistance, regardless of the basis on which this probability rests. B. "Domination" (*Herrschaft*) is the probability that a command with a given specific content will be obeyed by a given group of persons [...]. The concept of power is sociologically amorphous. All conceivable qualities of a person and all conceivable combinations of circumstances may put him in a position to impose his will in a given situation. The sociological concept of domination must hence be more precise and can only mean the probability that a command will be obeyed', Weber, *Economy and Society*: 53. 'Domination' thus implies a tendency to obey, that is, that commands are perceived as legitimate.

26. Weber, *Economy and Society*: 983, emphasis in the original.

27. Q13§36, in SPN: 186.

28. *Ibid.* (translation amended from 'functionaries' to 'officials').

29. Q8§55, in PN3: 268.

30. Q14§49, in SPN: 254 (translation amended from 'functionaries' to 'officials').

31. Weber, *Economy and Society*: 990–1.

32. *Ibid.*: 985, emphasis in the original.

33. *Ibid.*: 986. Weber uses the expression in reference to what he believes to be the first sign of bureaucratic organization: 'the substitution of the bureaucratic army for the self-equipped army of notables is everywhere a process of "passive" democratization, in the sense in which this applies to every establishment of an absolute military monarchy in the place of a feudal state or of a republic of notables' (*ibid.*). Shortly after, he adds: 'The modern army, finally, although it has everywhere been a means of breaking the power of the notables, has in itself in no way served as a lever of active, but rather remained an instrument of merely passive democratization' (*ibid.*: 987). This expression is also to be found in Weber's *Parliament and Government*, a work that Gramsci had certainly read, where Weber argues that a democracy without parliament, that is, without the selection of its leaders, and thus devoid of its political element, would produce a '*passive democratisation* [...] [that] would be the purest form of *uncontrolled bureaucratic rule*', Weber, *Parliament and Government in Germany*: 222.

34. Gramsci takes the term from the *Historical Essay* by Cuoco, where it is used to indicate, in fact, the lack of popular involvement in the revolution due to the differences between the 'leaders' and the people: 'our revolution was a passive revolution, and the only way for it to be successful would have been to win over popular opinion. But the patriots and the people did not hold the same views: they had different ideas, different customs, and even different languages', Vincenzo Cuoco, *Historical Essay on the Neapolitan Revolution of 1799*, translated by D. Gibbons, Toronto: University of Toronto Press, 2014 (1st ed. 1801): 91.

35. Cf. Q15§62, in SPN: 114.

36. Weber, *Parliament and Government in Germany*: 159, emphasis in the original.

37. Gramsci writes how 'the historico-political individual is not the "biological" individual but the social group', Q6§10, in PN3: 8.

38. Cf. Furio Ferraresi, *Il fantasma della comunità. Concetti politici e scienza sociale in Max Weber* [The Spectre of Community: Political Concepts and Social Science in Max Weber], Milan: Franco Angeli, 2003: 422.

39. Q7§33, in PN3: 183. This is the only note that explicitly foresees the emergence of a regulated society, which in this case could be seen as coinciding with Gramsci's perception of communism (almost all scholars do, in fact, see it this way: both those that interpret it positively, such as Thomas, *The Gramscian Moment*: 60–1, 87–92 and Coutinho, *Gramsci's Political Thought*: 201–3; and those who are critical thereof, such as Jean L. Cohen and Andrew Arato, *Civil Society and Political Theory*, Cambridge, MA-London: MIT Press, 1992: 156–9). All other references to a 'regulated society', however, are to be found within the context of a 'hypothetical' process of development. Rather than being used to foresee a conflict-free order (Gramsci, like Marx, does not provide 'recipes for the cook-shops of the future'), they indicate the direction taken by a process: 'the state *is conceived as surmountable* by 'regulated society', Q6§65, in PN3: 49; 'a theory that conceives of the State as *inherently liable* to wither away and dissolve into regulated society', Q6§88, in PN3: 75; '*It is possible to imagine* the state-coercion element withering away gradually, as the increasingly conspicuous elements of regulated society (or ethical state or civil society) assert themselves', *ibid*. (our italics).

40. Q8§195, in PN3: 347. The very notion of political party is reformulated here, with Gramsci perceiving it as including both mass structured organizations having a declared political purpose, and also that 'multiplicity of private associations [...] [that] prevails, relatively or absolutely, constituting the hegemonic apparatus of one social group over the rest of the population', Q6§136, in PN3: 107. Gramsci went on to state that: 'In the absence of centralized and organized parties, in Italy, one cannot ignore the newspapers: it is the newspapers, grouped in sets, that constitute the real parties', Q1§116, in PN1: 201. In this context, 'nobody is unorganized and without a party' (Q6§136, in PN3: 107) and the organization of society – not only that of the party's avant-garde – is the only way of organizing the revolution in the West.

41. Q8§21, in PN3: 247.

42. Q7§39, in PN3: 190.

43. Q2§75, in PN1: 323.

44. Robert Michels, 'Les Partis politiques e la contrainte sociale [Political Parties and Social Coercion]', *Mercure de France* [Mercury of France], 717, 1 May 1928: 513–35. For a detailed analysis of this note, cf. Corrado Malandrino, 'Gramsci e la "Sociologia del partito politico" di Michels [Gramsci and Michels' "Sociology of the Political Party"]', in S. Mastellone and G. Sola (eds), *Gramsci. Il partito politico nei 'Quaderni'* [Gramsci: The Political Party in the 'Prison Notebooks'], Florence: Centro Editoriale Toscano, 2001: 115–40.

45. Q7§77, in PN3: 209.

46. Q2§75, in PN1: 323.

47. Q11§25, in SPN: 429.

48. Michels places the focus on the tendency – inevitable in his view – of any party organization to replicate the organizational model whereby a tiny minority rule over the large majority. He thus formulates an 'Iron Law of Oligarchy' (Robert Michels, *Political Parties: A Sociological Study of the Oligarchical Tendencies of*

Modern Democracy, translated by E. and C. Paul, New Brunswick: Transaction Publishing, 1999 [1st ed. 1911]: 342), the causes of which lie not only with the political will of the leadership, but also with the objective nature of factors of organization, and of individual and collective psychology, as a result of which said law also governs those parties whose aim it is to guarantee the political participation of the greatest possible number of individuals. The bureaucratic character of all modern organizations, and thus of political parties as well, in Michels' view marks the end of all possible democratic prospects: 'Democracy is inconceivable without organization' (*ibid.*: 61), but at the same time 'Organization implies the tendency to oligarchy' (*ibid.*: 70). Bukharin was among those who placed the emphasis on the historicity, and thus the surmountable nature, of Michels' preconditions, when he wrote: 'what constitutes an eternal category in Michels' presentation, namely, the "incompetence of the masses" will disappear, for this incompetence is by no means a necessary attribute of every system; it likewise is a product of the economic and technical conditions, expressing themselves in the general cultural being and in the educational conditions', Bukharin, *Historical Materialism*.

49. If at first appearance the difference between the distinction ruling/ruled and that between leaders/led may appear elusive in the *Prison Notebooks*, in truth Gramsci uses such a distinction in an extremely specific manner. The relationship between the rulers and the ruled always arises on the basis of a class division, and is historically determined. The relationship between the leaders and the led, on the other hand, concerns an aspect of the workings of collective organisms that is ingrained in their very nature, and thus also regards those organisms that are not characterized by any class division within.

50. Cf. the note regarding fetishism, where Gramsci also remarks that 'What is surprising, and it is characteristic, is that this kind of fetishism should also be found in "voluntary" organisms, in other words those not of a "public" or state type, such as parties and trade unions', Q15§13, in QC: 1770, author's translation.

51. Q8§52, in PN3: 266.

52. In February 1926, Gramsci had already written, in his report on the Lyons Congress, that 'the working class is capable of taking action, and has shown, throughout history, that it is capable of performing its mission as the leading force in the struggle against capitalism, insofar as it is manages to express, from within, all those technical elements that are indispensable, in modern society, to the actual organization of those institutions in which the proletarian programme is to be achieved', 'Cinque anni di vita del partito [Five Years in the Life of the Party]', *L'Unità* [Unity], 24 February 1926 (CPC: 96).

53. Q8§52, in PN3: 266.

54. Q7§6, in PN3: 159.

55. Q13§27, in SPN: 221.

56. Q6§84, in PN3: 69.

57. *Ibid.*: 70.

58. Q15§4, in SPN: 146.

59. Cf. Gaetano Mosca, *The Ruling Class*, translated by H.D. Kahn, New York: McGraw-Hill, 1960; Vilfredo Pareto, *The Rise and Fall of Elites: An Application of Theoretical Sociology*, Totowa: The Bedminster Press, 1968.

60. Q13§30, in SPN: 192.

61. Q11§12, in SPN: 335.
62. Q8§191, in PN3: 345.
63. Cf. Q13§31, in SPN: 190–2.
64. Q14§70, SPN: 152–3.
65. Q8§195, in PN3: 346.
66. Q14§70, in SPN: 153 (translation modified for the second quote). On this question, Gramsci goes on to state: 'One speaks of generals without an army, but in reality it is easier to form an army than to form generals', Q14§70, in SPN: 152–3; and also that 'One might make use of this law metaphorically to understand how a "movement" or current of opinion becomes a party – i.e. a political force which is effective from the point of view of the exercise of governmental power: precisely to the extent to which it possesses (has developed within itself) cadres at the various levels, and to the extent to which the latter have acquired certain capabilities', Q13§31, in SPN: 191.
67. Q1§49, in PN1: 161.
68. Q3§56, in PN2: 56.
69. Q13§36, in SPN: 188–9.
70. Cf. Q14§34, in SPN: 155; Q14§38, in QC: 1695–6.
71. Q15§13, in QC: 1771, author's translation. Gramsci often refers to the metaphor of the orchestra: 'The command of the orchestra conductor: agreement reached in advance, collaboration; command is a distinct function, not imposed hierarchically', Q8§45, in PN3: 263.
72. Q15§13, in QC: 1771, author's translation.
73. Niccolò Machiavelli, *Discourses on Livy*, I-17-3, translated by H.C. Mansfield and N. Tarcov, Chicago-London: University of Chicago Press, 1996 (1st ed. 1531): 48.
74. Q11§25, in SPN: 429. Cf. Peter Ives, *Gramsci's Politics of Language: Engaging the Bakhtin Circle and the Frankfurt School*, Toronto: University of Toronto Press, 2004: 10–11.
75. Q11§25, in SPN: 428.
76. Cf. Benedetto Fontana, *Hegemony and Power: On the Relation between Gramsci and Machiavelli*, Minneapolis: University of Minnesota Press, 1993; Joseph V. Femia, *The Machiavellian Legacy. Essays in Italian Political Thought*, London-New York: Macmillan, 1998.
77. Louis Althusser, *Machiavelli and Us*, London-New York: Verso, 2000 (1st ed. 1994, writings from 1962 to 1986): 52.
78. Q8§84, in PN3: 283.
79. There are many arguments in these notes gathered together under the heading title 'Machiavelli': law, passion, the political class, relations of power, State life, foreign politics, military art, the bureaucracy, political parties, centralism, the war, ethics, natural law, sociology, political science, the passive revolution, the war of position, intellectuals. Prison Notebook 13, entitled *Noterelle sulla politica del Machiavelli* [Brief Notes on Machiavelli's Politics], comprises forty notes consisting almost exclusively of redrafted writings (c), with the exception of one.
80. Cf. Frederick II (King of Prussia), *Anti-Machiavel: Or, an Examination of Machiavel's Prince*, Gale Ecco, Print Editions, 2010 (1st ed. 1739); John Greville Agard Pocock, *The Machiavellian Moment: Florentine Political Thought and the Atlantic Republican Tradition*, Princeton: Princeton University Press, 1975.

81. Ugo Foscolo, *Sepulchres*, verses 156–8, translation by J.G. Nichols, London: One World Classics, 2010 (1st ed. 1807). Gramsci quotes them in Q4§4 (PN2: 144), Q8§44 (PN3: 262) and Q13§4 (QC: 1563).
82. Q13§25, in QC: 1617, author's translation.
83. Q13§20, in SPN: 135.
84. Cf. Maurizio Viroli, *Niccolò's Smile: A Biography of Machiavelli*, translated by A. Shugaar, New York: Farrar Straus Giroux, 2000 (1st ed. 1998).
85. Q14§33, in QC: 1690–1, author's translation.
86. Q13§25, in QC: 1618, author's translation.
87. Q13§20, in SPN: 136.
88. Q14§33, in QC: 1691, author's translation.
89. Q4§10, in PN2: 152.
90. Q8§21, in PN3: 247.
91. Q5§127, in PN2: 382.
92. Q8§21, in PN3: 247–8.
93. *Ibid.*: 247.

CHAPTER 4

1. Q10II§44, in SPN: 349.
2. Q11§25, in SPN: 429.
3. Q6§84, in PN3: 69 (the translation has been modified with regard to the term *conformazione* ['conformation'], which Buttigieg translates as 'adaptation', thus losing the semantic reference to the Italian *conformismo*).
4. Q16§9, in SPN: 396.
5. Q29§2, in CW: 181–2. With regard to the importance of the concept of 'organicity' in Gramsci's linguistics, cf. Ives, *Gramsci's Politics of Language*: 44–5; Niels Helsloot, 'Linguists of All Countries…! On Gramsci's Premise of Coherence', *Journal of Pragmatics*, 13, 1989: 547–66.
6. Q9§142, in QC: 1203, author's translation.
7. Respectively, in Q6§10 (PN3: 9) and Q7§83 (PN3: 213).
8. Q19§2, in QC: 1961, author's translation.
9. Q8§25, in PN3: 252 (the translation has been modified with regard to the term *disorganico* ['disorganic'], which Buttigieg translates as 'incoherent').
10. This is the case of the 'crisis of authority' of the ruling class: 'The crisis consists precisely in the fact that the old is dying and the new cannot be born', Q3§34, in PN2: 32–3.
11. Q13§23, in SPN: 210–18.
12. Q10I *Summary*, in FSPN: 329.
13. In addition to the previously mentioned work by Lacalu, see also Alessandro Pizzorno, 'Sul metodo di Gramsci: dalla storiografia alla scienza politica [On Gramsci's Method: From Historiography to Political Science]', in P. Rossi (ed.), *Gramsci e la cultura contemporanea* [Gramsci and Contemporary Culture], vol. 2, Rome: Editori Riuniti-Istituto Gramsci, 1969: 109–26 (also to be found in French and Spanish: 'A propos de la méthode de Gramsci, de l'historiographie à la science politique', *L'Homme et la Société*, 8, 1968; and *Sobre el método de Gramsci*, Córdova: Ediciones Pasado y Presente, 1972).

14. The fact that the life of the working class already alludes, in the existing order, to a potentially different organicity is also noted by Gramsci in his early works: 'The socialist State already exists, potentially, in the social institutions characteristic of the exploited working class', 'Democrazia operaia [Workers' Democracy]', *L'Ordine Nuovo* [The New Order], 21 June 1919 (PPW: 96).

15. Cf. Q6§138, in PN3: 109.

16. Q12§1, in SPN: 5.

17. Q4§49, in PN2: 200.

18. Q12§1, in SPN: 5.

19. Mannheim, *Ideology and Utopia*: 140.

20. Q12§1, in SPN: 5-7.

21. 'Indeed it happens that many intellectuals think that they are the State, a belief which, given the magnitude of the category, occasionally has important consequences and leads to unpleasant complications for the fundamental economic group which really is the State', *ibid.*: 16.

22. *Ibid.*: 7.

23. *Ibid.*: 17.

24. Q19§24, in SPN: 57.

25. Q12§1, in SPN: 15.

26. Q6§10, in PN3: 9.

27. Q9§21, in QC: 1109, author's translation.

28. Cf. Edward Hallett Carr, *A History of Soviet Russia. Vol. IV, The Interregnum: 1923-1924*, London: Macmillan, 1954.

29. Q22§2, in SPN: 285.

30. Q11§12, in SPN: 334.

31. According to Gramsci, 'Only the struggle and its outcome – which is not to say its immediate outcome but the outcome that manifests itself in a permanent victory – will reveal that which is rational or irrational, that which is "worthy" of victory because it continues the past in its own way and moves beyond it', Q6§10, in PN3: 8.

32. Q12§1, in SPN: 5.

33. Q12§3, in SPN: 9. *L'Ordine Nuovo* [The New Order] was a weekly (later becoming a daily) newspaper that Gramsci launched in Turin in 1919. Through journalistic work of the highest level, together with its persistent presence in the workplace and in places of political struggle, the paper contributed, with its workers' council-style approach, towards the organization of labour struggles during the 'Two Red Years' (1919-20). Cf. Darrow Schecter, *Gramsci and the Theory of Industrial Democracy*, Aldershot, Hants, UK: Avebury, 1991.

34. Q12§3, in SPN: 10 (the translation of the last part has been slightly modified). Weber as well had focused on 'the struggle of the "specialist" type of man against the older type of the "cultivated man", a struggle conditioned by the irresistibly expanding bureaucratization of all public and private relations of authority and by the ever-increasing importance of experts and specialised knowledge', Weber, *Economy and Society*: 1002. Gramsci was aware of this even before his period of imprisonment: 'In every country, the stratum of intellectuals has been radically modified by the development of capitalism. The old model of intellectual was the organizing element in a society with a prevalently peasant and artisanal basis […]. Industry has introduced a new model of intellectual: the technical organizer,

the specialist in applied science. [...] it is this second model of intellectual which has prevailed, with all its characteristics of order and intellectual discipline', *Some Aspects of the Southern Question*, in PPW: 328.

35. The difficult of reconciling the political function and the technical role also emerges in other areas of Gramsci's writings. For example, in regard to the 'deliberative and directive bodies' (Q4§49, in PN2: 209), or in his definition of *self-government* and of the class relations implicit in such (Q8§55, in PN3: 268).

36. Q10II§31, in FSPN: 385.

37. Q12§3, in SPN: 9.

38. Q6§88, in PN3: 75.

39. Q14§65, in CW: 130.

40. A field of study that Durkheim believes is defined by two theorems: the causal theorem, whereby *'To the same effect there always corresponds the same cause'* (Durkheim, *The Rules of Sociological Method*: 150, emphasis in the original), and the theorem of the homogeneity of cause and effect, whereby 'It is therefore in the nature of society itself that we must seek the explanation of social life' (*ibid.*: 128).

41. *Ibid.*: 56. By affirming so, Durkheim distances himself from the supporters of both evolutionary and contractual theories: in his view, while the former are mistaken in naturally deriving society from individuals, the second are wrong in defining society as an artificial construction, the result of individual wills. Both, however, grasp certain key aspects of the question: the evolutionists consider society to be a natural fact and not an artifice; those adopting a contractualist approach, on the other hand, place the emphasis on the coercive aspect of society (cf. *ibid.*: 142–3).

42. *Ibid.*: 43.

43. The use Durkheim makes of the French terms *coercition* and *contrainte* is of interest here. While in the first chapter of *The Rules of Sociological Method* he alternates them, with a certain preference for the term *coercition*, from the second chapter onwards Durkheim generally uses the term *contrainte* and its derivatives. The greater allusion to violence present in the term *coercition*, compared to the mediation of the social context alluded to in the term *contrainte*, will have persuaded Durkheim to choose the latter term more often than the former.

44. Q14§65, in CW: 130.

45. Cf. David Lockwood, *Solidarity and Schism. 'The Problem of Disorder' in Durkheimian and Marxist Sociology*, Oxford: Clarendon Press, 1992: 334.

46. Q7§12, in PN3: 164 (the translation has been modified with regard to the term *conformismo* ['conformism'], which Buttigieg translates as 'conformity').

47. *Ibid.*: 164–5.

48. Q22§11, in SPN: 302.

49. Q7§12, in PN3: 165.

50. *Ibid.*

51. Nicola Badaloni submits that it is 'difficult to believe that Emile Durkheim's anti-positivist argument, his anti-determinism, and above all his idea of collective man, had no effect on Gramsci's interpretation of Section IV of the first book of Marx's *Capital*', Nicola Badaloni, 'Antonio Gramsci. La filosofia della prassi come previsione [Antonio Gramsci: The Philosophy of Praxis as Prevision]', in E.J. Hobsbawm (ed.), *Storia del marxismo* [The History of Marxism], vol. 3, tome II, *Il marxismo nell'età della Terza Internazionale. Dalla crisi del '29 al 20°*

Congresso [Marxism in the Age of the Third International: From the 1929 crisis to the 20th Congress], Turin: Einaudi, 1981: 284). Alessandro Pizzorno as well mentions 'the Durkheimian effects that Gramsci must have unknowingly been subjected to, through Sorel who was strongly imbued with such', Pizzorno, *Sul metodo di Gramsci*: 117.

52. Q14§61, in CW: 124.
53. Q11§12, in SPN: 324 (the translation has been modified with regard to the term *uomo-massa* ['mass-man'], which SPN translates as 'man-in-the-mass', and with regard to 'men' instead of 'man').
54. Q7§12, in PN3: 166.
55. Q22§11, in SPN: 301–2.
56. See the discussion of Roman law in reference to the period of Italy's medieval Communes, to be found in Q3§87 (PN2: 86–90) and the interpretation of the law as an instrument with which the State conforms and educates society, in Q13§11 (SPN: 246–7).
57. Q8§62, in PN3: 272–3.
58. Q13§11, in SPN: 246.
59. Durkheim, *The Division of Labour in Society*: 68, emphasis in the original.
60. *Ibid.*: 77.
61. *Ibid.*: 70–1.
62. Q13§7, in SPN: 242.
63. *Ibid.*
64. 'This problem contains in a nutshell the entire "juridical problem", that is to say, the problem of assimilating the whole grouping to its most advanced fraction; it is a problem of education of the masses, of their "adaptation" according to the exigencies of the end pursued. This is precisely the function of law in the state and in society: through "law" the State renders the ruling group "homogeneous" and aims to create a social conformism that serves the purposes of the ruling group's line of development', Q8§84, in PN3: 69.
65. Q6§98, in PN3: 83–4.
66. Q19§24, in SPN: 57.
67. Q22§10, in SPN: 298.
68. Q14§65, in CW: 130.
69. Q11§52, in SPN: 410.
70. *Ibid.* In claiming the concept of determined market for critical economics, Gramsci defines it as 'the ensemble of the concrete economic activities of a particular social form, assumed according to the laws governing their uniformity, i.e. "abstracted" but without this abstraction ceasing to be historically determined', Q10II§32, in FSPN: 172. Cf. the letter dated 30 May 1932 that Gramsci sent to Tania (LP2: 177–9) and Gramsci's analysis of the concept of 'homo oeconomicus' in Q10II§15 (FSPN: 166–7) and Q10II§37 (FSPN: 165–6).
71. Q11§52, in SPN: 410.
72. *Ibid.*
73. *Ibid.*: 412.
74. Q11§14, in SPN: 437.
75. Q11§52, in SPN: 411.
76. Q11§14, in SPN: 437.
77. *Ibid.*

78. The problem remains unresolved as to the element permitting the transition from one determined market to another, from one organic to another; in other words, the way in which this element ceases to function as one of the factors of the existing equilibrium, to become the seed of a new equilibrium. This problem was subsequently to become a constant feature of most Marxist and post-Marxist thinking, in particular focusing on the questions of the distinction between labour power and the working class (Mario Tronti, *Operai e capitale* [Workers and Capital], Turin: Einaudi, 1966), of the aleatory encounter (Louis Althusser, *Philosophy of the Encounter: Later Writings, 1978–1987*, translated by G.M. Goshgarian, London-New York: Verso, 2006), of articulation (Laclau and Mouffe, *Hegemony and Socialist Strategy*) and of the event (Alain Badiou, *Being and Event*, translated by O. Feltham, London: Mansell Publishing, 2006 [1st ed. 1988]).

79. Q13§7, in SPN: 243. Gramsci thus seems to imply the need for a phase of movement, as in other revolutionary experiences, probably shorter than the one experienced in the Russian case, just as the latter was shorter than the equivalent phase during the French Revolution: 'In Europe from 1789 to 1870 there was a (political) war of manoeuvre in the French Revolution and a long war of position from 1815 to 1870. In the present epoch, the war of manoeuvre took place politically from March 1917 to March 1921; this was followed by a war of position whose representative – both practical (for Italy) and ideological (for Europe) – is fascism', Q10I§9, in SPN: 120.

80. Q10II§8, in FSPN: 179.

81. *Ibid.*

82. *Ibid.*

83. Q10II§57, in FSPN: 190.

84. Gramsci's need to formulate a notion of predictability that suits a given historical period, namely, that starting with the October Revolution, which radically enlarges the 'space of experience' and the possibility of a different timing, follows the same model adopted by the historical analysis of Lorenz Von Stein after the French Revolution (cf. the essay 'Historical Prognosis in Lorenz von Stein's Essay on the Prussian Constitution', in Reinhart Koselleck, *Futures Past: On the Semantics of Historical Time*, translated by K. Tribe, New York: Columbia University Press, 2004 [1st ed. 1979]: 58–71).

85. Q13§1, in SPN: 127.

86. Q11§26, in SPN: 426.

87. Q11§15, in SPN: 438.

88. Q11§38, in FSPN: 293.

89. Q11§15, in SPN: 438.

90. *Ibid.*

91. Q15§4, in SPN: 144.

92. Q11§25, in SPN: 428.

93. *Ibid.*: 429.

94. *Ibid.*

95. *Ibid.*

96. *Ibid.* In Gramsci's opinion, Fascism is also an aspect of this transition towards planned policies: 'a passive revolution takes place when, through a "reform" process, the economic structure is transformed from an individualistic one to an economy according to a plan (administered economy) and when the emergence

of an "intermediate economy" – i.e., an economy in the space between the purely individualistic one and the one that is comprehensively planned – enables the transition to more advanced political and cultural forms without the kind of radical and destructive cataclysms that are utterly devastating. "Corporativism" could be – or, as it grows, could become – this form of intermediate economy that has a "passive" character', Q8§236, in PN3: 378. Cf. Traute Rafalski and Michel Vale, 'Social Planning and Corporativism. Modernization, Tendencies in Italian Fascism', *International Journal of Political Economy*, 1, 1988: 10–64; and also Q8§216 (PN3: 365–7), Q14§68 (SPN: 240–1).

97. Q11§25, in SPN: 428.
98. *Ibid.*: 429 (the translation of the second quote has been modified).
99. *Ibid.*
100. Cf. Femia, *The Machiavellian Legacy*: 1–63, 80–125; Maurice A. Finocchiaro, *Beyond Left and Right: Democratic Elitism in Mosca and Gramsci*, New Haven: Yale University Press, 1999.

CHAPTER 5

1. Cf. Gwyn A. Williams, *Proletarian Order: Antonio Gramsci, Factory Councils and the Origins of Italian Communism, 1911–1921*, London: Pluto Press, 1975; Walter L. Adamson, 'Gramsci's Interpretation of Fascism', *Journal of the History of Ideas*, 4, 1980: 615–33.
2. 'La settimana politica [v]. La tendenza centrista [The Political Week (v). The Trend Towards Political Moderation]', *L'Ordine nuovo* [The New Order], 2 August 1919 (ON: 163), author's translation. Cf. James Martin, 'Hegemony and the Crisis of Legitimacy in Gramsci', *History of the Human Sciences*, 10, 1 February 1997: 37–56.
3. 'Il potere in Italia [Power in Italy]', *Avanti!* [Forward!], 11 February 1920 (ON: 411), author's translation.
4. 'Gli avventurieri della rivoluzione operaia [The Adventurers of the Workers' Revolution]', *Avanti!* [Forward!], 29 June 1920 (ON: 567), author's translation.
5. 'Il destino di Matteotti [Matteotti's Destiny]', *Lo Stato operaio* [The Workers' State], 28 August 1924 (CPC: 40), author's translation.
6. Q22§2, in SPN: 281. Gramsci correctly identifies 1929 as the year in which American capitalism began to establish its political hegemony. Prior to that date 'Hegemony here is born in the factory and requires for its exercise only a minute quantity of professional political and ideological intermediaries', *ibid.*: 285. Within this context 'the "structure" dominates the superstructures more immediately', because 'Up to the present (until the 1929 crash), there has not been, except perhaps sporadically, any flowering of the "superstructure". In other words, the fundamental question of hegemony has not yet been posed', *ibid.*: 285–6. The reference placed between parentheses '(until the 1929 crash)' can be found in text 'c', a redrafted version, dating from 1934, whereas it is absent in text 'a', the rough draft dating from early 1930 (cf. Q1§61, in PN1: 169). Clearly, the echo of the first important measures introduced by the New Deal alerted Gramsci to the beginning of a 'superstructural' development in the USA.
7. Gramsci's work reflects what appears to be a constant feature of Marxist thought, that is, the criticism and broadening of the Marxian concept of 'crisis' following a

period of genuine capitalist crisis. This rethinking, albeit in diverse forms, in fact emerged both during the 1970s (see Mario Tronti, *Soggetti, crisi, potere* [Subjects, Crisis, Power], Bologna: Cappelli, 1980), and more recently following the advent of the current financial and economic crisis in 2008 (see David Harvey, *The Enigma of Capital: And the Crises of Capitalism*, London: Profile, 2010; David Harvey, 'Crisis Theory and the Falling Rate of Profit', in T. Subasat and M.S. Kocman (eds), *The Great Financial Meltdown: Systemic, Conjunctural or Policy Created?*, Cheltenham: Edward Elgar, 2016).

8. Q4§38, in PN2: 177 (this is the English translation of Gramsci's Italian text, which in turn translates Marx's German text by memory). With regard to Gramsci's interpretation of the two Marxian principles, see Gerratana, *Gramsci. Problemi di metodo*: 99, 109 ff; Femia, *Gramsci's Political Thought*: 113–25.

9. Q13§23, in SPN: 211.

10. Q3§34, in PN2: 32–3.

11. Q11§15, in SPN: 438.

12. Q15§5, in FSPN: 220. Cf. Pasquale Voza, *Gramsci e la continua crisi* [Gramsci and the Continual Crisis], Rome: Carocci, 2008; Reinhart Koselleck, *Critique and Crisis: Enlightenment and the Pathogenesis of Modern Society*, Cambridge, MA: MIT Press, 1988 (1st ed. 1959).

13. Cf. Jean-Pierre Potier, 'La crisi degli anni Trenta vista da Antonio Gramsci [Antonio Gramsci's View of the 1930s Crisis]', in A. Burgio and A.A. Santucci (eds), *Gramsci e la rivoluzione in Occidente* [Gramsci and the Revolution in the West], Rome: Editori Riuniti, 1999: 69–81.

14. Q15§5, in FSPN: 219.

15. *Ibid.*

16. *Ibid.*

17. *Ibid.*: 219–20. Cf. Williams, *Proletarian Order*.

18. Q15§5, in FSPN: 220.

19. *Ibid.*: 220–1.

20. Gramsci's use of the 'language of equilibrium' when studying society and its crisis is probably a reference to his reading of Bukharin's *Historical Materialism*, three chapters of which were dedicated to the question of the theory of equilibrium. In the field of Marxism, the first to propose a theory of equilibrium in his writings was Bogdanov, one of the earliest Bolsheviks, a highly versatile scientist and a theoretician of organization (cf. *Empiriomonism* and *Tektology*, and Alexander Bogdanov, *Essays in Tektology*, translated by G. Gorelik, Seaside: Intersystem Publications, 1980). Bogdanov also took up a debate that at the end of the nineteenth century had seen the concept of equilibrium, in diverse forms, become a key element both of economic theory, with the establishment of marginalism, and of sociological theory with the emergence of functionalism.

21. Q15§62, in SPN: 114. Cf. John A. Davis (ed.), *Gramsci and Italy's Passive Revolution*, London: Routledge, 2014; Fabrizio Bracco (ed.), *Gramsci e la crisi del mondo liberale* [Gramsci and the Crisis of the Liberal World], Perugia: Guerra, 1980.

22. Q15§5, in FSPN: 220.

23. Q13§23, in SPN: 210 (the translation has been modified with regard to the term *gruppi* ['groups'], which SPN translates as 'classes').

24. *Ibid.*

25. *Ibid.*: 211.
26. Cf. Biagio De Giovanni, 'Crisi organica e Stato in Gramsci [Organic Crisis and State in Gramsci]', in F. Ferri (ed.), *Politica e storia in Gramsci* [Politics and History in Gramsci], vol. 1, Rome: Editori Riuniti-Istituto Gramsci, 1977: 248.
27. Q6§10, in PN3: 8–9.
28. Gramsci makes no mention of it, but this is the very pattern that the October Revolution followed, subsequent to previous experiences – both in the 1905 revolution and during the period from February to October 1917 – of the crisis of the preceding order.
29. Q4§38, in PN2: 177.
30. *Ibid.*
31. *Ibid.*
32. *Ibid.*: 177–8.
33. Rosa Luxemburg, *The Mass Strike, the Political Party and the Trade Unions*, translated by P. Lavin, 1906 (www.marxists.org/archive/luxemburg/1906/mass-strike).
34. Q7§10, in PN3: 161.
35. *Ibid.*
36. *Ibid.*: 161–2.
37. Gramsci wrote that 'this transition is only indirectly <mediately> related to what happened in the military field, although there is a definite and essential connection, certainly', Q6§138, in PN3: 109.
38. Q7§10, in PN3: 161.
39. Q13§24, in SPN: 234.
40. Q7§10, in PN3: 162.
41. Q7§16, in PN3: 168–9.
42. Q7§10, in PN3: 162.
43. Q13§17, in SPN: 184.
44. *Ibid.*
45. Q8§216, in PN3: 366.
46. *Ibid.*, emphases in the original.
47. *Ibid.*
48. Q13§23, in SPN: 210.
49. Q3§34, in PN2: 32.
50. Q1§158, in PN1: 235.
51. Q3§137, in PN2: 115. 'This transformism brings into sharp relief the contrast between culture, ideology, etc., and class power. The bourgeoisie is unable to educate its youth (generational struggle); the young allow themselves to be culturally attracted by the workers, and they even become <or try to become> their leaders (an "unconscious" desire to make themselves the bearers of the hegemony of their own class over the people), but during historical crises they return to the fold', Q3§137, in PN2: 115.
52. Q1§158, in PN1: 235.
53. *Ibid.*: 236.
54. Q22§11, in SPN: 303.
55. Q22§15, in SPN: 317.
56. Q13§17, in SPN: 185.

57. *Ibid.* Cf. Roger Simon, *Gramsci's Political Thought: An Introduction*, London: Lawrence & Wishart, 1991: 29 ff.
58. Q13§17, in SPN: 180–1
59. *Ibid.*: 181.
60. *Ibid.*
61. *Ibid.*
62. Q3§48, in PN2: 51.
63. *Ibid.*
64. *Ibid.*: 52.
65. *Ibid.*
66. Q6§138, in PN3: 109.
67. Q7§12, in PN3: 165.
68. Q13§17, in SPN: 184.
69. Q6§10, in PN3: 9.
70. *Ibid.* Here Gramsci is referring to 'Croce's address to the Philosophy Congress at Oxford [that] is in fact a political manifesto for an international union of the great intellectuals of all countries, especially the Europeans; and one cannot deny that this might become an important party and play a significant role', *ibid.*: 8.

CHAPTER 6

1. Cf. Badaloni, 'Gramsci and the Problem of the Revolution': 80–109. In the late 1960s, Althusser had criticized Gramsci on the basis of a reading of the *Prison Notebooks* heavily influenced by this political use: Louis Althusser and Étienne Balibar, *Reading Capital*, London: New Left Books, 1970 (1st ed. 1968): 126–38. The relationship between Althusser and Gramsci is more complex than this initial criticism led people to believe, however. Indeed, in 1965 Althusser also wrote: 'Who has *really* attempted to follow up the explorations of Marx and Engels? I can only think of Gramsci', Althusser, *For Marx*: 114. During the 1970s, Althusser returned once again to Gramsci in his work *Machiavelli and Us* (for the dating of the manuscripts, see the *Editorial Note* written by François Matheron: vii–ix).
2. The most well-known criticism of this temporal structure is that offered by Althusser: 'This means that the structure of the historical existence of the Hegelian social totality allows what I propose to call an *"essential section" (coupe d'essence)*, i.e., an intellectual operation in which a *vertical break* is made at any moment in historical time, a break in the present such that all the elements of the whole revealed by this section are in an immediate relationship with one another, a relationship that immediately expresses their internal essence', Althusser and Balibar, *Reading Capital*: 94, emphases in the original. This criticism of Gramscian historicism divulged through the PCI (Italian Communist Party) also led to the emergence of a difficult relationship between the Italian workerist tradition (*operaismo*) and the thought of Antonio Gramsci (cf. Mario Tronti, 'Tra materialismo dialettico e filosofia della prassi. Gramsci e Labriola [Between Dialectical Materialism and the Philosophy of Praxis: Gramsci and Labriola]', in A. Caracciolo and G. Scalia (eds), *La città futura. Saggi sulla figura e il pensiero di Antonio Gramsci* [The City of the Future: Essays on the Figure and Thought of Antonio Gramsci], Milan: Feltrinelli, 1959: 139–86; Antonio Negri, *Books for*

Burning: Between Civil War and Democracy in 1970s Italy, translated by A. Bove, E. Emery, T.S. Murphy and F. Novello, London-New York: Verso, 2005: 90 ff).

3. Cf. Peter Thomas, 'Gramsci e le temporalità plurali [Gramsci and the Plurality of Times]' and Fabio Frosini, 'Spazio-tempo e potere alla luce della teoria dell'egemonia [Space-time and Power in the Light of the Theory of Hegemony]', in V. Morfino (ed.), *Tempora multa: il governo del tempo* [Tempora Multa: The Governance of Time], Milan: Mimesis, 2013: 191–224, 225–54, who criticize the two interpretations of time in Gramsci's work made, respectively, by Althusser and Laclau.

4. Cf. Thomas' comparison of Gramsci's theory of personality and Deleuze's concept of 'disjunctive synthesis' (Thomas, 'Gramsci e le temporalità plurali': 208).

5. An example of this type is Gramsci's thoughts on subalterns: 'The history of subaltern social groups is necessarily fragmented and episodic. There undoubtedly does exist a tendency to (at least provisional stage of) unification in the historical activity of these groups, but this tendency is continually interrupted by the activity of the ruling groups; it therefore can only be demonstrated when an historical cycle is completed and this cycle culminates in a success', Q25§2, in SPN: 54–5.

6. Q10II§8, in FSPN: 179.

7. Alberto Burgio, *Gramsci storico: una lettura dei Quaderni del carcere* [Gramsci Historian: A Reading of the 'Prison Notebooks'], Rome-Bari: Laterza, 2003: 18–21; Alberto Burgio, *Gramsci: il sistema in movimento* [Gramsci: The Moving System], Rome: DeriveApprodi, 2014: 112–18.

8. Cf. Burgio, *Gramsci storico*: 122.

9. This interpretation of Gramscian time does not necessarily imply an 'aleatory' interpretation of his Marxism. The way in which political novelty is produced, in fact, remains an 'unspoken' feature of Gramscian discourse.

10. Q14§23, in SPN: 223.

11. Q14§76, in SPN: 256.

12. Q22§15, in SPN: 317.

13. Q10II§48, in SPN: 357 (the translation has been modified with regard to the term *mentalità* ['mentality'], which SPN translates as 'consciousness').

14. Q11§12, in SPN: 324.

15. According to Weber's famous definition: 'As intellectualism suppresses belief in magic, the world's processes become disenchanted, lose their magical significance, and henceforth simply "are" and "happen" but no longer signify anything. As a consequence, there is a growing demand that the world and the total pattern of life be subject to an order that is significant and meaningful', Weber, *Economy and society*, vol. 2: 506.

16. Cf. Thomas, 'Gramsci e le temporalità plurali': 208. The emphasis on plurality that characterizes this reading is linked to the pre-eminence of the 'immanentist' interpretative approach to the *Prison Notebooks*. In reading Gramsci's works solely in the light of the immanentist view of philosophy, history and politics, there is a risk, however, that the other elements, which we could call 'historically teleological', and which refer to another temporality, are ignored. On this point, Gramsci wrote that 'teleology [...] means something that, following Kant's qualifications, can be defended by historical materialism', Q7§46, in PN3: 194.

17. Q16§12, in QC: 1875, author's translation.

18. Q11§12, in SPN: 325.

19. Q11§12, in SPN: 324.

20. *Ibid.*: 328.

21. Q11§13, in SPN: 419.

22. Cf. Franco Lo Piparo, *Lingua, Intellettuali, Egemonia in Gramsci* [Language, Intellectuals and Hegemony in Gramsci], Bari: Laterza, 1979: 245. Also see the more recent studies by Ives, *Gramsci's Politics of Language* and by Alessandro Carlucci, *Gramsci and Languages: Unification, Diversity, Hegemony,* Leiden-Boston: Brill, 2013.

23. Q29§2, in SCW: 181.

24. *Ibid.*: 180.

25. *Ibid.* Gramsci wrote 'spontaneous' in inverted commas in order to emphasize the existence of a political line behind these movements as well: 'The elements of "conscious leadership" in the "most spontaneous" of movements cannot be ascertained, simply because they have left no verifiable document', Q3§48, in PN2: 49.

26. Here Gramsci criticizes both Manzoni's intellectualist plan for the Florentine vernacular to become the national language, that is, 'of returning to a Florentine hegemony using state means' (Q23§40, in SCW: 173), and the project to establish Esperanto as the lingua franca of international socialism (cf. Q11§45, in FSPN: 303–4 together with the article, 'La lingua unica e l'Esperanto [The Single Language and Esperanto]', *Il Grido del Popolo* [The Cry of the People], 16 February 1918 (SCW: 26–31).

27. However, this does not exclude his 'positive relationship with linguistic diversity [that] was crucial for his awareness of the perils inherent in imposing cultural and political unification', Carlucci, *Gramsci and Languages*: 15–16 (see also Ives, *Gramsci's Politics of Language*: 32).

28. Gramsci describes the difference between languages and dialects as follows: 'Someone who only speaks dialect, or understands the standard language incompletely, necessarily has an intuition of the world which is more or less limited and provincial, which is fossilized and anachronistic in relation to the major currents of thought which dominate world history. His interests will be limited, more or less corporate or economistic, not universal. While it is not always possible to learn a number of foreign languages in order to put oneself in contact with other cultural lives, it is at the least necessary to learn the national language properly. A great culture can be translated into the language of another great culture, that is to say a great national language with historic richness and complexity, and it can translate any other great culture and can be a world-wide means of expression. But a dialect cannot do this', Q11§12, in SPN: 325.

29. Q7§16, in PN3: 169 (cf. Chapter 5, section 'The multiple meanings of "crisis"').

30. Cf. Adam David Morton, *Revolution and State in Modern Mexico. The Political Economy of Uneven Development,* Lanham, MD: Rowman & Littlefield, 2011.

31. Q10II§12, in SPN: 365–6.

32. Cf. Buci-Glucksmann, *Gramsci and the State*: 261–4; Stephen Cohen, *Bukharin and the Bolshevik Revolution: A Political Biography, 1888–1938,* New York: Random House, 1975 (1st ed. 1973). On the question of the relationship between Gramsci and Bukharin, permit me to refer to a previous work of mine, Filippini, *Una politica di massa* [Mass Politics]: 103–49.

33. Cf. Henri de Man, *Au-delà du marxisme* [Beyond Marxism], Bruxelles: L'Églantine, 1927 (Gramsci had a 1929 Italian translation of this book when he was in prison); Dirk Pels, 'Hendrik de Man and the Ideology of Planism', *International Review of Social History*, 32, 1987: 206–29.

34. This observation holds for many of the most important concepts contained in the *Prison Notebooks*: 'hegemony' is taken from Lenin (cf. Thomas, *The Gramscian Moment*: 57–8), 'civil society' from the classical economists and from Marx (cf. Jacques Texier, 'Gramsci, Theoretician of the Superstructures. On the Concept of Civil Society', in Mouffe (ed.), *Gramsci and Marxist Theory*: 48–79), 'historical bloc' from Sorel (cf. note 63 to Chapter 1), 'intellectual and moral reform' from Renan (*La réforme intellectuelle et morale*), 'modern Prince' from Machiavelli (*The Prince*), 'philosophy of praxis' from Labriola (cf. Antonio Labriola, letter to G. Sorel, 14 May 1897, in *Socialism and Philosophy*, translated by E. Untermann, 1907 (www.marxists.org/archive/labriola/works/al04.htm) [here translated as 'philosophy of practice']), 'Fordism' from the European debate on the question (Friedrich von Gottl-Ottlilienfeld, *Fordismus: Paraphrasen über das Verhältnis von Wirtschaft und technischer Vernunft bei Henry Ford und Frederick W. Taylor* [*Paraphrases about the Relationship Between the Economy and Technical Rationality from Henry Ford and Frederick W. Taylor*], Jena: G. Fischer, 1924). Cf. Anne Showstack Sassoon, 'Gramsci's Subversion of the Language of Politics', in P. Ives and R. Lacorte, *Gramsci, Language, and Translation*: Lanham, MD: Lexington Books, 2010: 243–54.

35. Q4§57, in PN2: 232.

36. Q10I§9, in FSPN: 349.

37. Q8§225, in PN3: 372.

38. Q8§25, in PN3: 252.

39. Q15§25, in SPN: 113. Cf. John A. Davis and Paul Ginsborg (eds), *Society and Politics in the Age of Risorgimento. Essays in Honour of Danis Mack Smith*, Cambridge: Cambridge University Press, 1991.

40. Q19§24, in SPN: 57.

41. *Ibid.*: 60.

42. *Ibid.*: 57.

43. *Ibid.*: 63.

44. Q19§27, in SPN: 102.

45. Q19§24, in SPN: 63.

46. *Ibid.*: 61.

47. Q19§26, in SPN: 101.

48. Q19§24, in SPN: 63.

49. *Ibid.*: 79.

50. *Some Aspects of the Southern Question*, in PPW: 313–37.

51. Q19§24, in SPN: 58–9. Cf. Raffaella Gherardi, *L'arte del compromesso. La politica della mediazione nell'Italia liberale* [The Art of Compromise. The Politics of Mediation in Liberal Italy], Bologna: Il Mulino, 1993.

52. Q15§11, in SPN: 109.

53. Q13§1, in SPN: 132.

54. Q19§27, in SPN: 103.

55. Q19§53, in QC: 2075, author's translation.

56. *Ibid.*

57. Walter Benjamin, 'On the Concept of History', translated by H. Zohn, in *Selected Writings*, vol. 4, Cambridge, MA: Harvard University Press, 2003 (1st ed. 1950): 394–5.

58. The theses were written between 1939 and 1940, and were conceived as an introduction to the Passagen-Werk: cf. Gianfranco Bonola and Michele Ranchetti, 'Introduzione [Introduction]' and 'Sulla vicenda delle tesi "sul concetto di storia" [On the Vicissitude of the Theses "On the Concept of History"]', in Walter Benjamin, *Sul concetto di storia* [*On the Concept of History*], Turin: Einaudi, 1997: vii–xix, 5–13. The *Prison Notebooks* and the *Theses*, despite being very different writings from many points of view, nevertheless share certain specific characteristics: both are unfinished and were not published by their respective authors; both were written in dangerous situations, under the looming Fascist and Nazi regimes; and both were the last works written by their respective authors.

59. Benjamin, *On the Concept of History*: 395.

60. *Ibid.*: 396. See Benedict Anderson's use of this Benjaminian concept in regard to the construction of nationalism, in *Imagined Communities: Reflections on the Origin and Spread of Nationalism*, London-New York: Verso, 2006 (1st ed. 1991): 24–6.

61. Benjamin, *On the Concept of History*: 396.

62. Q13§1, in SPN: 132, our italics. Gramsci repeats on several occasions in this note his thoughts on the precocious Jacobinism of Machiavelli: 'Machiavelli did not merely abstractly desire the national unification of Italy; he had a programme, and it was one which revealed his "precocious Jacobinism"', *ibid.*: 123.

63. *Ibid.*: 130, 123. The same temporal structure also emerges in the following passage: 'there is the "passion" of the "Jacobin" in Machiavelli, and that is why he must have been so popular with both the Jacobins and the followers of the Enlightenment', Q17§27, in QC: 1929, author's translation.

64. In Thesis VI, Benjamin writes that: 'Articulating the past historically does not mean recognizing it "the way it really was". It means appropriating a memory as it flashes up in a moment of danger. Historical materialism wishes to hold fast that image of the past which unexpectedly appears to the historical subject in a moment of danger. The danger threatens both the content of the tradition and those who inherit it. For both, it is one and the same thing: the danger of becoming a tool of the ruling classes every age must strive anew to wrest tradition away from the conformism that is working to overpower it', Benjamin, *On the Concept of History*: 391.

65. Gramsci in fact points out that 'Without the agrarian policy of the Jacobins, Paris would have had the Vendee at its very doors', Q19§24, in SPN: 79.

66. *Ibid.*: 64.

67. *Ibid.*

Bibliography

Websites last accessed 1 September 2016.

OVERVIEW

Introductions to Gramsci's thought

Bambery, Chris, *A Rebel's Guide to Gramsci*, London: Bookmarks, 2006.

Fiori, Giuseppe, *Antonio Gramsci: Life of a Revolutionary*, translated by T. Nairn, London-New York: Verso, 1990 (1st ed. 1966).

Hoare, George and Sperber, Nathan, *Antonio Gramsci: An Introduction to Antonio Gramsci: His Life, Thought and Legacy*, London: Bloomsbury Academic, 2015.

Joll, James, *Gramsci*, London: Fontana Paperbacks, 1977.

Jones, Steve, *Antonio Gramsci*, London: Routledge, 2006.

Levy, Carl, *Antonio Gramsci*, Cambridge: Polity, 2013.

Martin, James, *Gramsci's Political Analysis: A Critical Introduction*, Basingstoke: Macmillan; New York: St Martin's Press, 1998.

Ransome, Paul, *Antonio Gramsci: A New Introduction*, New York-London: Harvester Wheatsheaf, 1992.

Salamini, Leonardo, *The Sociology of Political Praxis: An Introduction to Gramsci's Theory*, London: Routledge & Kegan Paul, 1981.

Santucci, Antonio A., *Antonio Gramsci*, translated by G. Di Mauro and S. Engel-Di Mauro, New York: Monthly Review Press, 2010 (1st ed. 1987).

Schwarzmantel, John, *The Routledge Guidebook to Gramsci's Prison Notebooks*, London-New York: Routledge, 2015.

Simon, Roger, *Gramsci's Political Thought: An Introduction*, London: Lawrence & Wishart, 1991.

In-depth studies and analyses

Adamson, Walter L., *Hegemony and Revolution: A Study of Antonio Gramsci's Political and Cultural Theory*, Berkeley: University of California Press, 1980.

Bellamy, Richard and Schecter, Darrow, *Gramsci and the Italian State*, Manchester-New York: Manchester University Press, 1993.

Boggs, Carl, *The Two Revolutions. Gramsci and the Dilemmas of Western Marxism*, New York: South End Press, 1984.

Buci-Glucksmann, Christine, *Gramsci and the State*, translated by D. Fernbach, London: Lawrence & Wishart, 1980 (1st ed. 1975).

Burgio, Alberto, *Gramsci storico: una lettura dei Quaderni del carcere* [Gramsci Historian: A Reading of the 'Prison Notebooks'], Rome-Bari: Laterza, 2003.

Coutinho, Carlos Nelson, *Gramsci's Political Thought*, translated by P. Sette-Camara, Leiden: Brill, 2012 (1st ed. 1989).

Femia, Joseph V., *Gramsci's Political Thought: Hegemony, Consciousness, and the Revolutionary Process*, Oxford: Clarendon Press, 1981.

Germino, Dante, *Antonio Gramsci: Architect of a New Politics*, Baton Rouge: Louisiana State University Press, 1990.

Gerratana, Valentino, *Gramsci. Problemi di metodo* [Gramsci: Problems of Method], Rome: Editori Riuniti, 1997.

Hoffman, John, *The Gramscian Challenge: Coercion and Consent in Marxist Political Theory*, Oxford-New York: Blackwell, 1984.

Joseph, Jonathan, *Hegemony: A Realist Analysis*, London-New York: Routledge, 2002.

Kiros, Teodros, *Toward the Construction of a Theory of Political Action. Antonio Gramsci: Consciousness, Participation and Hegemony*, New York: University Press of America, 1985.

Liguori, Guido, *Gramsci's Pathways*, translated by D. Broder, Leiden: Brill, 2015 (1st ed. 2006).

Morera, Esteve, *Gramsci's Historicism: A Realist Interpretation*, New York: Routledge, 1990.

Nemeth, Thomas, *Gramsci's Philosophy: A Critical Study*, Brighton: Harvester, 1980.

Paggi, Leonardo, *Gramsci e il moderno principe: nella crisi del socialismo italiano* [Gramsci and the Modern Prince: In the Crisis of Italian Socialism], Rome: Editori Riuniti, 1970.

——, *Le strategie del potere in Gramsci: tra fascismo e socialismo in un solo paese, 1923–1926* [Power Strategies in Gramsci: Between Fascism and Socialism in One Single Country, 1923–1926], Rome: Editori Riuniti, 1984.

Thomas, Peter D., *The Gramscian Moment: Philosophy, Hegemony, and Marxism*, Leiden: Brill, 2009.

Influential critiques

Althusser, Louis, *On the Reproduction of Capitalism: Ideology and Ideological State Apparatuses*, translated by G.M. Goshgarian, London-New York: Verso, 2014: 10–13 (1st ed. 1970).

Althusser, Louis and Balibar, Étienne, *Reading Capital*, London: New Left Books, 1970: 126–44 (1st ed. 1968).

Anderson, Perry, 'The Antinomies of Antonio Gramsci', *New Left Review*, 100, 1976: 5–78.

Asor Rosa, Alberto, *Scrittori e popolo: saggio sulla letteratura populista in Italia* [Writers and People: An Essay on Populist Literature in Italy], Rome: Samonà e Savelli, 1965.

Bobbio, Norberto, 'Gramsci and the Concept of Civil Society', in J. Keane (ed.), *Civil Society and the State: New European Perspectives*, London: Verso, 1988: 73–99 (1st ed. 1976).

Day, Richard J.F., *Gramsci is Dead: Anarchist Currents in the Newest Social Movements*, London: Pluto Press; Toronto: Between the lines, 2005.

Negri, Antonio, *Books for Burning: Between Civil War and Democracy in 1970s Italy*, translated by A. Bove, E. Emery, T.S. Murphy and F. Novello, London-New York: Verso, 2005: 90 ff.

Tronti, Mario, 'Alcune questioni intorno al marxismo di Gramsci [Certain Questions Regarding Gramsci's Marxism]', in E. Garin, P. Togliatti, C. Luporini et al. (eds), *Studi gramsciani* [Gramscian Studies], Rome: Editori Riuniti, 1958: 305–21.

——, "Tra materialismo dialettico e filosofia della prassi. Gramsci e Labriola [Between Dialectical Materialism and the Philosophy of Praxis. Gramsci and Labriola]", in A. Caracciolo and G. Scalia (eds), *La città futura. Saggi sulla figura e il pensiero di Antonio Gramsci* [The City of the Future: Essays on the Figure and Thoughts of Antonio Gramsci], Milan: Feltrinelli, 1959: 139–86.

Riechers, Christian, *Gramsci e le ideologie del suo tempo* [Gramsci and the Ideologies of his Time], Genova: Graphos, 1993 (1st ed. *Antonio Gramsci: Marxismus in Italien*, Frankfurt am Main: Europaische Verlagsanstalt, 1970).

Collections of essays

Baratta, Giorgio and Liguori, Guido (eds), *Gramsci da un secolo all'altro* [Gramsci from One Century to the Next], Rome: Editori Riuniti, 1999.

Burgio, Alberto and Santucci, Antonio (eds), *Gramsci e la rivoluzione in Occidente* [Gramsci and the Revolution in the West], Rome: Editori Riuniti, 1999.

Davis, John A. (ed.), *Gramsci and Italy's Passive Revolution*, London: Routledge, 2014.

Ferri, Franco (ed.), *Politica e storia in Gramsci* [Politics and History in Gramsci], 2 vols, Rome: Editori Riuniti-Istituto Gramsci, 1977.

Francese, Joseph (ed.), *Perspectives on Gramsci. Politics, Culture and Social Theory of Gramsci: A Multidisciplinary Perspective*, New York: Routledge, 2009.

Frosini, Fabio and Liguori, Guido (eds), *Le parole di Gramsci. Per un lessico dei 'Quaderni del carcere'* [The Words of Gramsci: Toward a Lexicon of the 'Prison Notebooks'], Rome: Carocci, 2004.

Garin, Eugenio, Togliatti, Palmiro, Luporini, Cesare et al., *Studi gramsciani* [Gramscian Studies], Rome: Editori Riuniti, 1958.

Green, Marcus E. (ed.), *Rethinking Gramsci*, London: Routledge, 2010.

Howson, Richard and Smith, Kylie (eds), *Hegemony: Studies in Consensus and Coercion*, New York: Routledge, 2008.

Martin, James (ed.), *Antonio Gramsci*, 4 vols, London: Routledge, 2002.

Mastellone, Salvo (ed.), *Gramsci: i Quaderni del carcere. Una riflessione politica incompiuta* [Gramsci: The Prison Notebooks. An Unfinished Political Reflection], Turin: Utet, 1997.

Mastellone, Salvo and Sola, Giorgio (eds), *Gramsci. Il partito politico nei 'Quaderni'* [Gramsci: The Political Party in the 'Prison Notebooks'], Florence: Centro Editoriale Toscano, 2001.

McNally, Mark (ed.), *Antonio Gramsci*, New York: Palgrave Macmillan, 2015.

Mouffe, Chantal (ed.), *Gramsci and Marxist Theory*, London: Routledge & Kegan Paul, 1979.

Rossi, Pietro (ed.), *Gramsci e la cultura contemporanea* [Gramsci and Contemporary Culture], 2 vols, Rome: Editori Riuniti-Istituto Gramsci, 1969.

Sbarberi, Franco (ed.), *Teoria politica e società industriale: ripensare Gramsci* [Political Theory and Industrial Society: Rethinking Gramsci], Turin: Bollati Boringhieri, 1988.

Showstack Sassoon, Anne (ed.), *Approaches to Gramsci*, London: Writers and Readers Publishing Cooperative Society, 1982.

Tega, Walter (ed.), *Gramsci e l'Occidente. Trasformazioni della società e riforma della politica* [Gramsci and the West: Social Transformations and Political Reform], Bologna: Cappelli, 1990.

Tosel, André (ed.), *Modernité de Gramsci?* [Gramsci's Modernity?], Paris: Les belles lettres, 1992.

Vacca, Giuseppe (ed.), *Gramsci e il Novecento* [Gramsci and the 20th Century], 2 vols, Rome: Carocci, 2009.

USING GRAMSCI

Political science and international relations

Ayers, Alison J. (ed.), *Gramsci, Political Economy, and International Relations Theory: Modern Princes and Naked Emperors*, New York: Palgrave Macmillan, 2008.

Bieler, Andreas and Morton, Adam David (eds), *Images of Gramsci: Connections and Contentions in Political Theory and International Relations*, London: Routledge, 2006.

Bieler, Andreas, Bonefeld, Werner, Burnham, Peter and Morton, Adam David (eds), *Global Restructuring, State, Capital and Labour: Contesting Neo-Gramscian Perspectives*, New York: Palgrave Macmillan, 2006.

Cox, Robert, 'Gramsci, Hegemony and International Relations: An Essay on Method', in R. Cox and T. Sinclair (eds), *Approaches to World Order*, Cambridge: Cambridge University Press, 1996: 49–66.

Germain, Randall D. and Kenny, Michael, 'Engaging Gramsci: International Relations Theory and the New Gramscians', *Review of International Studies*, 24(1), 1998: 3–21.

Gill, Stephen (ed.), *Gramsci, Historical Materialism and International Relations*, Cambridge: Cambridge University Press, 1993.

'Gramsci and International Relations Theory', special issue of *Critical Review of International Social and Political Philosophy*, 4, 2005.

McNally, Mark and Schwarzmantel, John (eds), *Gramsci and Global Politics: Hegemony and Resistance*, London: Routledge, 2009.

Morton, Adam David, *Unravelling Gramsci: Hegemony and Passive Revolution in the Global Political Economy*, London-Ann Arbor, MI: Pluto Press, 2007.

Rupert, Mark, 'Reading Gramsci in an Era of Globalising Capitalism', *Critical Review of International Social and Political Philosophy*, 8, 2005: 483–97.

Education and pedagogy

Adamson, Walter L., 'Beyond "Reform or Revolution": Notes on Political Education in Gramsci, Habermas and Arendt', *Theory and Society*, 3, 1978: 429–60.

Borg, Carmel, Buttigieg, Joseph and Mayo, Peter (eds), *Gramsci and Education*, Lanham, MD: Rowman & Littlefield, 2002.

Coben, Diana, *Radical Heroes: Gramsci, Freire, and the Politics of Adult Education*, New York-London: Garland Publishing, 1998.

Entwistle, Harold, *Antonio Gramsci: Conservative Schooling for Radical Politics*, London: Routledge & Kegan Paul, 1979.

Hill, Deb J., *Hegemony and Education: Gramsci, Post-Marxism, and Radical Democracy Revisited*, Lanham, MD: Lexington Books, 2007.

Mayo, Peter, *Gramsci, Freire and Adult Education: Possibilities for Transformative Action*, London-New York: Zed book, 1999.

—— (ed.), *Gramsci and Educational Thought*, Oxford: Blackwell, 2009.
——, *Hegemony and Education Under Neoliberalism: Insights from Gramsci*, London: Routledge, 2015.

Political theory and philosophy

Althusser, Louis, *Machiavelli and Us*, London-New York: Verso, 2000 (1st ed. 1994, writings from 1962 to 1986).

Finocchiaro, Maurice A., *Gramsci and the History of Dialectical Thought*, Cambridge: Cambridge University Press, 1988.

Frosini, Fabio, *La religione dell'uomo moderno* [The Religion of Modern Man], Rome: Carocci, 2010.

Golding, Sue, *Gramsci's Democratic Theory: Contributions to a Post-liberal Democracy*, Toronto: University of Toronto Press, 1992.

Holub, Renate, *Antonio Gramsci: Beyond Marxism and Postmodernism*, London-New York: Routledge, 1992.

Kahn, Beverly L., 'Antonio Gramsci's Reformulation of Benedetto Croce's Speculative Idealism', *Idealistic Studies*, 15, 1985: 18–40.

Laclau, Ernesto and Mouffe, Chantal, *Hegemony and Socialist Strategy: Towards a Radical Democratic Politics*, London-New York: Verso, 2011 (1st ed. 1985).

——, *New Reflections on the Revolution of our Time*, New York: Verso, 1990: 193–5.

Mouffe, Chantal, 'Hegemony and Ideology in Gramsci', in Chantal Mouffe (ed.), *Gramsci and Marxist Theory*, London: Routledge & Kegan Paul, 1979: 168–204.

Showstack Sassoon, Anne, *Gramsci and Contemporary Politics: Beyond Pessimism of the Intellect*, London: Routledge, 2000.

West, Cornel, *The American Evasion of Philosophy*, Madison: University of Wisconsin Press, 1989: 211–35.

Language

Boothman, Derek, *Traducibilità e processi traduttivi. Un caso: A. Gramsci linguista* [Translatability and Processes of Translation. A Case-study: A. Gramsci, Linguist], Perugia: Edizioni Guerra, 2004.

——, 'Gramsci's Interest in Language: The Influence of Bartoli's Dispense di Glottologia (1912–13) on the Prison Notebooks', *Journal of Romance Studies*, 3, 2012: 10–23.

Carlucci, Alessandro, *Gramsci and Languages: Unification, Diversity, Hegemony*, Leiden-Boston: Brill, 2013.

Helsloot, Niels, 'Linguists of All Countries …! On Gramsci's Premise of Coherence', *Journal of Pragmatics*, 13, 1989: 547–66.

Ives, Peter, *Language and Hegemony in Gramsci*, London: Pluto Press; Winnipeg: Fernwood Publishing, 2004.

——, *Gramsci's Politics of Language: Engaging the Bakhtin Circle and the Frankfurt School*, Toronto: University of Toronto Press, 2004.

Ives, Peter and Lacorte, Rocco, *Gramsci, Language, and Translation*: Lanham, MD: Lexington Books, 2010.

Lo Piparo, Franco, *Lingua, Intellettuali, Egemonia in Gramsci* [Language, Intellectuals and Hegemony in Gramsci], Bari: Laterza, 1979.

Cultural studies

Briziarelli, Marco and Martìnez Guillem, Susana, *Reviving Gramsci: Crisis, Communication, and Change*, London: Routledge, 2016.

Hall, Stuart, 'Politics and Ideology: Gramsci', in S. Hall, B. Lumley and G. McLennan (eds), *On Ideology. Working Papers in Cultural Studies*, Birmingham: Centre for Contemporary Cultural Studies, 1977: 45–76.

——, 'Cultural Studies: Two Paradigms', *Media, Culture and Society*, 2, 1980: 57–72.

——, 'Gramsci's Relevance for the Study of Race and Ethnicity', *Journal of Communication Inquiry*, 10(2), 1986: 5–27.

——, 'The Problem of Ideology: Marxism Without Guarantees', *Journal of Communication Inquiry*, 10(2), 1986: 28–43.

——, 'Gramsci and Us', in S. Hall, *The Hard Road to Renewal: Thatcherism and the Crisis of the Left*, London-New York: Verso, 1988: 161–75.

Harris, David, *From Class Struggle to the Politics of Pleasure: The Effects of Gramscianism on Cultural Studies*, London-New York: Routledge, 1992.

Landy, Marcia, *Film, Politics, and Gramsci*, Minneapolis: University of Minnesota Press, 1994.

Nelson, Cary and Grossberg, Lawrence (eds), *Marxism and the Interpretation of Culture*, Urbana: University of Illinois Press, 1988: 17–33, 35–73.

Williams, Raymond, 'Base and Superstructure in Marxist Cultural Theory', in R. Dale, G. Esland and M. Macdonald (eds), *Schooling and Capitalism: A Sociological Reader*, London: Routledge & Kegan Paul, 1976.

——, *Marxism and Literature*, Oxford: Oxford University Press, 1977: 108–14.

Subaltern and postcolonial studies

Arnold, David, 'Gramsci and Peasant Subalternity in India', *Journal of Peasant Studies*, 11(4), 1984: 155–77.

Chatterjee, Partha, *Nationalist Thought and the Colonial World: A Derivative Discourse*, Minneapolis: University Of Minnesota Press, 1993: 29–30, 43–9.

Green, Marcus, 'Gramsci Cannot Speak: Presentations and Interpretations of Gramsci's Concept of the Subaltern', *Rethinking Marxism*, 14(3), 2002: 1–24.

Guha, Ranajit, *Dominance Without Hegemony: History and Power in Colonial India*, Cambridge, MA: Harvard University Press, 1997.

Modonesi, Massimo, *Subalternity, Antagonism, Autonomy: Constructing the Political Subject*, translated by A.V. Rendon Garrido and P. Roberts, London: Pluto Press, 2014.

Pasha, Mustapha K., 'Islam, "Soft" Orientalism and Hegemony: A Gramscian Rereading', *Critical Review of International Social and Political Philosophy*, 4, 2005: 543–58.

Said, Edward W., *Reflections on Exile and Other Literary and Cultural Essays*, Cambridge, MA: Harvard University Press, 2000.

Spivak, Gayatri Chakravorty, 'Can the Subaltern Speak?', in C. Nelson and L. Grossberg (eds), *Marxism and the Interpretation of Culture*, Urbana: University of Illinois Press, 1987: 271–313 (1st ed. 1983).

Srivastava, Neelam and Battacharya, Baidik, *The Postcolonial Gramsci*, New York: Routledge, 2012.

Anthropology and geography

Crehan, Kate, *Gramsci, Culture and Anthropology*, London: Pluto Press, 2002.

Ekers, Michael (ed.), *Gramsci: Space, Nature, Politics*, Chichester: Wiley-Blackwell, 2013.

De Smet, Brecht, *Gramsci on Tahrir. Revolution and Counter-revolution in Egypt*, London: Pluto Press, 2016.

Kurtz, Donald V., 'Hegemony and Anthropology: Gramsci, Exegeses, Reinterpretations', *Critique of Anthropology*, 16(2), 1996: 103–35.

Morton, Adam David, *Revolution and State in Modern Mexico: The Political Economy of Uneven Development*, Lanham, MD: Rowman & Littlefield, 2011.

Pizza, Giovanni, *Il tarantismo oggi. Antropologia, politica, cultura* [Current-day Tarantism: Anthropology, Politics and Culture], Rome: Carocci, 2015: 126–72.

Ruberto, Laura E., *Gramsci, Migration, and the Representation of Women's Work in Italy and the U.S.*, Lanham, MD: Lexington Books, 2007.

Schirru, Giancarlo (ed.), *Gramsci, le culture e il mondo* [Gramsci, Culture and the World], Rome: Edizioni Viella, 2009.

Comparisons

Finocchiaro, Maurice A., *Beyond Left and Right: Democratic Elitism in Mosca and Gramsci*, New Haven: Yale University Press, 1999.

Fontana, Benedetto, *Hegemony and Power: On the Relation Between Gramsci and Machiavelli*, Minneapolis: University of Minnesota Press, 1993.

Giglioli, Matteo Fabio Nels, *Legitimacy and Revolution in a Society of Masses: Max Weber, Antonio Gramsci and the Fin-de-siècle Debate on Social Order*, New Brunswick-London: Transaction, 2013.

Kreps, David and Gill, Stephen (eds), *Gramsci and Foucault: A Reassessment*, Farnham: Ashgate, 2015.

Radhakrishnan, Rajagopalan, 'Toward an Effective Intellectual: Foucault or Gramsci?', in B. Robbins (ed.), *Intellectuals: Aesthetics, Politics, Academics*, Minneapolis: University of Minnesota Press, 1990: 59–99.

Yanarella, Ernest J., 'Whither Hegemony?: Between Gramsci and Derrida', in J.P. Jones III, W. Natter and T.R. Schatzki, *Postmodern Contentions: Epochs, Politics, Space*, New York: Guilford Press, 1993: 65–98.

OTHER BOOKS MENTIONED

Adamson, Walter, 'Gramsci's Interpretation of Fascism', *Journal of the History of Ideas*, 4, 1980: 615–33.

Althusser, Louis, *For Marx*, translated by B. Brewster, London-New York: Verso, 2005 (1st ed. 1965).

——, *Philosophy of the Encounter: Later Writings, 1978–1987*, translated by G.M. Oshgarian, London-New York: Verso, 2006.

Anderson, Benedict, *Imagined Communities: Reflections on the Origin and Spread of Nationalism*, London-New York: Verso, 2006 (1st ed. 1991).

Anderson, Benedict and Balakrishnan, Gopal (eds), *Mapping the Nation*, London: Verso, 1996.

Ansaldo, Giovanni, 'La democrazia tedesca nel pensiero di Max Weber [German Democracy in the Thought of Max Weber]', *Rivoluzione liberale* [Liberal Revolution], 4, 1923: 13–15.

Arato, Andrew and Cohen, Jean L., *Civil Society and Political Theory*, Cambridge, MA-London: MIT Press, 1992.

Badaloni, Nicola, 'Antonio Gramsci. La filosofia della prassi come previsione [Antonio Gramsci: The Philosophy of Praxis as Prevision]', in E.J. Hobsbawm (ed.), *Storia del marxismo* [The History of Marxism], vol. 3, tome II, *Il marxismo nell'età della Terza Internazionale. Dalla crisi del '29 al 20° Congresso* [Marxism in the Age of the Third International: From the 1929 Crisis to the 20th Congress], Turin: Einaudi, 1981: 251–340.

Badiou, Alain, *Manifesto for Philosophy*, translated by N. Madarasz, New York: State University of New York Press, 1999 (1st ed. 1989).

——, *Being and Event*, translated by O. Feltham, London: Mansell Publishing, 2006 (1st ed. 1988).

Benjamin, Walter, 'On the Concept of History', translated by H. Zohn, in *Selected Writings*, vol. 4, Cambridge MA: Harvard University Press, 2003: 389–400 (1st ed. 1950).

Bernstein, Eduard, *The Precondition of Socialism*, Cambridge: Cambridge University Press, 1993 (1st ed. 1899).

Bogdanov, Alexander, *Essays in Tektology*, translated by G. Gorelik, Seaside: Intersystem Publications, 1980.

Bonola, Gianfranco and Ranchetti, Michele, 'Introduzione [Introduction]' and 'Sulla vicenda delle tesi "sul concetto di storia" [On the Vicissitude of the Theses "On the Concept of History"]', in Walter Benjamin, *Sul concetto di storia* [*On the Concept of History*], Turin: Einaudi, 1997: VII–XIX, 5–13.

Bracco, Fabrizio (ed.), *Gramsci e la crisi del mondo liberale* [Gramsci and the Crisis of the Liberal World], Perugia: Guerra, 1980.

Bukharin, Nikolai, *Historical Materialism: A System of Sociology*, 1921 (www.marxists. org/archive/bukharin/works/1921/histmat/index.htm).

Burgio, Alberto, *Gramsci: il sistema in movimento* [Gramsci: The Moving System], Rome: DeriveApprodi, 2014.

Carr, Edward Hallett, *A History of Soviet Russia. Vol. IV, The Interregnum: 1923–1924*, London: Macmillan, 1954.

Cohen, Stephen, *Bukharin and the Bolshevik Revolution: A Political Biography, 1888–1938*, New York: Random House, 1975 (1st ed. 1973).

Cuoco, Vincenzo, *Historical Essay on the Neapolitan Revolution of 1799*, translated by D. Gibbons, Toronto: University of Toronto Press, 2014 (1st ed. 1801).

Davis, John A. and Ginsborg, Paul (eds), *Society and Politics in the Age of Risorgimento: Essays in Honour of Danis Mack Smith*, Cambridge: Cambridge University Press, 1991.

De Man, Henri, *Au-delà du marxisme* [Beyond Marxism], Bruxelles: L'Églantine, 1927.

Destutt De Tracy, Antoine-Louis-Claude, *A Treatise on Political Economy (To Which is Prefixed a Supplement to a Preceding Work on the Understanding or Elements of Ideology)*, translated by T. Jefferson, Auburn, AL: The Ludwig Von Mises Institute, 2009 (1st ed. 1822).

Durkheim, Émile, 'Lo stato attuale degli studi sociologici in Francia [The Present State of Sociological Studies in France]', *Riforma sociale* [Social Reform], 2, 1895: 607–22, 691–707.

——, 'Il suicidio e l'instabilità economica [Suicide and Economic Instability]', *Riforma sociale* [Social Reform], 7, 1897: 529–57.

——, 'Il suicidio dal punto di vista sociologico [Suicide from a Sociological Viewpoint]', *Rivista italiana di sociologia* [Italian Journal of Sociology], 1, 1897: 17–27.

——, 'La sociologia e il suo dominio scientifico [Sociology and its Scientific Field]', *Rivista italiana di sociologia* [Italian Journal of Sociology], 4, 1900: 127–48.

——, *The Rules of Sociological Method*, translated by W.D. Halls, New York-London-Toronto-Sydney: The Free Press, 1982 (1st ed. 1895).

——, *The Division of Labour in Society*, translated by W.D. Halls, London: Macmillan, 1984 (1st ed. 1893).

——, *On Suicide*, translated by R. Buss, London: Penguin Books, 2006 (1st ed. 1897).

Eagleton, Terry, *Ideology: An Introduction*, London-New York: Verso, 1991.

Eley, Geoff and Grigor Suny, Ronald (eds), *Becoming National: A Reader*, New York: Oxford University Press, 1996.

Femia, Joseph V., *The Machiavellian Legacy. Essays in Italian Political Thought*, London-New York: Macmillan, 1998.

Ferraresi, Furio, *Il fantasma della comunità. Concetti politici e scienza sociale in Max Weber* [The Spectre of Community: Political Concepts and Social Science in Max Weber], Milan: Franco Angeli, 2003.

Filippini, Michele, *Una politica di massa. Antonio Gramsci e la rivoluzione della società* [Mass Politics: Antonio Gramsci and the Revolution of Society], Rome: Carocci, 2015.

Foscolo, Ugo, *Sepulchres*, translated by J.G. Nichols, London: One World Classics, 2010 (1st ed. 1807).

Foucault, Michel, *The Order of Things: An Archaeology of the Human Sciences*, New York: Pantheon Books, 1970 [1st ed. 1966].

Frederick II (King of Prussia), *Anti-Machiavel: Or, an Examination of Machiavel's Prince*, Gale Ecco, Print Editions, 2010 (1st ed. 1739).

Freeden, Michael, *Ideology: A Very Short Introduction*, Oxford: Oxford University Press, 2003.

Gervasoni, Marco, *Antonio Gramsci e la Francia. Dal mito della modernità alla 'scienza della politica'* [Antonio Gramsci and France: From the Myth of Modernity to the 'Science of Politics'], Milan: Unicopli, 1998.

Gherardi, Raffaella, *L'arte del compromesso. La politica della mediazione nell'Italia liberale* [The Art of Compromise: The Politics of Mediation in Liberal Italy], Bologna: Il Mulino, 1993.

Gill, Stephen and Mittelman, James H. (eds), *Innovation and Transformation in International Studies*, Cambridge: Cambridge University Press, 1997.

Gottl-Ottlilienfeld (von), Friedrich, *Fordismus: Paraphrasen über das Verhältnis von Wirtschaft und technischer Vernunft bei Henry Ford und Frederick W. Taylor* [Paraphrases about the Relationship Between the Economy and Technical Rationality from Henry Ford and Frederick W. Taylor], Jena: G. Fischer, 1924.

Harvey, David, *The Enigma of Capital: And the Crises of Capitalism*, London: Profile, 2010.

——, 'Crisis Theory and the Falling Rate of Profit', in T. Subasat and M.S. Kocman (eds), *The Great Financial Meltdown: Systemic, Conjunctural or Policy Created?*, Cheltenham: Edward Elgar, 2016.

Hegel, George Wilhelm Friedrich, *Elements of the Philosophy of Right*, translated by H.B. Nisbet, Cambridge: Cambridge University Press, 1991 (1st ed. 1820).

Hobsbawm, Eric J., 'Per capire le classi subalterne [Understanding the Subaltern Classes]', *Rinascita – Il contemporaneo*, special issue 'Gramsci nel mondo [Gramsci in the World]', 8, 28 February 1987: 15–34.

Karsenti, Bruno, *La société en personnes: études durkheimiennes* [Society in Person: Durkheimian Studies], Paris: Economica, 2006.

Kennedy, Emmet, '"Ideology" from Tracy to Marx', *Journal of the History of Ideas*, 3, 1979: 353–68.

Koselleck, Reinhart, *Critique and Crisis: Enlightenment and the Pathogenesis of Modern Society*, Cambridge, MA: MIT Press, 1988 (1st ed. 1959).

——, *Futures Past: On the Semantics of Historical Time*, translated by K. Tribe, New York: Columbia University Press, 2004 (1st ed. 1979).

Labriola, Antonio, *Socialism and Philosophy*, translated by E. Untermann, 1907 (www.marxists.org/archive/labriola/works/al03.htm).

Laclau, Ernesto, *On Populist Reason*, London: Pluto Press, 2005.

Lenin, Vladimir Ilyich, *What is to be Done?*, translated by J. Fineberg and G. Hanna, 1901 (www.marxists.org/archive/lenin/works/1901/witbd).

Lockwood, David, *Solidarity and Schism: 'The Problem of Disorder' in Durkheimian and Marxist Sociology*, Oxford: Clarendon Press, 1992.

Lovett, Clara Maria, *The Democratic Movement in Italy, 1830–1876*, Cambridge, MA: Harvard University Press, 1982.

Lukács, György, *History and Class Consciousness: Studies in Marxist Dialectics*, translated by R. Livingstone, Cambridge, MA: MIT Press, 1971 (1st ed. 1923).

Luxemburg, Rosa, *The Mass Strike, the Political Party and the Trade Unions*, translated by P. Lavin, 1906 (www.marxists.org/archive/luxemburg/1906/mass-strike).

Machiavelli, Niccolò, *Discourses on Livy*, translated by H.C. Mansfield and N. Tarcov, Chicago-London: University of Chicago Press, 1996 (1st ed. 1531).

——, *The Prince*, translated by P. Bondanella, Oxford: Oxford University Press, 2005 (1st ed. 1532).

Mack Smith, Denis, *The Making of Italy, 1796–1866*, London: Macmillan, 1988.

Malagodi, Giovanni, *Le ideologie politiche* [Political Ideologies], Bari: Laterza, 1928.

Mannheim, Karl, *Ideology and Utopia: An Introduction to the Sociology of Knowledge*, translated by L. Wirth and E. Shils, London-Henley: Routledge & Kegan Paul, 1998 (1st ed. 1929).

——, *Essays on the Sociology of Knowledge*, translated by P. Kecskemeti, London: Routledge, 1998 (1st ed. 1952).

Martin, James, 'Hegemony and the Crisis of Legitimacy in Gramsci', *History of the Human Sciences*, 10, 1 February 1997: 37–56.

Marx, Karl, *Theses on Feuerbach*, translated by C. Smith, 1845 (www.marxists.org/archive/marx/works/1845/theses).

—— *Thesen über Feuerbach*, 1845 (www.marxists.org/deutsch/archiv/marx-engels/1845/thesen/thesfeue-or.htm).

——, 'Preface' to *A Contribution to the Critique of Political Economy*, translated by S.W. Ryazanskaya, 1859 (www.marxists.org/archive/marx/works/1859/critique-pol-economy/preface.htm).

——, *Lohnarbeit und Kapital. Zur Judenfrage und andere Schriften aus des Frühzeit* [Wage Labour and Capital. The Jewish Question, and Other Early Writings], Leipzig: Philipp Reclam, 1920.

Marx, Karl and Engels, Friedrich, *The German Ideology*, translated by C. Dutt, 1845 (www.marxists.org/archive/marx/works/1845/german-ideology).

Michels, Robert, 'Les Partis politiques e la contrainte sociale [Political Parties and Social Coercion]', *Mercure de France* [Mercury of France], 717, 1 May 1928: 513–35.

—— (ed.), *Politica ed economia* [Politics and Economics], Turin: Utet, 1934.

——, *Political Parties: A Sociological Study of the Oligarchical Tendencies of Modern Democracy*, translated by E. and C. Paul, New Brunswick: Transaction Publishing, 1999 (1st ed. 1911).

Morfino, Vittorio (ed.), *Tempora multa: il governo del tempo* [Tempora Multa: The Governance of Time], Milan: Mimesis, 2013.

Mosca, Gaetano, *The Ruling Class*, translated by H.D. Kahn, New York: McGraw-Hill, 1960.

Moss, Howard, *Gramsci and the Idea of Human Nature*, Farnham: Ashgate, 1997.

Oestreich, Gerhard, *Neostoicism and Early Modern State*, translated by D. McLintock, Cambridge: Cambridge University Press, 2008: 258–73 (1st ed. 1969).

Paine, Thomas, *Rights of Man, Common Sense and Other Political Writings*, Oxford: Oxford University Press, 1998.

Paladini Musitelli, Marina (ed.), *Gramsci e la scienza. Storicità e attualità delle note gramsciane sulla scienza* [Gramsci and Science: The Historicity and Actuality of Gramsci's Notes on Science], Trieste: Istituto Gramsci del Friuli Venezia Giulia, 2008.

Pareto, Vilfredo, *The Rise and Fall of Elites: An Application of Theoretical Sociology*, Totowa: The Bedminster Press, 1968.

Pels, Dirk, 'Hendrik de Man and the Ideology of Planism', *International Review of Social History*, 32, 1987: 206–29.

Pocock, John Greville Agard, *The Machiavellian Moment: Florentine Political Thought and the Atlantic Republican Tradition*, Princeton: Princeton University Press, 1975.

Rafalski, Traute and Vale, Michel, 'Social Planning and Corporativism: Modernization, Tendencies in Italian Fascism', *International Journal of Political Economy*, 1, 1988: 10–64.

Ragazzini, Dario, *Leonardo nella società di massa: teoria della personalità in Gramsci* [Leonardo in Mass Society: The Theory of Personality in Gramsci], Bergamo: Moretti & Vitali, 2002.

Rehmann, Jan, *Theories of Ideology: The Powers of Alienation and Subjection*, Leiden-Boston: Brill, 2013.

Renan, Ernest, *La réforme intellectuelle et morale* [Intellectual and Moral Reform], Paris: Michel Lévy Frères, 1871.

Ricciardi, Maurizio (ed.), *Ordine sovrano e rivoluzione in età moderna e contemporanea* [The Sovereign Order and Revolution in the Modern and Contemporary Ages], Bologna: Clueb, 2003.

——, *La società come ordine. Storia e teoria politica dei concetti sociali* [Society as Order: The History and Political Theory of Social Concepts], Macerata: Eum, 2010.

——, 'L'ideologia come scienza politica del sociale [Ideology as a Political Science of the Social]', *Scienza & Politica*, 52, 2015 (http://scienzaepolitica.unibo.it/article/view/5282).

Ricciardi, Maurizio and Scuccimarra, Luca, 'L'ideologia e la sua critica [Ideology and its Critique]', *Scienza & Politica*, 47, 2012: 5–9 (http://scienzaepolitica.unibo.it/article/view/3835).

Romano, Santi, *Lo Stato moderno e la sua crisi: saggi di diritto costituzionale* [The Modern State and its Crisis: Essays on Constitutional Law], Milan: Giuffrè, 1969.

Rossi-Landi, Ferruccio, *Marxism and Ideology*, translated by R. Griffin, Oxford: Clarendon Press, 1990 (1st ed. 1978).

Santoro, Emilio, *Autonomy, Freedom and Rights: A Critique of Liberal Subjectivity*, Dordrecht: Kluwer Academic, 2003 (1st ed. 1999).

Schecter, Darrow, 'Two Views of the Revolution: Gramsci and Sorel, 1916–1920', *History of European Ideas*, 5, 1990: 637–53.

——, *Gramsci and the Theory of Industrial Democracy*, Aldershot, Hants, UK: Avebury, 1991.

Schiera, Pierangelo, *Il laboratorio borghese. Scienza e politica nella Germania dell'Ottocento* [The Bourgeois Laboratory: Science and Politics in 19th Century Germany], Bologna: Il Mulino, 1987.

Scott, David, *Gilbert Simondon's Psychic and Collective Individuation: A Critical Introduction and Guide*, Edinburgh: Edinburgh University Press, 2014.

Simmel, Georg, *Sociology: Inquiries into the Construction of Social Forms*, translated by A.J. Blasi, A.K. Jacobs and M. Kanjirathinkal, 2 vols, Leiden: Brill, 2009 (1st ed. 1908).

Simondon, Gilbert, *L'individuation psychique et collective* [Psychic and Collective Individuation], Paris: Aubier, 1989.

Sorel, Georges, *Le Procès de Socrate. Examen critique des thèses socratiques*, Paris: Alcan, 1889 (partial translation 'The Trial of Socrates', in J. Stanley (ed.), *From Georges Sorel: Essays in Socialism and Philosophy*, Oxford: Oxford University Press, 1976: 62–70).

——, *Contribution à l'étude profane de la Bible* [Contribution to a Secular Study of the Bible], Paris: A. Ghio, 1889.

——, 'L'Ancienne et la nouvelle métaphysique [The Old and the New Metaphysics]', Ère nouvelle [The New Era], March 1894: 329–51; April 1894: 461–82; May 1894: 51–87; June 1894: 180–205.

——, 'Les théories de M. Durkheim' [Mr. Durkheim's Theories], *Le Devenir social* [The Social Becoming], 1, April 1895: 1–26; 2, May 1895: 148–80.

——, 'Germanesimo e storicismo di Ernesto Renan. Saggio inedito di Georges Sorel [The Germanism and Historicism of Ernesto Renan: An Unpublished Essay by Georges Sorel]', *Critica sociale* [Social Critique], 1932, instalments II, III, IV, V: 110–44, 139–207, 358–67, 430–44.

——, *Lettere a un amico d'Italia* [Letters to an Italian Friend], Bologna: Cappelli, 1963.

——, *Scritti politici e filosofici* [Political and Philosophical Writings], Turin: Einaudi, 1975.

——, *Le teorie di Durkheim e altri scritti sociologici* [Durkheim's Theories and Other Sociological Writings], translated by P. Reale, Naples: Liguori, 1978.

——, *Reflections on Violence*, Cambridge: Cambridge University Press, 1999 (1st ed. 1908).

Steinberg, Hans-Josef, *Sozialismus und deutsche Sozialdemokratie: zur Ideologie der Partei vor dem 1. Weltkrieg* [Socialism and German Social Democracy: The Ideology of the Party before the First World War], Hannover: Verlag für Literatur und Zeitgeschehen, 1967.

Taylor, Charles, *The Malaise of Modernity*, Toronto: House of Anansi Press, 1991.

Taine, Hippolyte, *The Origins of Contemporary France*, translated by J. Durand, New York: P. Smith, 1931 (1st ed. 1875–93).

Togliatti, Palmiro, *Scritti su Gramsci* [Writings on Gramsci], edited by G. Liguori, Rome: Editori Riuniti, 2001.

Tronti, Mario, *Operai e capitale* [Workers and Capital], Turin: Einaudi, 1966.

——, *Soggetti, crisi, potere* [Subjects, Crisis, Power], Bologna: Cappelli, 1980.

Viroli, Maurizio, *Niccolò's Smile: A Biography of Machiavelli*, translated by A. Shugaar, New York: Farrar Straus Giroux, 2000 (1st ed. 1998).

Voza, Pasquale, *Gramsci e la continua crisi* [Gramsci and the Continual Crisis], Rome: Carocci, 2008.

Weber, Max, *Economy and Society: An Outline of Interpretive Sociology*, translated by E. Fischoff, H. Gerth, A.M. Henderson, F. Kolegar, C. Wright Mills, T. Parsons, M. Rheinstein, G. Roth, E. Shils and C. Wittich, 2 vols, 1968: 1148–56 (1st ed. 1922).

——, *Political Writings*, translated by R. Speirs, Cambridge: Cambridge University Press, 1994.

——, *The Protestant Ethic and the Spirit of Capitalism*, London-New York: Routledge, 2001 (1st ed. 1905).

Williams, Gwyn A., *Proletarian Order: Antonio Gramsci, Factory Councils and the Origins of Italian Communism, 1911–1921*, London: Pluto Press, 1975.

Index

Printed and bound by CPI Group (UK) Ltd, Croydon, CR0 4YY

13/04/2025

14656490-0001